"MACO"

The Malcolm Marshall Story

by Pat Symes

The Parrs Wood Press
MANCHESTER

First Published 2000

THE PARRS WOOD PRESS
St Wilfrid's Enterprise Centre
Royce Road, Manchester, M15 5BJ

© Pat Symes 2000

ISBN: 1 903158 07 9

Front and back cover photographs courtesy of Harry Herd

This book was produced by Andrew Searle, Ruth Heritage and Bob Wells of The Parrs Wood Press and Printed in Great Britain by:

Fretwell Print and Design
Healey Works
Goulbourne Street
Keighley
West Yorkshire BD21 1 PZ

ACKNOWLEDGEMENTS

This is a book that ought not to have been written for many more years but, after his untimely death from cancer in November 1999, it was time to pay Malcolm Marshall proper tribute, the tribute he deserves as one of cricket's greatest talents.

I am indebted to Andy Searle of The Parrs Wood Press for nurturing the idea and for seeing the project through with the sort of care and devotion expected of a man rapidly earning the reputation as one of the most ambitious of the smaller independent publishers. He's also a cricket nut.

Statistical detail is the province of Jim Baldwin, who met all his deadlines with his usual calmness and enthusiastic good nature. For the photographs that appear in this book I'd like to express my gratitude to Harry Herd, Mick Young and Hampshire County Cricket Club's Marketing Manager, Mike Taylor. And for the additional material I needed from Barbados, my thanks go to Mike Vimpany.

Lastly, I would also like to thank my wife, Lin, for her greater computer knowledge when it looked as if 90,000 words had disappeared into cyberspace.

About the author

Patrick Symes first saw cricket as a schoolboy at Dean Park, Bournemouth in September 1961 and came away believing Hampshire always won the County Championship. Now he gets paid to watch cricket and football for a living and like all journalists cannot believe his luck. He first came across Malcolm Marshall in 1979 and remembered how long it took the languid West Indian to get from the dressing room to the crease when it was his turn to bat. It appeared to take him even longer to go back again! Later they co-operated for the production of 'Marshall Arts' (Queen Anne Press, 1987) and for Marshall's regular column in the Daily Mirror. Now too close for comfort to 50 and running a news agency, Pat Symes lives with his wife Lin and two over-indulged Jack Russells in Southsea, Hampshire and keeps a paternal eye on grown-up children Paul, Aimee and John.

For all cancer-sufferers and those who suffer with them.

CONTENTS

PART ONE

1.

The Death

MALCOLM DENZIL MARSHALL died peacefully in a hospital bed in his beloved home island of Barbados on a warm and tranquil Caribbean evening on Thursday, November 4, 1999. He was 41 years and six months old and his death sent shockwaves through an entire sporting community.

Within minutes, the news of his premature demise was being relayed across the cricketing world, among his many, many friends and those who simply remembered him as the sunny face of a game he loved and a game which loved him. There were tears in Barbados, Bournemouth, Bangalore and Brisbane and all stops in between; everywhere in fact he had ever ventured in one of cricket's most distinguished and remarkable careers. Malcolm Marshall was no ordinary cricketer and no ordinary man and the outpouring of grief that followed his death manifestly reflected both those facets.

Hurricane Lenny had left a trail of devastation across the Caribbean not long before Marshall had lost his grim battle against cancer of the colon, but in many respects the effects were similar. Not since the death of another great cricketing icon, Sir Frank Worrell from leukaemia some 32 years before and at only a year older, had Barbados been plunged into such a state of despair and disbelief.

Among those at his bedside when he passed away were his new wife, Connie, and the Rev. Wes Hall, himself another of the great gifts to cricket from the tiny island of Barbados. Connie had been Marshall's companion for some 12 years and their nine year old son, Mali, was within hours of his father's death to write a moving prayer tribute which was read on his behalf at the funeral by family friend, Dr Rudi Webster. Hall and Marshall were all but blood brothers; they came from the same part of the island, from disadvantaged backgrounds, raised by single parents and rose

3

to become fast bowlers of exceptional quality. It was Hall who had put Marshall on the path to stardom and who had overseen a career in many ways even more significant than his own. It was fitting therefore that his first major sermon as a recently installed minister of the church should be at the funeral some ten days after Marshall's death. It was a thunderous sermon, one which brought a lump to the throat and a tear to the eye to those many friends and former teammates who attended the moving ceremony at Barbados' Sir Garfield Sobers Gymnasium.

That a 41 year old in the prime of life should have succumbed to colon cancer so quickly after it had been diagnosed makes the Malcolm Marshall story all the more tragic and sad. Doctors around the world have a high success rate in the treating of cancer of the colon, providing it is identified and treated at an early stage. In Marshall's case, it was not. For three years, in growing discomfort and obvious pain, he had gone around the cricketing globe in his capacity as West Indies' coach and coach also to the Hampshire county team in England. It was thought he might have had an ulcer or that he might have been suffering from indigestion. Only when the pain became too awful to carry on was he admitted to hospital in Edgbaston, Birmingham during the 1999 World Cup, where tests were conducted and the awful truth revealed.

That was in May. Within six months he was gone. Some 14 cancerous inches of his intestinal colon were removed on the surgeon's table and he was released to his home near Southampton only after being warned that the survival odds in his favour were merely 60-40. "Better than the other way around," he quipped with typical optimism. What followed was a long and tortuous series of chemotherapy sessions throughout the English summer. It's not an easy journey to Birmingham from the south coast for a man with a death sentence hanging over him. He coped bravely and as vigorously as he could but it became apparent that for all his determination to recover and the best of medical facilities and knowledge this was one obstacle too many. He accepted his fate with quiet dignity and good grace, never letting on to those around him that time was running out.

His occasional visits to the cricket at Southampton's County Ground revealed a proud man grown weary and thin by a desperate struggle to live. Countless well-wishers noticed the horrific change in his physical appearance but the smile never disappeared. "Not too bad," was his

4

standard reply to the obvious question, but he never let on. Even his wife was never sure how he was feeling or how the treatment was progressing. In a television interview in the aftermath of her husband's death, she said: "For three years he had the cancer and it was never treated. Only when he got to England and it all got so bad did they discover what it was. As soon as I found out I got the first plane to England and went to Birmingham. I had been held up in traffic and he would not go in for his operation until I had arrived. When anyone asked him how he was, he never gave much of a reply, not even to me. He was very strong and self-contained and regarded the cancer as his problem. If anyone wanted to talk about cricket, that was different. He opened up."

He was able to play some golf and bowl a few gentle deliveries to Mali in the garden but the zest had gone and when the wedding was announced for September his friends and the outside world began to realise that perhaps his treatment was not going so well, that here was a man getting his house in order. Connie Earle and Malcolm Marshall were married at All Saints Church, Eastleigh, a small town known best for its railway yards a few miles outside Southampton. The bride was given away by her father, Vince Earle of New York, and the best man was Marshall's former Barbados and West Indies teammate, Desmond Haynes. Those who attended the simple service remembered it as both sorrowful and happy. There were tears among the confetti because Marshall's frail and emaciated body was a shadow of the sturdy frame that had carried him so stoutly through a Test career of 376 wickets and earned him a reputation as the greatest fast bowler of his generation.

Among the guests were Clive Lloyd, who had captained the West Indies when Marshall was such an integral part and was now its manager. With him was his wife, Waveney, and there also were performance consultant and fellow Barbadian, Dr Webster. From Hampshire came Robin Smith, Adrian Aymes and Shaun Udal, and significantly also the surgeon who had removed the cancer from his colon, Tariq Ismail.

There were good days and bad, as with most cancer-sufferers, and a few rounds of golf with Haynes and his Hampshire friends suggested strength enough to cope with his ordeal. Haynes recalled: "It was as if he knew it was going to be his last round of golf with me and he was determined to enjoy it." But as the English season ended and the warmth of summer gave way to the falling leaves of Autumn, Marshall grew weaker and more tired by the day. It was decided to head for home, Barbados and the house he'd had built overlooking the glistening Caribbean. It was here that Wes Hall reintroduced him to religion and where he found God again to help comfort him through what everyone had come to accept were his final weeks. As Robin Smith noted: "No one wanted to believe it, but we felt he was heading home to die and it was then that it hit us. He wasn't going to get better." As his own account indicates, Marshall had lapsed as a Christian in youth and early manhood, but as his time approached Hall said he found great solace in the the teachings of the Bible. Two of his favourite passages were read at the funeral, Psalm 46: verses 6-10 by Clive Lloyd and Philippians 3: verses 6-10 by his cousin, Errol Yearwood. Old colleagues, Haynes and Gordon Greenidge also took part in Hall's Bible classes, easing their friend's path to its inevitable and imminent conclusion.

Soon he was being taken to hospital in Bridgetown for the final chapter in the Malcolm Marshall story. By now he was down to six stones and there was little about him to indicate the formidable athlete he had once been. His wife, Connie, vividly recalls the final moments. "At the end he gave his life to Jesus. The Reverend Hall helped him. On his last day I went to see him in the Queen Elizabeth Hospital and he was so weak he could not speak. There was fluid running down his face, but they were not tears. Wes Hall said his body was cleansing. I got the impression he wanted to say something but couldn't. I leant across and said, 'what is it, Malcolm? Do you want to say something?' As he struggled, I said : 'I love you.' And he summoned just enough strength to reply: 'And I love you too.'" He puckered for a kiss and having kissed his new bride, never spoke again. He was certified dead soon afterwards.

The tightly-knit world of cricket was soon mourning as it hadn't mourned before. It is used to its heroes dying of old age or simply fading away, but somehow Marshall's death had been different. It was not his relative youth or the fact that no bowler had taken more Test wickets in the 1980s, though both such things mattered. It was that he was a great man, a special man, as his Hampshire captain Mark Nicholas pointed out in his eulogy, and it was the loss of him as a person which so shocked and appalled. Within hours of his quiet exit in a hospital bed becoming known, international cricketers in places as far-flung as Brisbane and Harare were wearing black armbands as a mark of respect. In neither case were the West Indies involved.

Immediately Connie and the Marshall family, his mother and step-father, step-brothers and sisters, had to decide what to do about a funeral. Should it be a small and private affair with perhaps a memorial service at some later date? Or should it be a grand affair to mark the passing of an important personality? Cricket will be grateful for the choice of the latter. It was decided firstly that the body should lie in state, in repose at Bridgetown's St Michael's Cathedral. So many people in the island wanted to pay their final respects to a man perhaps many of them had only known by repute. He was the international face of Barbados, as were many cricketers, and they wanted to say goodbye in a proper and reverential manner because as their ambassador he had been an unprecedented success. Whenever he was home he had time for everyone; a ready smile and a firm handshake. He knew how much he meant to them and how he perhaps represented their own repressed ambitions and hopes. Now it was pay-back time. The Clyde B Jones Funeral Directors of Top Road, Christchurch dressed his body in his best suit and tie and it was taken to the cathedral where huge queues braved the unremitting sunshine and heat. Later, funeral director Ken Jones looked back on his busiest few days before and during the occasion. "As an ardent cricket fan it was hard to do but it had to be done."

It was estimated that several thousand people filed past the body to offer little prayers and thanks for a life well spent. Again there were tears, but often only sadness. There had been so much more he was ready to offer and in normal circumstances would have fulfilled. Symbolically, a shiny red new cricket ball was placed in his lap, held by hands shrunken by the wretched disease he fought so valiantly but in vain to overcome. So great was the demand among Bajans to say farewell that the lid was only placed on the coffin just before it was taken to the gymnasium for the funeral. It was the last the world would see of him.

2.

The Funeral

MALCOLM MARSHALL'S funeral on Saturday, November 13 was not designated a state occasion, but it was as close to one as it was possible to be. Governor-General Sir Clifford Husbands, acting prime minister David Simmons, opposition leader David Thompson and many members of the Barbadian cabinet attended the two-hour service in the hanger-like gymnasium that carries the name of another great Barbados icon, Sir Garfield Sobers, at Wildey outside Bridgetown. But while the presence of civic leaders gave some indication of Marshall's importance to Barbados as a nation and its government, it was the countless number of players, past and present, who wept openly or hid their grief behind dark glasses who gave a clearer indication of his importance to cricket. As those players, all of them resplendent in blazer and tie denoting their own cricketing background, gathered to discuss the shock and suddenness of his death, two words cropped up again and again. The first was 'special' and the other was 'love'. Malcolm Marshall was regarded as a special person and he had that rare quality to be genuinely loved by those who knew him well. Mark Nicholas referred to both of those qualities later in his eulogy.

As the body was taken from the cathedral to the gymnasium, the roads were lined by islanders bowing their heads or simply staring in disbelief. One or two applauded. To greet the funeral cortege was a veritable galaxy of stars, a Who's Who of West Indian cricket. Sir Viv Richards, Sir Clive Lloyd, Gordon Greenidge, Desmond Haynes, Richie Richardson, Collis King, Gus Logie, David Murray, Roger Harper, Andy Roberts, Joel Garner, Ezra Moseley, Michael Holding, Colin Croft, Wayne Daniel and Sylvester Clarke were all contemporaries. Present-day players included then captain Brian Lara, Courtney Walsh, Curtly Ambrose and Nixon McLean, while Phil Simmons interrupted his season in the South African domestic competition to travel back to the Caribbean to pay his respects. From previous eras came cricketing knights Sir Everton Weekes, Sir Clyde Walcott and Sir Conrad Hunte and others who had played just before his time: Seymour Nurse, Wes Hall, Charlie Griffith, David Holford, John Shepherd, Robin Bynoe, Maurice Foster, and Richard Edwards. The West Indies Cricket Board understandably sent their top men in a delegation led by its president, Pat Rousseau, chief executive officer Steve Camacho, executive secretary Andrew Sealy, director of coaching Reg Scarlett and chairman of selectors Mike Findlay. From the Barbados Cricket Association came Stephen Alleyne and Tony Marshall. Oddly the only major name missing was Sir Garfield Sobers, who was away in South Africa and unable to get back in time. If there was one name bigger than Marshall's in the annals of Barbados cricket it was surely Sobers, the greatest all-rounder of all time.

But the true measure of Marshall the man was the number of mourners from overseas, particularly Hampshire, where he was equally revered. His captain, Nicholas, Robin Smith, Tim Tremlett, Cardigan Connor and physiotherapist David Newman had scrambled on to last-minute flights, while John Stephenson had made his own way from the United States. Paul-Jan Bakker had come from Holland. They all wanted to give him the send-off he deserved. The family were also strongly represented: his wife Connie, son Mali, daughter Shelly, 14, from a previous relationship, mother Eleanor, grandmother Lilian Welch and many step-brothers, step-sisters and cousins.

Two of the mourners would themselves be dead within a month. Sir Conrad Hunte was 67 when he died of a heart attack in Sydney. A high class opening batsman in his time, Hunte went on to become prominent in the Moral Rearmament movement and was one of the pallbearers as the coffin was carried from the gymnasium. Sylvester Clarke was a month short of his 45th birthday. After a career of almost 1,000 first class wickets, many for Surrey, Clarke had returned to Barbados and was still playing club cricket not long before his death, also from a heart attack. While the deaths of such good men were shocking in their own right it is fair to say that neither made the impact of Marshall's.

The gymnasium was chosen as the venue for the funeral because it is one of the biggest arenas on the island, yet it was only a third full when Rev Basil Yarde of the Abundant Life Assembly called the congregation to worship at ten o'clock on a bright, sparkling morning. The coffin, which had been brought into the gymnasium by Vincent Nurse, Errol Yearwood, Michael Marshall, Roland Holder, Courtney Walsh, Stephen Farmer, Cardigan Connor and Clive Lloyd, was placed on the stage draped in the maroon colours of West Indies' cricket against a royal blue-curtained background and the whole proceedings were broadcast across a bereaved Caribbean. There was a hymn, 'Lead us, Heavenly Father, Lead Us', prayers from the Dean of St Michael's Cathedral, the Very Rev Harold Crichlow, and a bible reading (from Psalm 46) by Clive Lloyd. This was followed by a musical rendition from the Abundant Life Assembly choir, supported by the Police Band, and the second lesson (from Philippians 3), read by Marshall's cousin Errol Yearwood.

Then came one of the highlights of the entire ceremony, the reading by Dr Rudi Webster of a prayer written by Mali Marshall, aged nine, within minutes of hearing of his father's death. It brought tears to the eyes of many in the congregation and at the insistence of a priest got a generous round of applause afterwards. Entitled, My Little Prayer, it read:

'O, Lord, I love my father.
And I know he is fighting inside.
Connie and Daddy love you very much.
God, Bless my father.
I want you to know that Daddy loves Mummy and I, I love my father;
He was the best father I had in the world.
Father; I love you and Mummy very, very much.
God bless all of us.
God, take care of my father.
For I love him very much.
God, bless all of us;
Love Mali, Daddy and Mummy.
Goodbye Father. That was the last time I saw you.
God bless Malcolm for me please,
Love, Your son, Mali Marshall.
We love Malcolm Marshall.
Take care of him for me and mummy, Lord.
Love, Mali. God bless.'

It was some time before the service could be resumed after Dr Webster had taken his seat again and the applause had subsided. Calypso king, the dreadlocked Mighty Gabby, was visibly upset before the funeral began and feared his voice might break with emotion. But he gave what the Barbados Sunday Advocate described as an 'inimitable, hair-raising rendition of The Lord's Prayer that ended with an Amen so powerful it stunned the congregation into silence by its sheer vocal force and beauty'. Mighty Gabby, whose calypsos were so enjoyed by Marshall, admitted later: "The only other time I felt I might not be able to sing was at my mother's funeral last year."

Marshall's great friends, former agent Vincent Nurse and Sir Viv Richards, gave their appreciations of the man they knew. Vincent Nurse told the congregation: "Malcolm knew his enormous strengths and recognised his weaknesses. Never did he try to mask those frailties with those strengths. He faced the realities of his life with thanks and humility. He was happy to take his rightful place in the line and he did not try to buy favours with the currency of fame." Sir Viv Richards said he had the mental toughness and professionalism necessary for top flight cricket and had now gone to "that final series. I can see him now, saying to me: 'Cappy, these conditions are good for fast bowling.'"

Mark Nicholas, now a television commentator and journalist, admitted he had been honoured when Connie had asked him to deliver the eulogy, and befitting someone as eloquent as the former Hampshire captain, he did not let his audience down in a superb 20 minute speech which brought laughter and sobs in equal measure. With an insight gleaned from a decade or more of being teammate, captain, friend and confidante, Nicholas made the very best of his opportunity and was roundly praised for giving a cherished view of the whole man:

"Many years ago, my mother suggested to me in reference to a splendid school-teacher who had just left us, that in life one came across only a few truly special people. Lots of good ones, she said, plenty of fabulous folk, but only a few who are special. Malcolm Marshall was one of those special people. Not so much because he was extraordinarily good at cricket but because of the way he applied the various gifts, and cricket amongst them, which were given to him. Malcolm was no waster, not of time, not of talent, nor a shirker of any situation or challenge which confronted him. Malcolm

11

maintained excellence without ever a hint of arrogance, he earned respect without ever assuming respect, and he displayed confidence and self-assurance within his immense humility.

"For as long as perhaps the last two months he knew deep down I think that the game was up. But he was damned if he would let us know. He was a stubborn fellow and - Connie would know that and any of us who played with him would know that. It was as if he was more concerned with the suffering of those around him, those few intensely close friends that were kept by this very private man. The qualities of thoughtfulness and caring, of courage and of bravery - and he showed that so often in his play - were among his finest. For all the flamboyance and bravado of Malcolm he was never one to over dramatise off the field. He resolved that his dreadful illness would be his own problem and as it escalated he was determined not to panic others with its potential end.

"For everyone who lives here on this magical island, the name of Malcolm Marshall is synonymous with the style of the place; with the game of cricket in its purest calypso form, but also in its more modern professional form; with fun and sun, with the good and simple living that is typical here and with the honesty and generosity of spirit that characterises the people of Barbados. It is clear to all of us who visit that his loss has stunned this nation, yet his death has echoed around the world. Volley upon volley of shock is stabbing at friends wherever the game is treasured. Among the first calls I received was from Shaun Pollock in Natal, South Africa who attributes much of his success from the guidance he received from Malcolm, from Barry Richards and from Martin Crowe, the New Zealander who called him 'the finest opponent of them all - furious but fair and fantastic value in the bar.' Even Ian Botham was for once unable to speak, so sad was he at not being able to say goodbye.

"It was funny to watch opponents greet Malcolm on the morning of matches at county grounds after he had joined Hampshire. The greats, his peers, would relish the moment with hand-slapping glee and then they would go out in the middle and tear the life out of each other. The less good used to whisper among themselves if Malcolm was late, which he often was, incidentally, saying : 'No sign of Maco today? Phew'. And then when he arrived wrapped in gold chains - and boy did he dress fancy - their faces would fall with horror. Ray East and David Acfield, two of the Essex county spinners, and let me tell you bunny rabbits, terrified tail-enders, used to wait by his car and offer to carry his bags to the dressing room. 'Why?' Malcolm asked. 'Well, Mr Marshall,' said Ray East, 'we thought you might consider a couple of half volleys and if they're nice and straight we promise to miss them.'

The Malcolm Marshall Story

"He was a lethal bowler - that skidding bouncer it homed in on its target like a Scud missile - and he was revered after play when he drank those beloved brandies, when his sharp mind chewed the cud of the game and when he boasted about his batting. How he loved his batting. He had time for everyone after play, everyone. So at the moment, then, we have a universally loved and respected character who is unselfish and warm, and a man of supreme skill. But we mustn't forget his sense of humour, the extravagant plans for each batsman and those often hysterical, detailed field settings. I remember Chris Lewis waiting to face him - a wicket had fallen, it was a run out - and Lewis was at the striker's end while Malcolm practised bowling on a side pitch with our wicket-keeper Bobby Parks. He said to me: 'Watch this skipper,' and he bowled an outswinger and said, 'See'. I said, 'What?'. He told me to watch again. Another outswinger. 'See,' he said. Once more I asked him what he was trying to show me. Then he explained. 'I'll show you now. I'll bowl Lewis the inswinger.' Lewis had also watched the outswingers and thought he would leave the first delivery he faced. Big inswinger, middle stump, boom, boom, boom and he followed through and he punched the air and then he stopped and he turned to me and went: 'Oh la-la, easy game.'

"Not much got his back up. I'll tell you what he didn't like. He didn't like sloppiness from cricketers or from people in general. He didn't like people meddling with his cricket case. It was so immaculate that if you nicked a tee-shirt out of it, huh, you would have thought an atomic bomb had gone off. No, he didn't like sloppiness. He didn't suffer indifference either. He was strict with indifference and he could not stand bad manners. He had immaculate manners. He was beautifully brought up. Oh, he liked to get his own way, did our Maco. And you know why these things frustrated him? Because he cared. He cared so much about standards, about commitment to his chosen cause. About quality in all things. Even before his operation he would be bowling in the nets, inswing and outswing, appeals and exasperation, smiles and scowls and so much joy. That's Maco for me. A man of joy and delight in all he did and in others around him. The endless chatter. The laughter with his head thrown skywards, those dancing, happy eyes and that welcoming ripper of a smile. And the unbridled enthusiasm for a determined march on all the challenges of life. It didn't matter what they were, simple things even such as a round of golf, hand of backgammon, a night on the town. All those things met with equal relish and hope.

'He is a man we must, must celebrate for he gave life all that he had and from him came an unforgettable warmth and always a sense of direction. The Hampshire captain of the 60s, colourful character Colin Ingleby-Mackenzie, said: 'We

13

can only assume the great maestro in the sky was short of a class all-rounder.' Not only does the maestro in the sky now have a great all-rounder, he has the greatest enthusiast for the game that I have ever known. They will probably be partying with each other now, looking upon us and in time we shall party too. He would hate it if we didn't smile from within each time we thought of him for the Malcolm Marshall memory is one to treasure. Malcolm always referred to himself as 'a lucky man' for the gifts he had and his life. I reckon we are the lucky ones to have known him. What a privilege it has been."

If Nicholas's eulogy had been fair, compassionate and compelling, the sermon from Wesley Hall was full of passion, fire and brimstone. It followed a warm and personal address in a prayer for the family from Rev Keith Griffith and a hymn, 'It Is Well With My Soul'. Wes Hall delivered his sermon with all the fury he summoned as a great fast bowler in the 50s and 60s. It was the first time the former minister of sport had been seen in his clerical collar, but if he was nervous or uncertain on his debut it did not show. Hall had played a prominent part in many of Marshall's major career-forming decisions, helping him into the West Indies team, to Hampshire and then at the end leading him back to his Christian faith. Hall had been at the hospital bedside, praying for him as he breathed his last. He told his audience that he had induced him to salvation two weeks before his death. "Malcolm Denzil Marshall is safe and all is well with his soul." Hall called him the greatest fast bowler in history with deference to all fast bowlers, but added: "If there is one thing I think I know, I think I know about fast bowling. I am letting the process of elimination prevail and therefore I say without contradiction that Maco was the best."

Maria Bradshaw of the Sunday Sun, Barbados commented: "Hall evoked smiles and frowns, laughs and amens, then finally applause as he spent 20 minutes on his sermon which addressed ultimate love, ultimate death and ultimate hope. His biblical language, his Latin phrases and his famous quotations were interspersed with typical Wes Hall humour. At the height of the sermon he even turned to Bishop Rufus Brome and Dean Harold Crichlow for confirmation of his scriptural assertions". Hall said that as the end neared Marshall had "shown the same indomitable spirit in the face of death as he had displayed on the cricket field." His calls for a permanent monument to be erected were warmly greeted.

The Lord Bishop of Barbados, Dr Brome, gave the final prayers and benediction and a hymn, 'Be Thou My Guardian and My Guide', closed a ceremony which alternated from the sombre to the optimistic in violent swings of emotion. The finale was as fitting as it could be: a phalanx of raised crickets bats as the coffin draped in the West Indian flag was taken from the gymnasium by pallbearers Dr Webster, Haynes, Greenidge, Richards, Hall, Lara, Sir Conrad Hunte and Patrick Rousseau. Former colleagues from the West Indian teams, Barbados and Hampshire all lifted bats in salute as the coffin was wheeled out for the last journey in a unique and touching tribute.

And so to the final resting place; the pretty little church of St Bartholomew's, nestling uncomfortably close to the Grantley Adams airport. A different set of mourners had emerged as the last group of pallbearers - Joel Garner, Bobby Goodman, Peter Inniss, David Trotman, Nixon McLean, Robert Earle, Robin Smith, David Newman, Tim Tremlett and Philo Wallace - delivered the coffin in the noon-day heat. A guard of honour was presented at the graveside by pupils from Marshall's alma mater, Parkinson School, many of them too young to have seen any of his prodigious exploits. Shakena Marshall, an eleven year old chosen by the school to help form the guard of honour, confessed to the Sunday Sun that she had never seen him in action. "All I know is that he was a great bowler." Gravedigger Carrington Smith had spent three days preparing the ground for the mahogany casket, still draped on arrival in the maroon flag. "I knew all about him of course and followed his career but I never met him. It is hard enough even for those who have lived a full life but this man was still so young. I don't like preparing to bury the young."

There were so many people, ordinary Bajan folk, who had missed the funeral service at the gymnasium but made their way instead by bus and on foot to the graveside, determined to pay their respects. So many in fact that some clung to branches of swaying trees to get a better look, others sat on the wall - any vantage point they could find. Eighty year old Adin Greene left home in Coconut Grove in the distant parish of St Joseph at 6am, some six hours before the internment, to be sure of getting a place as near to the ceremony as possible. "I would not have missed the funeral for anything. He was a great man." Orwin Lashley sat on a rock as he watched the dignified final proceedings. "I never knew Maco but I see him on the

15

cricket field and if anybody deserve honour, it is him. Look how some other cricket teams see how good he is and get him to coach them. That is why everybody beating the West Indies now, cause they don't see what they have and use it. But I tell you, these days are funny nights and I know all of the people out here will never forget Saturday, November 13 cause that is when a good man get put down in the ground." The only woman in the subdued crowd, Mabeline Thompson, said: "I was here from nine am and there ain't nothing that could stop me from seeing my boy go down in that hole today. Nothing."

The church was familiar to Connie Marshall. It was where she was taught as a girl and where Mali now attended Sunday school. Police made sure nobody from the gathering throng pushed too far forward as the Rev. Mark Harewood committed the body to the ground and the flag was slowly folded and handed to the widow. The church choir sang 'Lead us, Heavenly Father Lead us', and roses were placed on the casket. The Sunday Advocate reported: "By the time it was electronically lowered amid strains of 'Love Divine, All Loves Excelling', Malcolm's coffin was covered with red roses. Then the tears which had been threatening to fall from red and swollen eyes began to flow and it was a mixture of family, friends and fans who openly showed their sorrow.

Robin Smith recalled: "Joel Garner and I just looked at each other. This was the end and we both knew it. We were both very emotional. No words were spoken, there was nothing more to say. It was the end of one of the most profound experiences of my life - one I hope never to repeat." Marshall's mother, Eleanor, was overwhelmed by the tide of worldwide condolences. "I am sad but very proud," she said. Gayle Alleyne, a writer with the Sunday Sun, remembered the graveside scene. She wrote: "Almost uncannily, just before the cortege arrived there, the noisy departure of a Concorde from the nearby Grantley Adams International Airport drew much attention. Upon reflection, its action - slicing through brilliant skies - seemed a unique salute to one who shared a passion for speed and precision." At 12.13, it was all over.

PART TWO

Malcolm Marshall wrote 'Marshall Arts' (1987) to encompass his life from its start until 1986 when he was at his peak. It was partly a commercial decision to produce a ghosted autobiography while he was still only 28 to take advantage of his pre-eminence in world cricket at a time when many of the game's followers wanted to know more about him. At that stage he was writing a regular column in the Daily Mirror and his views were always strongly-held but completely fair, typical in fact of the man himself.

We reproduce 'Marshall Arts' here with additional, updated comments and tributes from friends and former opponents after each chapter, giving valuable insights into the man and the way he led his sadly shortened life. In the first chapter, for instance, Marshall writes of growing up in Barbados, his obsession with cricket, his lack of scholarly inclination and, perhaps most surprisingly, his apparent lack of ambition. If others had not recognised his potential and nurtured it he might never have surfaced as others of equal talent, he claims, did not. This is all the odder because Marshall earned a reputation for determination and a fierce competitiveness in all matches, great or small. Even allowing for teenaged angst and indifference, there was nothing about his early life which suggested a driven man, as Marshall certainly was.

1.

Surprise Selection

THE RADIO WAS ON, loud and clear. Pop music helped the long, tedious days in the storeroom of Banks Breweries pass a little quicker. Today was just another counting bottles and dreaming of cricket. The music stopped. It was news time. I hardly ever listened to the news; as far as I was concerned it merely interrupted the music which eased my boredom. This time, though, it was different. The news reader suddenly grabbed my attention. 'Major shocks in the West Indies touring party for India,' he said. Out came the names, one by one, and there in the middle was Marshall of Barbados. I have never been so staggered, so utterly transfixed. Was I dreaming? Was it a mistake? Had they got the wrong man? Had my fantasies, fuelled by hours and weeks of mind-numbing repetition, finally got the better of my brain? I desperately wanted the newsman to say it all again. I just could not take in the sheer enormity of the announcement.

I knew, of course, that West Indian cricket had been thrown into turmoil by the Packer affair. World Series had claimed all our best players and the Caribbean cupboard was decidedly bare in 1978, but never in my wildest dreams did I imagine a raw novice like me would be on the plane to India. To be honest, I had no idea where India was! Geography had not been a strong point at school; after all, I had not expected really ever to leave the tiny confines of my native island. That was my world, the beginning and end of it, yet now I was on my way to a place I knew nothing about - as a professional cricketer. I had no right even to be considered. Of course I wanted to play for the West Indies. I thought about and planned little else in my life. It was my ultimate ambition; everything I lived for, but in my estimation it was all a long, long way off.

I was still staring, absolutely shell-shocked when a ringing phone

19

brought me temporarily back to reality. I picked it up, my hands still shaking. 'Congratulations,' said the voice at the other end. It was the great Wes Hall, a legend in the West Indies, a god in Barbados and public relations officer for Banks Brewery. 'Get yourself together, you're on your way.' I was too stunned to make much of a reply. At least he was able to confirm I had not been going mad. Why me? was the sum total of my reaction. What other nation would pick a player with just one first class match under his belt? That was the limit of my experience. No wonder I was so dazed. Could you imagine England choosing a player with only one county match behind him? Or Australia beckoning forward a 20 year-old rookie with a single state game to his name? There was no time to gather my thoughts: Ready or not, I was about to become an international cricketer.

The West Indies Board of Control defended such an outrageous choice by telling the world that the young Marshall, who bowled slightly above medium pace and could bat in the middle order, was 'a player for the future', a phrase which has stuck with me ever since. Not surprisingly, my elevation from nowhere provoked a storm of reaction, particularly from other islands where, even allowing for the dearth of available talent, there were players who might have been thought to have prior claim to my place.

The phone in the storeroom scarcely stopped ringing once the composition of the touring party had become public knowledge. It was hard for me to make much of a comment, or one that made much sense. I was too overwhelmed to say anything other than that I was delighted and shocked all at the same time. I floated home that night to tell my mother and family. They could hardly believe it either. But even in the sanctuary of our little home in the St Michael district of Barbados there was no respite. The phone was red-hot with friends, relatives and well-wishers congratulating me. Reporters soon tracked me down, as they had done at the brewery, and all I could promise was 100 per cent effort. I had no intention of letting such a golden opportunity, presented when it was least expected, slip from my grasp.

Once I had been able to gather my thoughts and my wits, I decided to celebrate, but not in the way players elsewhere in the world might have done. There was no champagne - I hardly knew such a substance existed - nor a night on the town. Instead I relaxed and came to terms with the news in the manner I enjoyed best, by playing cricket. With a palm tree as a wicket, I played bare-footed among my friends with a softball in nearby Queens Park. I don't suppose many other future Test players have greeted their selections in such a way but this was how I spent much of my spare time and most of my evenings - and tonight was no different. My pals shook my hands and slapped my back and then redoubled their efforts to get me out on our improvised strip. That's the way things happen in Barbados and had Test cricket not intruded, I would probably still be playing that type of game and enjoying every minute of it, as I did that warm Caribbean evening as the sun slowly dropped behind the palm trees and beyond the sea.

As I made my way back home again, my mind was still full of questions. I was still mystified. One match for Barbados was all that I had to offer and a century for my club, Banks, two days before the announcement could have had no bearing on my selection. But I was not complaining. There was no happier cricketer in the world that night.

Cricket had been my life ever since I could stand upright and hold a cricket bat - or at least our home-made apology built from anything which remotely looked like one. I played morning, noon and night every day of my life. Not even school could get in the way of my obsession with the game. There was no question of us playing football or any other game for very long. It was cricket, cricket and more cricket. Our matches, played in the streets, in the parks and on any piece of wasteland, were automatically transformed into Tests at Lord's or Sydney, although we had no idea what those sort of places were really like. That just didn't matter. Sides were drawn up, with the West Indies against England the most popular, and our struggles were every bit as real to us as the Tests themselves were to the big names.

Yet it was my first encounter with Gary Sobers which lit the fuse of what was much later to become a burning ambition to play for the West Indies in something other than my imagination. Like Wes Hall, Sobers was an absolute deity in Barbados. He could do no wrong; a national hero loved by every one of the island's 250,000 population.

Like thousands of other cricket-mad youngsters I crammed into the Kensington Oval in Barbados to see him in action in March, 1972 as a highly-impressionable 13-year-old when he lead the West Indies against the visiting New Zealanders. The record books show how the West Indies were all out for 133 in the first innings in spite of 35 from Sobers and New Zealand had every reason to anticipate a comfortable win when they rattled up a massive 422 in reply. But then, right on cue, Sobers stepped from the pavilion to save the match with a truly majestic performance. I will remember it to my dying day. He and Charlie Davis of Trinidad took apart the New Zealand attack. Davis had a fantastic technique and he made a fine 183 but it was Sobers I shall treasure. That casual walk with the collar turned up. What a sight he was to us boys! Where Davis did everything by the textbook, correct and orthodox, Sobers produced all the shots - frequently from a textbook of his own. Every run was greeted with a roar; this was how cricket should be played. The great man was dropped when he had scored 87 and he went on to make 142 of the best runs I have ever seen.

In my estimation an ordinary left-hander can look awkward. Not so Sobers. Here was genuine class and I lapped up his every languid movement. The outcome was one of the most exciting days of my young life as Sobers and Davis helped the West Indies reach 564 for eight, thereby ensuring a draw. For weeks afterwards I wore my collar turned up and practised for ages to perfect the Sobers walk. Clive Lloyd sometimes thinks I have never shrugged off my idolatry. When I lapsed back into my Sobers step he would wake me up by calling me 'Sobey'. Clive knew about my love of the great man. 'Come on, Sobey,' he would say. 'Your turn to bowl'.

Barbados is not a very big island - about the same size as the Isle of Wight - but we have a proud reputation for producing top-class cricketers, of whom Sobers is still regarded as our greatest gift to the game. The West Indies team is packed with Barbadians and there is always a great feeling of national pride if we win the inter-island Shell Shield competition.

Despite being a loyal Barbadian though, as far as I am concerned there can be no greater achievement than to play for the West Indies and I shall fight for the right to do so for as long as my body will stand up to the rigours of playing virtually 12 months a year all around the world. I can't see myself playing county cricket much beyond the age of 30, however, not because I don't enjoy it, but because as a fast bowler my bargaining power will begin to diminish. Although I sincerely want to keep my place in the West Indies squad for a few years more the last thing I want is to turn into a medium paced bowler simply to keep my career going into the late 30s.

I am at the peak of my powers as a cricketer and yet there have been many times when I might well have fallen by the wayside. For a start the golden beaches of Barbados, a magnet for tourists, almost claimed my life on no fewer than three occasions. Even now I don't like swimming, much as I love the beach itself. But when it comes to entering the water then that's a different matter because I begin to feel decidedly uneasy if my feet are not touching the ground. My nervousness stems from two incidents at the Acquatic Beach and one at the harbour pier in Bridgetown. They still provoke terrifying nightmares. The nearest scrape was when I was having swimming lessons, ironically enough. My lifejacket came off and the swimming coach, unaware of my distress, told me to fight against the cramp which suddenly seized my body. I tried. I fought and fought but I started to swallow water and to sink. It was only as I thought I was about to drown that he plunged in to rescue me.

My fear of the water, however tempting it looks to everyone else, has lived with me to this day and it is a phobia I am unlikely ever to conquer. I preferred dry land as a boy and that meant cricket. Growing up in the St Michael's district, I must admit that I never thought I was in any way exceptional as a cricketer. There were many of my contemporaries whom I considered every bit as good as me but, for one reason or another, simply failed to carry on the promise of their childhood and youth and have the luck to become, as I have, an international cricketer making a living out of what was once a hobby.

I had one great advantage. I was fortunate enough to come from a happy, close-knit home - and I suppose looking back now, I was a bit spoilt as a child. My mother, Eleanor, brought me up and we lived with my grandparents after the death of my father, Denzil, when I was only a year old. He was a policeman and he broke his neck in a motorbike crash. My mother subsequently remarried and I now have a half-brother, Michael, who's a tiler by trade, and Cheryl-Anne, a half-sister. My mother was, of course, a big influence in my life and I am delighted to say she has recently been planning her first trip to England to see my home near Southampton and to keep an eye on me. My grandparents doted on me and it was they who watched over me while my mother went to work as a cashier at Moses' store in Bridgetown's Swan Street.

We lived in a four-bedroomed wooden house on a main road and though all the facilities like toilets were outside, like most houses in that part of the island, I cannot ever remember thinking we were poor in any way. Having tasted more luxurious accommodation around the world I suppose it is fair to say it was all a bit rudimentary but with two aunts and an uncle also living in the same house, it was always a lively place and always full of laughter. My Aunt Shirlene, now living in the United States, has a curious claim to fame because she was the first woman bus driver in Barbados: We were all very proud of her!

With so many adults around I got everything I wanted, much to the irritation of my grandparents, Lillian and Oscar, who tried to keep me out of trouble. The kids in the area had a reputation for fighting and they did not want me getting caught up in their dubious activities, but the temptation was always too great and there was no doubt I deserved the occasional lashing I received from my mother when she got home from work, tired by a hard day at the store. I was small for my age, indeed I'm no giant now, but the bigger boys showed me no mercy when it came to playing cricket as we frequently did using bark from the palm trees for stumps. I may have had a natural aptitude for the game but that counted for nothing against superior physical strength, and their philosophy was a simple one when it came to bowling at me: the quicker I was hurt, the quicker I was out. We played all day and there is no question that those street games certainly toughened me and, in a way, I am grateful for that, however unpopular it made me with my mother.

David Murray, the wicket-keeper, was from the same district but Wes Hall was our best known cricketer. He was an inspiration to us because we knew that if he could make it to the top there was no reason why other boys could not emulate him. We all wanted to be Wes Hall in our street games unless, of course, it was my turn to be Sobers.

It may come as a surprise to many people and, I hope, a disappointment to many batsmen when I reveal that I nearly chose to become a wicket-keeper. Even now I wish sometimes I was in Jeff Dujon's place behind the stumps for the West Indies, especially when I am feeling tired after a long bowling stint in the heat. As a schoolboy, before I started taking the game more seriously, I was always the wicket-keeper, partly because I loved the constant involvement and partly because I was so much smaller than the other participants in our street and school games. The older boys were much stronger than I was and when I first went to St Giles Boys' School, using a soft ball for our inter-class matches, I considered myself a batsman and wicket-keeper.

At 5ft 10 1/2 inches and 174lbs I'm hardly in the classic mould of powerfully built fast bowlers, and as a nine and 10-year old I was always just about the smallest boy in the class. Fast bowling was for the bigger boys and I was quite happy diving and sprawling about as wicket-keeper. What's more, fast bowling looked distinctly like hard work and if I was ever pressed into turning my arm over, it was always with a great deal of reluctance. Even at that age, though, I had developed the shoulder action which has been my trademark in world cricket and which has been the major reason why I have been able to generate so much of my pace. St Giles was responsible for beginning my real interest in the game, I suppose. Every break-time was spent playing our own improvised versions and every games lesson was devoted to yet more cricket. My home was two miles from school and at the end of each day I would run home to join the hastily assembled games anywhere within the vicinity of our house. Errol Yearwood, a cousin who still plays club cricket in Barbados for Texaco, and my grandfather Oscar Welch encouraged my passion though, like me, they saw my future in the game as a wicket-keeper/batsman and certainly not as a quick bowler. It was only after I graduated to Parkinson Comprehensive, elsewhere in St Michael, that I finally emerged from my squatting position as wicket-keeper to begin my career in its more familiar form.

At the comprehensive school my involvement became even more intense: There was not a spare moment when we were not playing cricket: To us there was simply nothing else in the world and certainly not school-work. Each lunchtime was spent playing cricket in the playground and it was not uncommon to go three or four days without getting a knock because the natural excellence of so many batsmen made it impossible to dismiss them and our rules stipulated a boy batted until he was out. This is probably the reason I became a bowler. I became so exasperated not getting a bat that I figured the only way to get a chance was to get up and bowl a few people out myself. I soon found I was good at it.

Sometimes our games carried on long after we were supposed to be back at our desks; school bells fell on deaf ears, particularly if you had just got to the crease after four days of waiting for your turn. Lunchtime food was completely ignored, our hunger was only for cricket - even if it did get us into trouble with our teachers. As a result I confess I am no academic. I loved Maths - in fact I still do - and I was good enough at English Language to pass both subjects before school and I parted company when I was 15. Subjects like History and Geography bored me to tears. History seemed so ancient and irrelevant and since I had no anticipation of ever leaving my own paradise, the rest of the world failed to matter. My disenchantment with both disciplines must have been obvious to my teachers and, in retrospect, I have every sympathy with them. I was not an ideal pupil. Not surprisingly, they often resorted to throwing me out of the class for talking too much or playing around when I should have been paying attention, but even then that worked in my favour. Freed from having to listen to subjects which didn't interest me, I would step out into the sunshine and - wait for it - played cricket, either by myself, reliving every Sobers shot, or with other boys despatched from their classes for a similar inability to listen.

Errol Lorde was my best friend and, like me, a cricket fanatic. Errol was probably a better player than I was. He had enormous natural talent and I have no doubt that he could have been playing with me for the West Indies had he pursued his schoolboy interest in the game. Like many Barbadians the harsh realities of making a living got in the way of his dreams and he was never able to fulfil his tremendous ability. He later became a born-again Christian and cricket is little more than a pleasant memory of his childhood now. Indeed the church plays a big part in life in Barbados and although I have lapsed in the meantime, religion was my only diversion from cricket when I was growing up. As a committed Christian myself, I regularly attended the 8.30 service every Sunday morning and in the afternoon, between 3.00 and 6.00, there was Sunday School. The full implications of the religious teachings may have passed me by but there was one overriding compensation which made those three hours absolutely compulsory. We played cricket. Needless to say, I never missed Sunday School, bible in one hand and cricket ball in the other.

But my knowledge of the game, its tactics and its exponents was still limited and I was getting by on natural ability alone, though I was never short of top class club cricketers and teachers, who had played the game, to offer me advice. To Nolan Clarke I owe more than most.

When I eventually joined a club called Spartan I was still a batsman occasionally bowling a bit of medium pace, mostly outswingers. I suspect I was nothing out of the ordinary except for my shoulder action which provided the potential which Nolan was quick to spot. Nolan was typical of many Barbadians, rich himself in potential but never able to be in a position to exploit it. In my opinion, and I don't say this lightly, I believe he had more ability than Viv Richards but the farthest he got for one reason or another was to play for Barbados. Nolan noted how I always looked down as I was about to bowl and recognised it as a technical deficiency. He implored me to bowl faster, as quickly as I could. Then he told me to look upon bowling in the same way that I would a long jump. He used to put down a piece of paper or something similar near the stumps and told me to approach like I was a Carl Lewis - with increasing speed and to hit like I was about to take off. It was a sound piece of advice and I still think of it even now if I run into no-ball problems. Once I had mastered this new approach and moving in at a far greater pace, I was able to ally my new technique to my natural shoulder action and I was soon reaping the rewards at club level.

This was long after I had begun to make my mark in organised schools cricket, though my impetuosity and my stubborn inability to heed well-intentioned advice from schoolteachers almost killed off my career before it had got beyond its infancy. At 13 I was considered good enough to play for the school side in the Ronald Tree Cup at under-15 level. The following year, as number five batsman and medium-pace bowler, I was in the team on a regular basis but in those days I refused to be told anything. I thought I knew it all and that my natural ability would always see me through any crisis. My fondness for hooking and pulling cost me dearly in those school matches, much to the annoyance of my games teacher, Maurice Morrison. Virtually every game I needlessly sacrificed my wicket exercising my favourite shots. In the end he could tolerate my disobedience no longer. He warned me in the strongest possible terms than unless I cut out the hook and pull from my repertoire I would not be part of any team he organised. I thought I knew best and in the next match was caught hooking. He was as good as his word. For the next school match, against Foundation, I was dropped. To say the least, I was stunned. I was too proud to apologise and too shocked to plead for another chance. I felt ashamed and angered and only went along to the match to watch; left to sit on the boundary line to contemplate my folly.

Just before the start, Mr Morrison emerged looking agitated. One of his players had failed to show up. 'Marshall you will have to play instead,' he told me. Trying not to look too enthusiastic, I jumped at the chance, a wiser man for my punishment. If ever a man had learned his lesson it was me. I got my head down, eliminated the hook and the pull, tempted though I was at times, and scored my first ever hundred in a competitive match. Mr Morrison did not know whether to laugh or cry but I'm sure he was as delighted as I was. 'Good,' he said when I returned from the crease. 'You can get plenty of big scores if you don't play across the line'. For once, I heeded his advice, held my place for the rest of the season and scored three more, textbook half-centuries. I had arrived.

Schools cricket in Barbados was very competitive and most of our rivals had an exceptional player or two in their ranks. Thelston Payne, who earned himself a place in the West Indies squad after some consistent displays for Barbados, was a contemporary while he attended Princess Margaret High School. Desmond Haynes was a year ahead of me, a pupil at the Federal High School; but there was one boy we all dreaded facing. Even then Wayne Daniel was a fearsome proposition. Wayne is a big man nowadays and at 14 and 15 he was not much smaller. Wayne was far bigger than any of his contemporaries and the prospect of having to take him on, bowling fast even then, led to many a late withdrawal from prospective opponents who had decided discretion was a better bet than a broken limb or two. I enjoyed my schools cricket when not confronted by someone like Wayne but, at 16 and with my Maths and English exam passes, I was tipped into the big, wide world on an island with high unemployment and I still had no real idea what I wanted to do with my life.

As a schoolboy I had had a holiday job as a cash-boy in Harrison's store in Bridgetown but that soon disappeared and I started to look for something more permanent. Eventually I joined a little company which made tiles and I can't say I much enjoyed the experience. It was hard work and it was not very well paid. I had been there six laborious months when I was goaded by a group of my workmates into going to the boss, cap in hand, to ask for a collective pay rise. Ian Whelan, the manager, was staggered by my cheek and, accusing me of being the ringleader and a trouble-maker, refused point blank. Calling his bluff, I walked out and for the best part of three or four years, never got another job. I never regretted my action. I didn't like the job and I far preferred my freedom, idly playing cricket all day long with my friends, most of whom, like me, were unemployed and with no realistic chance of getting any work. To be honest, we didn't look very hard for anything which might distract us from our life of ease. My sloth was worsened by my doting family. Not that I needed much, but my hard-working mother and my grandparents always made sure I had some money because Barbados has no dole system. They need not have felt sorry for me, doing exactly what I wanted in such idyllic circumstances. To supplement my meagre ration of cash I would play games of road tennis, a sort of table tennis, for money and I soon became a champion.

My non-stop involvement in our street and parks cricket was interrupted only by night classes in commerce and accounts but I don't believe I really thought they would ever lead to anything. At least it showed my family that I was willing to do something other than spend my days lapping up the sunshine and wasting my time on frivolous pleasures. When I was not playing cricket I would disappear into the countryside with my girlfriend, Beverley Holder, but, looking back on it, I suppose I might have made a bit more effort to find something worthwhile to do. Life, though, was easy. I didn't need much money and my friends and I saw no reason to chain ourselves to jobs we did not enjoy while we could be having fun. It was a wonderful, carefree time and the only thing I took seriously was cricket. Even so, I was not keen to get involved in any organised club cricket because I felt it would be too restrictive. Such was my lack of ambition that I would rather have played knock-about games with my friends than join a club. Everyone in Barbados wants to bat and where club games are played over two Sundays it is not uncommon for one side to bat on both days if the opposition fail to get them out. Extraordinary as it may seem, one side would bat right through every session of play, amassing a huge total and the other side might never get an innings at all. The thought of bowling and fielding for two days did not appeal to me. In our rough and tumble affairs I could be guaranteed as many as five innings a weekend, which was much more my idea of how the game should be played. Then one Sunday a cousin persuaded me to turn out for Texaco 2nd XI against St Catherine rather against my wishes. St Catherine had two bowlers, Cox and Walcott, who bowled a lot of quite quick and short deliveries but, remembering the lessons I had learnt at school, scored 80 or so batting at number three. Not surprisingly, the club wanted me to continue and after a lot of consideration I decided to carry on with Texaco but only after my cousin volunteered to pay my monthly membership fee of six dollars. Had he not done so I dare say I would have gone back to the streets and parks with my mates.

Once I became used to club cricket I began to enjoy it and for 1974 and 1975 I worked my way through the Texaco club sides before deciding a change of scene might benefit my game. For the first time I began to realise I had talent above the ordinary and after being selected for the Barbados Youth squad in 1975 I was in demand from other clubs. I went for a trial match with Empire in 1976, broke two stumps with my only three deliveries and then changed my mind by going to Spartan, a club laden with the island's top players. My promotion at Spartan was rather quicker than I had anticipated and it made me a very nervous man when, on the first day of the season, I was hastily summoned into the first team to play Wanderers when I had been expecting to make my debut in the less demanding intermediate match. The call came as quite a shock.

David Murray had been injured, hence my late call-up. Emmerson Trotman was in the team. So, too, Wayne Daniel and Alvin Greenidge while the vastly experienced David Holford, the former West Indian Test player, was our captain.

I was overawed and felt out of my depth surrounded by so many big names, to such an extent that I would rather have been anywhere else. I figured it would be best for me to hide away in the field and maybe bat at number eleven. Far from it: Holford threw me the new ball and told me to get on with it. These days I have strong views about setting my field and have frequent tactical conferences with captains, but on this particular day I was so nervous I simply agreed to every suggestion made by Holford about where they should all be placed. If he had told me to have nine slips, I would have said 'yes'. What made my discomfort even worse was the sight of the batsman. It was Robin Bynoe, another ex-Test player, who must have been relishing the prospect of taking advantage of such an ill-at-ease teenage rookie. I came in for my first ball at little more than medium as I desperately tried to conquer my nerves and bowled Bynoe a rank long hop. I waited for him to crack it to the boundary, as it deserved, but instead he flashed at this inviting present, got an outside edge and was caught behind.

I smiled weakly and felt much, much better. After that I became a regular member of the first team even though I was only 18, batting at number eight, one place below Holford, and gradually learning to bowl faster. The club was undergoing a torrid spell in which Collis King, feeling he had been made a scapegoat, had left and there were opportunities for new talent. I enjoyed my time at Spartan, batting at five when the wicket was wet because none of the bigger names relished the conditions, and gaining experience by the match. I was on my way and for the first time could see that I might actually make some sort of living from the game I so adored.

* Games teacher Dennis Depeiza told the Barbados Advocate about the powerful influence Maurice Morrison had on the young Marshall: "Maurice was a very good player and would put a coin on top of the stumps and dare youngsters to knock it off. If someone bowled him and knocked off the coin it would be given to the successful bowler. Most of the time the boys couldn't bowl him. Marshall bowled him a lot." At the passing of his old schoolfriend, Errol Lorde was a laboratory assistant at Harrison College, Barbados and on his way to work would pass Queens Park where he and Marshall used to play cricket on their own, if there were no others around. "As boys Malcolm was a better batsman than bowler. We kept in touch; if we passed each other on the road we would honk our horns at each other". Lorde did not play first class cricket. As for Marshall's mathematics, he had an encyclopaedic knowledge of his own bowling statistics however distantly they had been obtained and however trivial the occasion.

2.

Success and Access

FROM THE MOMENT I first saw David Gower in action as a curly-haired youth with the looks of a choirboy I realised that here was a player of exceptional talent. I did not have to be a clairvoyant to see that this willowy teenager was going to have a big future in cricket provided he maintained his stunning promise. My first encounter with a man against whom I have played many times since was for Barbados Youth when he was playing for the touring England Youth team which also included Mike Gatting and Bill Athey. Gatting looked, as he does now, an attacking batsman when he has time to get on the front foot. He has improved his back-foot play since then, of course, but here he did not look happy unless he could lunge forward at every ball. Athey was the most technically correct, more so even than Gower but when it came to class, flair and the ability to improvise when required, Gower was simply streets ahead of his contemporaries that day. Hartley Alleyne is no mean performer with a new ball and I should imagine he must have seemed pretty quick to the English boys as they struggled to cope with the different conditions the Caribbean provided. But twice Alleyne strayed a little in length and line and Gower belied his frail looks by punishing him with searing boundaries. I turned to a crestfallen Hartley - and I take no credit for my remarks - and I told him: 'This boy will play for England'.

We have both matured and developed since then and there is no doubt Gower has been able to confirm those outstanding first impressions of mine. I have always enjoyed my battles with him. There is little need for me to say that he is now a world-class batsman, the one player we in the West Indies camp know we have to get out. Ian Botham can destroy any attack - ours included - if he gets the opportunity; Allan Lamb is a fine player and there are plenty of capable cricketers in the England side but

Gower, in our estimation, holds the key to the England performance and his is always the crucial wicket. Little did either of us realise, that day in Barbados, how we would be pitting our wits against each other in the future. While Gower's path into the England Youth squad was being smoothed by his precocious talent, my own path to the top was by no means as comfortable. It took me more than a year to be sure of a position in the Barbados team, such was the fierce competition for places. In 1975, for instance, I was called up for the trial matches for the Barbados Youth team and I was immediately aware how many good players were available to the selectors. I was aware also that I was going to have to wait for my chance to break through.

Wayne Daniel, the big boy of his generation, was already being regarded as a Test prospect and was our number one bowler. Desmond Haynes was installed as an opening batsman while Emmerson Trotman was also in the team. The best I could hope for that year was a place in the middle order. The best I achieved was 12th man, and a reluctant one at that, for all three inter-island matches. Someone, though, must have noted my potential because Ian Clark, a benefactor to many sportsmen in Barbados, offered to give me a job at Banks Brewery, of which he was managing director. Mr Clark was an Englishman who died in 1982 but will always be remembered for his assistance and encouragement to so many young Barbadian cricketers. In return for employment and plenty of time off to play representative cricket, all he asked from us was to play for his club side. Gordon Greenidge and Vanburn Holder both at various times played and worked for Banks and now it was my turn to receive his offer.

Looking back on it now, it is hard to understand my own arrogance and stupidity. Here I was, a teenager with no job - or prospect of one - and desperate to succeed as a cricketer; yet I turned him down. 'No thank you', I said, 'I would rather stay unemployed and play street cricket or road tennis with my mates.' Mr Clark must have been shocked after showing me around the brewery to have his well-intentioned offer slapped back in his face. He had only my interests at heart because, as a talent-spotter, he saw that I might possibly develop into an above average cricketer. I was definitely not going to make Banks Brewery any more profitable, that was for sure. I doubt if anyone had ever flatly rejected an offer from him in the past and I shudder to realise now that it could have been the end of me as a serious cricketer; I could have been consigning myself to oblivion. In truth I really did not like the idea of swapping my freedom, albeit in poverty, for the daily grind of hard labour in a factory. It would have meant money in my pocket and all the time I needed to develop my career, as Mr Clark pointed out, but I simply said no and walked away into the sunshine. Luckily I came to my senses when once more he threw me a lifeline, at last awakening some ambition in me. I suppose I was a day-dreamer, longing for the day when I could be Sobers in front of thousands of adoring fans. It was another matter altogether taking positive steps to turn those dreams into reality even though Mr Clark was not the only one to tell me I had the ability to go far in the game. I don't think I doubted my own talent; it was not a question of being a shrinking violet. At that stage of my life, a happy-go-lucky teenager still coming to terms with the world, I doubted my desire to reach the top. It all seemed too much like hard work. Now, it is a different matter. I have grown up, acknowledge the need for hard work, and there could not be a more ambitious cricketer.

What had coincided with Mr Clark's offer was my development in 1976. I was in the Barbados Youth team on merit from the start and I never looked back after that awkward first year with the squad. My biggest fear had nothing to do with cricket. What paralysed me with worry was flying. I had never flown before but our games took us to the other islands and that meant, of course, boarding a plane. I used to go very silent while all around me were excited and expectant faces. I prayed all the time, suddenly rediscovering those prayers I had learnt at Sunday school and forgotten again just as quickly when it was time to play cricket. Above all, I hoped I could somehow manage not to be sick - and sometimes my prayers were not always answered. Travelling gave me the chance to discover how fortunate I was to be living in the comparatively affluent surroundings of Barbados. There are many things wrong with Barbados, as there are with any country, but it was like heaven to my mind as I compared it with the shock of Guyana's poverty where the incessant tropical rain lashed down on the shanty towns. Timur Mohamed, Andrew Lyght and Mark Harper, brother of Roger, were prominent members of the Guyana team while Winston Davis and Ignatius Cadette - later to tour with me on the West Indies Under-26 trip to Zimbabwe m 1981 - were in the Windward Island side. It was only then, playing in all three matches that I could look at my contemporaries around the Caribbean and gauge for myself the extent of what I might be able to achieve and to what I could rightfully aspire.

It was the following year that Mr Clark, undeterred by my attitude, came back a second time and offered me the same, highly flattering deal. This time, as captain of the Barbados Youth team, I agreed to take the job and to transfer my club allegiance from Spartan to Banks. It was a small sacrifice to make considering what I would be getting out of it. The prestige they received by having the Barbados Youth captain in their ranks was nothing compared to the advantages it held for me, eager though I had been to snub them a year before. During my time at Banks, when I was able to devote my attentions more fully to club cricket, I was batting at number six, bowling medium-fast and, with the team rarely out of the top three, thoroughly enjoyed myself. My progress was unchecked and I was selected to play in the one-day international against England for the West Indies youth side at Guaracara Park in Trinidad. I cannot remember having much success in that particular match but it gave me another glimpse of Gower, Gatting and Athey and the chance also to see, for the first time, Chris Cowdrey, Ian Gould and Paul Allott, all of whom have gone on to play for England. I was also considered good enough to warrant a place in the squad for the one 'Test' between the sides but my hoodoo struck again - I was named as 12th man and once more, feeling opportunity was slipping me by, I did not relish the experience.

Much as I enjoyed my cricket at the brewery, the same could not be said for the job. I derived plenty of satisfaction from my batting - more so than my bowling, in fact - but not even a top score of 109 could hide the increasing boredom I felt at Banks. My first job was as a production-line worker, watching bottles wend their inexorable way around the factory. It was not a task which required much in the way of skill or brain-power and I could go the best part of a day without seeing anyone with whom I could chat about cricket. I was earning between £35 and £40 a week but as I stared at the sunshine through the windows, it hardly compensated me for the loss of my liberty. I should have been grateful for what the job enabled me to do but, with the perversity of youth, I was not and there were times when I came near to packing it all in and returning to another favourite pastime of my teenage years - doing nothing. Eventually I could stand it no more, the sight of those brown bottles all arranged in military precision, and I went to see the kindly Mr Clark to point out how dissatisfied I was with my daily lot. He was sympathetic as usual but disappointed I had chosen to look his particular gift horse in the mouth. I can hear his words now: 'You have to start somewhere,' he told me. 'You cannot expect to walk into the best jobs without any experience.' It was advice well-meant but he could sense I might yet walk out for good and it was then that he put me out of my misery by offering me a job in the storeroom. To be honest, it was only marginally more interesting and demanding than my previous role but at least it gave me the chance to meet other people to ease the pain of each working day that separated the cricket-filled bliss of the weekends.

It is only since his untimely death back in his native England that I have felt some form of guilt for the way I failed to respond properly to the generosity of Mr Clark's spirit. Barbados cricket owes him a huge debt for the way he gave his time and his money so freely. Without him I would go so far as to say that as an island we may never have reached our present ascendancy and, bearing in mind the number of Barbadians who have played for the West Indies in recent years, the repercussions for the national team are obvious. Many people have contributed to the simultaneous rise in the fortunes of Barbados and West Indies cricket and, because he kept to the background, perhaps Mr Clark's contribution is in danger of being overlooked. But he was always fair and generous to me and without his persistence I, among others, might never have emerged from my own backyard. For I began my job at Banks the day after my 19th birthday in April 1977 as an impoverished nobody and just eighteen months later I was playing Test cricket in faraway India. The story in between reflects little credit on me or, I believed at the time, the selectors who chose the Barbados Shell Shield team.

By the start of the 1977-78 season in Barbados I was a man who felt he was ready to make an impact. Suddenly my diffidence gave way to unadulterated determination to make something of my cricket career. After two or three years when I had failed to comprehend my own potential, I was in a hurry to make up for lost time. I knew Wayne Daniel, by now a Test player, was in his prime and there were plenty of other quick bowlers in Barbados, but I saw myself as a batting all-rounder and I felt I should be able to force my way in batting at, say, six or seven and being prepared to do my share of bowling when the ball became old. To this day I have retained my love of the old ball. Some fast bowlers lose interest once the shine has disappeared; it is as if all their power rubs away with the gloss. I firmly believe a good fast bowler should be able to use the old ball as effectively as the new, even allowing for the obvious diminished movement. Most of the quick men around the world would fall over each other to use the new ball and for both the West Indies and Hampshire I am expected now to make the best of the shine, yet I have never been scared of being made to use an old one. Sometimes I think the amount of shine on a ball can produce a psychological block for batsman and bowler alike, depending on how much of it remains. Anyhow, that was the role I saw for myself in the Barbados team and I was more than a little aggrieved when the teams were announced for the early Shield matches and I was only 12th man - again.

My attitude, possibly as a result of not being in the team at the outset, was not what it should have been and my first-class career all but came to an abrupt end even before it had begun. Cammie Smith was the manager of the Barbados team and we were in St Lucia for a match. We were told by Mr Smith to be ready to catch the team bus at a certain time. Four of us missed our deadline and the manager was not very happy at this lack of discipline. As he prepared to deliver us a lecture about punctuality, he spotted a sheepish smirk on my face. If it was a gesture of defiance, it was badly mis-timed. 'What are you laughing at, youth?' he shouted at me. Being summoned in such a fashion did not have its desired effect. On the contrary, being called 'youth' hurt my pride and when he demanded an apology for my demeanour, he didn't get it. 'You will pay for it if you don't say you are sorry,' he told me. Once more, I refused. And pay for it I did. Upon our return to Barbados I was dropped from the squad for disciplinary reasons and I was left to reflect on the incident time and again as I played on for Banks in club competitions. Having had a little taste of the first-class scene I was anxious to have another and yet it looked as if I had blown my chances before I had even been given the opportunity to show what I could do. I realised I had made a grave error of judgement and since I was not going to apologise I resigned myself to the belief that my career might already be over.

While I was left to kick my heels, Greg Armstrong got in ahead of me for the match against Trinidad and there seemed no way I could now get in, even though Sylvester Clarke and myself were far more successful in club matches. Then, just when I was prepared to give up hope, I was called in, duly forgiven I suppose, for the one-day game against Jamaica. It was not a particularly auspicious occasion. I took no wicket for 12 runs in eight overs, contracted cramp and took no further important part in the proceedings. With the St Lucia incident behind me thankfully and, I had hoped, forgotten by the Barbadian selectors I had my sights on the Barbados match against the touring Australians, a high spot in the season and as far as I would have been concerned, the highlight of my whole career to date. It would also have given me the chance to find out just how good I was against fully-fledged Test players in the knowledge that some success against them ought to have guaranteed me a regular place, if nothing else. But just when I had my hopes raised, I was left out again in favour of Wayne Daniel, our island's champion bowler of the time. It was a bitter disappointment, particularly as Daniel was not at his best and proving expensive. My only consolation was the equally unexpected call to play in the Shell Shield match against Jamaica, the last Shield match of the season and, at 19 years of age, my first class debut. I won't have been the first future Test player to begin with a nought. It happened to me in my only innings of the match but I did at least make a far greater impression with my bowling. My figures were impressive with six for 77 in one innings and one for 20 in the other, a very respectable haul from my first match and I went home feeling pleased with my efforts.

I was sure now the selectors would have to take me seriously the following season and when I returned to my job in the brewery my sights were set no more firmly than on looking forward to the next year and the chance to establish myself in the Barbados team. That was my only objective as I settled down again to my life in the island, wondering, as everyone else was, who would be in the West Indies team to tour India later that year. The Packer men were out of contention and there was a lot of conjecture about the composition of the team. So it was against this background that I suddenly received my call to tell me I was to be a member of that squad. I have emphasised the shock and the way that one radio bulletin was to change my whole life. What made it more incredible in retrospect is that I was convinced that the cricket establishment held me in very low esteem. I thought my brushes with authority would always be held against me and might possibly bar me from the Barbados team, let alone the West Indies. I knew I had the ability to make the top but I was not at all sure those in a position of authority shared my sentiments. I would not have been the first talented sportsman to have disappeared without trace for no other reason than upsetting the wrong people.

After my selection it was some days before I was able to sit back and take in exactly who would be sharing my life on this trip to India. The West Indian selectors had precious little to take with them in terms of experience and proven ability at the highest level. Shorn as they were of all their big names, they were forced to fulfil the obligation of the tour with next to nothing in terms of star quality. There was no Lloyd, no Richards, no Roberts, no Holding; none of the great players who had so excitingly put West Indies cricket on top of the world in three short years since the debacle of the five-one drubbing in Australia at the hands of the Chappell brothers and Lillee. Drawing up a tour party bereft of such men must have been an awesome task and one in which they must have known that the majority of people they were to choose would never really bridge the huge gulf between the Shell Shield and Test cricket. That is why my selection was all the more incredible. They might so easily have chosen someone perhaps not as successful as I have subsequently become, but at least with some experience behind them. In the end the tour party had a distinctly second-rate look about it and I mean that as no disrespect to those who went to India and fought so bravely against the likes of Kapil Dev, Gavaskar, Viswanath and the spinners Venkat and Chandra on their own soil and in front of their own partisan supporters. It was a daunting job we were asked to undertake and in the circumstances we did admirably to lose a six-match series only one, closely contested, Test to nil.

Ours was a curious looking line-up. Alvin Kallicharran, the one top-grade batsman not to defect to Packer, was our captain and on whom so much depended. There was precious little to support him. Larry Gomes, later to become a vital ingredient in the West Indies team, had not by that time emerged as anything other than promising, but runs were expected from him. Faoud Bacchus, another with some genuine Test pretensions, was also included but of the others, like Basil Williams of Jamaica and Alvin Greenidge of Barbados, the selectors had gone for players who had performed consistently in Shield cricket and who normally would never have got anywhere near the Test team. I'm sure they would be honest enough to agree with that assessment, as would Herbert Chang of Jamaica and Norbert Phillip of Essex and the Windward Islands, two highly capable players but not at the forefront of discussions about potential Test cricketers. We still had the faithful old warrior, Holder, to take the new ball even though he was now 33 and slightly beyond his prime. Sylvester Clarke had not yet developed his fearsome reputation much away from the Caribbean and in the spinning department Raphick Jumadeen, Derick Parry and Sew Shivnarine had all enjoyed success for their islands but were little known elsewhere. David Murray, faithful deputy to Deryck Murray, was still available with Randall Lyon of Trinidad as his number two. There was also the young Jamaican all-rounder Errol Brown, another without a cap, and add those to my own total inexperience and you have a squad which could scarcely have frightened the Indians when they first saw it. They would have been grateful, though, that the West Indian Board of Control were determined to stand up to Packer and to carry on without Lloyd and his boys. I think it helped me thinking there were many others in the tour party as new to big-time cricket as I was. Had it been laced with top-class players who had travelled the world time and again, I dare say I would have become very nervous, but with the blind optimism of my tender age, I knew no real nerves - only genuine elation and excitement.

My first job, and it may seem curious to relate, was to get myself some playing gear. I had little or none of my own. I needed shirts, shoes, trousers, pads, bats, enough of everything to last a long tour when my mother would not be around to do my washing for me. Luckily all that was quickly taken care of for me by Geoffrey Greenidge, the former Sussex and West Indies opener who was an agent for Gray-Nicholls in Barbados. He soon got me a contract to supply me exclusively with his company's equipment and at last I began to feel and look like something other than an enthusiastic amateur cricketer with pretensions to grandeur - I was later to learn I had been chosen primarily as a bowler, still medium-fast, who could bat a bit when required.

I had either met or knew about all the other players and it was with great and mounting anticipation that I boarded the plane for London where we were staying for three days before continuing our journey to India and the great unknown. I had heard so much about London, one of the supreme capitals of the world, from other Barbadians who had either gone there to live and work or who had been there as visitors. They all told of its vastness; of its endless suburbs and its nightlife. As a wide-eyed boy from a little Caribbean island, I was especially keen to sample the nightlife. London was cold and gripped by a northern winter but I was immediately fascinated. It was hard to know which way to look. No sooner had we booked into a Lancaster Gate hotel than Parry, Greenidge, Clarke and myself were on our way out again in search of the famous clubs of London. Remember I was a non-drinker, non-smoker and the only girls I knew were from the same rural background as myself. It was all a bit too much to comprehend. The four of us found ourselves at the Twilight Club, a whirl of all that I had hoped for in a London club and pretty girls and drinks I had never even heard of to be discovered in all directions. We bought three jugs of beer between us and I took to its intoxicating taste with increasing relish. The girls became more attractive by the minute as the drink slipped down smoothly!

Like giggling schoolboys at our first party, we summoned enough Dutch courage to approach four highly desirable young ladies we had been eyeing across the club for some time. They saw us coming... and how! As we swayed across to chat them up, they were ready to welcome us with open arms - provided we were prepared to buy them their favourite drink, which just happened to be the very best champagne! I had heard about this famous French drink and was fairly keen to have a drop or two myself. We bought a bottle, and then another, and then another. In the end we got through four bottles of the stuff at the little matter of £23 a time. The girls must have thought it was Christmas. By the end of the evening we were hardly in a position to contradict them. Somehow, with the girls in tow, we staggered back to the hotel to take the evening an exciting step or two further. Alvin got out some brandy and that too quickly disappeared and, for the first time in my life, I was well and truly drunk. Just as I was ready to offer one of the girls the comforts of my room my plans took a nasty tumble - literally! With the lounge twisting and turning around me, I fell across a table and lapsed into a state of alcohol-induced unconsciousness. When I finally opened my eyes many hours later, the room was still, the girls had gone and my head hurt like it had never hurt before.

For the rest of our stay in London, I paid dearly for my night out.

MACO

My pockets were empty and I spent the best part of the next three days staring into a toilet bowl as I gradually eased my way back into the world of the living. It was a painful way to learn the lessons of London's sophisticated clubland. Even when we headed off to India, I was with the party in body only as I desperately fought to get into shape once more. The others got over their night out much quicker than I did and I'm afraid I had rather let myself down again. They must have wondered who they had taken on as a tour companion as I fell in and out of sleep and in and out of the bathroom. I was very inexperienced when it came to cricket and when it came to life in general, I was no less naive. When we arrived in India I was not much better and it was another two days before I shrugged off the last vestiges of my excesses. All in all it was quite a way to start my life as an international cricketer.

* If Kerry Packer's infamous World Series had not creamed off the very best how long would it have taken Marshall to be recognised at international level? He always believed that he was pitched forward a year and possibly two prematurely. Of those who represented the West Indies in 1978-79 in India only Gomes, Bacchus and Marshall went on to enjoy prolonged Test careers and only Marshall achieved true greatness. Most of the others, Kallicharran and the ageing Holder aside, were sampling only a fleeting moment in the spotlight. It was a feature of Marshall that he was always looking for players who, like himself, could be similarly promoted from nowhere. When established inter-island players failed at Test level, Marshall was perhaps influential as coach in the likes of Patterson Thompson, Corey Collymore and Pedro Collins being projected into the Test side with little first class experience behind them. As for alcohol, his first foray into London did not put him off for long. Brandy was his tipple and opponents were known at the end of a day's play to ply him with a drop or two in the hope that he might look more kindly on them or dissipate his powers next day, but it never did. He was too professional for that.

3.

Birth of a Vendetta

MY FIRST TEST MATCH innings was a miserable experience. I was cheated out and I cried all the way back to the pavilion. It is a moment I will never forget. Nor will I ever forgive the Indians, player and umpire, for what happened to me that hot and sultry day in Bangalore. The occasion was the second Test, in December 1978. I was still a boy in a man's world and I was about to learn a cruel lesson. As with every ground in India, this one was packed to the rafters with spectators clinging from every vantage point. It was a scaring place to be; a hostile environment which would have tested the nerve and moral strength of Lloyd and his troops almost as much as it did such a group of novices as ourselves.

It was my turn to bat with the West Indies poised at 383 for seven in the first innings and the crowd growing more impatient by the minute. I was batting at nine on the second morning and I was not so much nervous as relishing the opportunity of taking on a tiring Indian attack. Within a few minutes I was on my way back, sobbing to myself and swearing vengeance. Chandrasekhar was the bowler and he knew a rookie when he saw one. With his first or second ball to me there was a loud appeal for a bat and pad catch by Vengsarkar. I could hardly believe my ears. I had never got anywhere near the ball. In my short career I had never come across any form of gamesmanship; now I was about to find out the hard way how much a part of Test cricket it is. In the same over, having survived that nasty little moment, I played the ball firmly into my pads as I stepped forward to Chandra's spin. Once more the appeals spilled forward in a near-hysterical crescendo and to my astonishment the umpire raised his finger to give me out. The crowd roared their approval and the Indian players engulfed the successful bowler. I stayed my ground in sheer, utter disbelief. Surely this was a bad dream. I would wake up soon. But no, this was very real - and I

43

was out. I simply could not comprehend that I had been given out when I had so positively hit the ball. The rules stated you could not be out bat before wicket. I had hit the ball all right, and the Indian players knew it. I had been the victim of a con trick and the umpire merely smiled at me in a rather embarrassed fashion from the other end of the wicket. I wanted to remonstrate with him but I knew I was in a hopeless situation. I burst into tears as I made the long and painful journey to the pavilion. The crowd soon sensed my pathetic response and rose from their seats to pile on the agony as I made my way up the steps. Some laughed, some swore at me but the one comment which I still remember, hurts to this day. One vitriolic little man screamed at me in derision: 'Poor little boy. Look, he has not lost his mother's features yet.' His friends roared with laughter to make my abject misery all the more complete. I had been humiliated.

I don't think I have ever been more glad to see the inside of a dressing-room where I was able to continue my grief in private. Countless big names have been out without scoring in their debut innings but not many, I would suggest, dismissed in such an outrageous manner. I knew I was not out. The Indians knew it also. I vowed to get my own back one day and in that respect they chose the wrong man. I can bowl very fast, particularly when I have something to prove or a point to make. Indeed it was another four years before I got my chance and the Indian players got wind of my lingering desire for revenge. Vengsarkar was my main target - but that's another story I shall reveal later. Suffice to say, a grudge was born that day as I contemplated in my lonely silence the iniquities of life.

What hurt more even than the insult hurled at me as I fought back my tears on the pavilion steps was the way the umpire had so blatantly given what I believed was a false decision. This was Test cricket, the highest level the game could be played and yet here was an umpiring decision so laughable, in my opinion, that it would have been regarded as ludicrous by my mates had we been playing under the palm trees of Barbados. I believed in my naiveté that the standards of umpiring would match those of the players. I assumed, obviously wrongly, that Test cricket was played in the best of spirits. I had never known cheating or gamesmanship in club, schools or, in my limited experience, first class cricket. I had certainly not expected any of it in front of so many people and on such a grand occasion as a Test match. I am not, incidentally, accusing this umpire, whose name I don't know or want to know, of cheating. Indian umpires are not the best in the world. That's an understatement and it's possibly because they encounter so little top class cricket. Unfortunately Test players from every other country know they have to knock the stumps out of the ground before they will get a decision in their favour. Years later I met that umpire again. He was still smiling. 'Marshall,' he said. 'I knew you would become a good player'. Praise indeed. With a few more decisions like his my career would have been stillborn.

My growing-up process had been hastened, however, and, after all, I was fortunate even to be playing in the Test match, only my fifth first class game. As the youngest member of the touring party I had not really expected to be playing much, if any, Test cricket and to be called up in the second game of the series was an achievement in itself. My career had developed so fast from complete obscurity I had no time to feel nervous or any sense of success. Some players, better qualified than me, go through their entire cricketing lifespan without getting a cap. Yet here was I, a Test player after five matches. I should have been delighted.

For the record, we made 437 with Bacchus top-scoring on 96 and only myself and Sylvester Clarke, batting at number 11, failing to reach double figures. Now it was our turn to bowl and with Clarke dismissing Gavaskar without a run on the board our hopes were high, but on an easy-paced wicket India's famed batting-in-depth came to the fore. I bowled first change and had two spells of nine overs each in which I did little of note, conceding 53 runs, but allowing Chetan Chauhan to become the first of what I hoped would be many more Test wickets. He had scored 15 when he guided a wide-ish delivery of mine to the safe hands of Parry at third slip.

I was, of course, elated but as India ground on, I was constantly aware of the big gap between Test cricket and other sections of the first class game. Here were international players, selling their wickets dearly on a pitch which suited batsmen. In the circumstances we did well to restrict them to 371, thereby giving us a first innings lead of 66. It was a triumph for Clarke whose hostility earned him five for 126 from nearly 35 overs. I'm afraid I fared no better with the bat in the second innings and I could not even blame the umpire this time. I had made five when I was bowled by Ghavri and with one day to go, the match was interestingly poised. We were

200 for eight and with every prospect of an exciting finish looming. But we never reached the wicket that last day. The former prime minister, Mrs Gandhi, had been imprisoned and many of her subjects had taken it badly. They rioted in Bangalore and the match was abandoned as a draw because it would have been dangerous to have even contemplated attempting to start the fifth day. It was all rather an anti-climax but a firm reminder how precariously cricket survives in such prevailing conditions. In India anything can happen at any time.

The first Test in Bombay had also been a high scoring affair inevitably ending in a draw, and though I had obviously taken no part in it myself, it was all part of my education as I took in the sheer squalor and colour of such a huge and awe-inspiring city. I knew India was bigger than Barbados but that was about all I did know. I had simply not expected such poverty, such dirt and such noise. To put it bluntly, I was rather frightened by the place. There were beggars outside our hotel, proffering stumps where once there had been hands, arms and legs. It was still more alarming to discover that very often these limbs had been severed deliberately to aid their begging. We did not stir far from our hotels, the standard of which were in palatial contrast to the despair a few yards outside. To say the least, it was all experience.

In spite of my very moderate debut performance I played in two more Test matches in that series, the third at Calcutta and the sixth at Kanpur. It was in the fourth at Madras that India scraped home by three wickets for the only decisive result, but as far as I was concerned I was learning all the time. Once the novelty of the sub-continent had worn off I soon realised we were not going to get far with Kallicharran as our captain. Alvin led from the front with scores of 187 and 98 at various venues but when it came to leadership and inspiration he was not seen at his best. Even he would probably admit he was not by nature a captain. As a batsman with an instinctive feel for the game he might have amassed a prodigious number of Test runs had he not been lured to South Africa. As our captain on a difficult and demanding tour he left a lot to be desired. He would argue that he had little in the way of experience at his disposal and, of course, he would be right. But what resources he did have he used poorly in my estimation and some of our team selections were strange. Vanburn Holder was his vice captain and the two of them would retreat to slip where they spent their time conferring. Vanburn never gave less than 100 per cent for the West Indies, Worcestershire or whoever and, remembering that he was carrying the brunt of the bowling long before the West Indies were able to gather such a fearsome array of fast bowlers, his final record of 109 wickets in 40 Tests is testimony to his value. But I doubt that even his best friends would describe him as an obvious slip fielder. Mind you, I was hardly an asset at that stage of my career as I felt my way up the ladder. I was content to take in the many treasures of India, visiting the Taj Mahal, buying cheap silks and diamonds for my family and sampling some of the hotel nightclubs - with the caution of a man who had learned a valuable lesson.

In retrospect I should never have played at Calcutta, the Test which brought the curtain down on 1978, the most momentous year in my short life. It was a spinner's wicket but after taking 11 wickets in a state game I was retained and did not do a bad job, although the record books might suggest otherwise. I scored only a single in each innings and took only one wicket for a combined total of 89 runs.

My tally of wickets should have been higher but once more I ran into Indian umpires at their most bigoted. I know every batsman thinks he is not out when the umpires give him out lbw and every bowler is convinced the umpire has erred when he fails to give an lbw decision in his favour. I realise also this will sound like the bleating of yet another disappointed bowler but, to my dying day, I will remain certain that I twice had Gavaskar out leg before. It may also smack of sour grapes when those same record books show how the Indian captain went on to score 107 and 182 not out, but the feeling of indignation remains with me even now. As 12th man in Gavaskar's home town of Bombay, I noticed how he had got away with a blatant lbw but in my naiveté I had put it down to sheer bad luck. It was only after my own brush with Indian authority in Bangalore that I came to realise how little luck had to do with it. I am positive I had Gavaskar leg before but each time our appeals, loud and long, were rejected and the little maestro did not often need another invitation to go on and compile a huge score. When the second of my appeals was turned down, Kalli was moved to desert his post at slip to remonstrate with the umpire concerned. The official merely smiled back at him as they always do. I have no grudge against Gavaskar. He has scored runs all around the world on all types of wickets. He does not need such protection because, as his formidable number of Test runs shows, he can look after himself quite well enough. But I rapidly formed the impression - and it has never left me - that in his home country it is as easy to get an lbw decision against him as it is to steal the Taj Mahal. It is not easy, either, to recover from such a setback. Nowadays I would shrug off the disappointment and get on with the game all the more determined to make sure the batsman was not at the crease for much longer. As a youth, new to what I thought was obvious bias, it was a different matter.

I was lucky, though, on my first tour that more experienced players were always ready to help me, offering advice where it was needed and providing a calming influence in times of strife. Vanburn was particularly kind in this respect, since they must all have realised I was still very much a beginner at my trade. Cricket spread over five days is an altogether different concept to the three or four day game, as big a difference in fact as it is from a one-day match. That may sound like stating the obvious but until you play Test cricket over five days it is sometimes difficult to appreciate the wide gulf. The gulf was all the wider in my case because I had played so little first class cricket before sampling life at the top. It was obviously almost as much as I could do to take it all in and certainly my lack of success in my first two Tests would appear to confirm the colossal gap. Even so, I should have played in the fourth Test at Madras on a green wicket which would have suited my type of bowling. Instead I was left out to make way for an extra batsman, Herbert Chang, who was making his only Test appearance. It was a comparatively low-scoring match with India winning by three wickets after being left only 125 to win. Once India get their noses in front in a series it is difficult to pull back the deficit and with two matches to go they realised they only had to avoid risks to make sure we went home to the Caribbean as a beaten side. It was a situation tailor-made for their batsmen and in those last two Tests, at Delhi and Kanpur, six of them scored centuries against us, quietly strangling the series in the process. I was obliged to sit it out at Delhi but was recalled for Kanpur with the West Indies desperately needing victory.

Kanpur represented our last chance and, without making it sound like the dice were loaded against us, we were very unfortunate there. Gavaskar was dropped three times off my bowling before I eventually had him caught behind for 40. By then, though, the damage had been done, the

Indian batsmen profited from our errors and our chances gradually subsided as Viswanath, Gaekwad and Amarnath all scored centuries in a massive total of 644 for seven declared. There was no chance of us winning from that position and although Bacchus hit a magnificent 250 in our reply, the match petered out into the tamest of draws without either side batting a second time. It was a dull, meaningless way to end the tour and my own contribution of one for 123 and one not out hardly had me as a candidate for man of the match. My final Test record does not bear close scrutiny. In three Tests I scored eight runs at an average of two and my three wickets cost the little matter of 88.33 each.

Undoubtedly, though, I came away from India a wiser and better bowler. I had learned about flat, lifeless wickets and about the depth of out-standing batsmen ready to gorge themselves at every available opportunity on those wickets and against inexperienced bowling. I had learned also about one-eyed umpiring, fanatical crowds and the need to work hard for anything I achieved. In three short months I grew up after a crash course in the life of a professional cricketer. I acknowledge I had been lucky to get on the tour in the first place and my performance at Test level confirmed how much I had still to learn. In my own defence, if I failed to make an impact in the Tests at least I gave the selectors the right to feel justified by my displays in the other first class matches in India. In six matches I took 34 wickets at 13.29 each, including 11 in one match, and I also hit my first half-century. There was their confirmation in my promise for the future. I picked up five more cheap wickets when we moved on to Sri Lanka for a short stop but it was back in Barbados that I suddenly burst forward.

I arrived home to discover the Packer affair had been resolved and all our top players were available again to play for their islands and, of course, the West Indies. This meant Holding, Croft, Garner, Roberts and Daniel - a formidable array of talent - were all in line to take my place and I was not happy about the prospect of being consigned to oblivion so soon after tasting the fruits of touring as a full-blown West Indian cricketer. I was determined to hold on to my place even with these people, my heroes, now ready to take over again. Just to underline the depth of competition, I could not even be sure of holding down a place in the Barbados team, let alone the West Indies. Daniel and Garner were automatic choices for Barbados and Sylvester Clarke was now, like myself, a Test player in his own right. My first job was going to be getting into the Barbados team; with a limited number of matches I had to make a good impression quickly.

It was not as though I had a glittering record behind me for Barbados. I had played just once for them in a first class fixture and my rivals all had claims for getting in ahead of me. Luckily, although peace had broken out, the Packer boys did not arrive back from Australia until towards the end of the Shell Shield season. As a result Garner played only twice and Daniel once, which meant Clarke and I did the bulk of the fast bowling for Barbados. Clarke took 14 wickets but, with so much at stake, I went far better, taking 25 wickets at 16.04, twice recording five wickets in an innings and in the course of a fantastic personal run set a Barbadian record for the most wickets in a season. In the light of how little I had played it was a tremendous achievement, I suppose, and it showed the value of my hard, largely unrecorded graft on those dead Indian wickets. I found I had learned to control the ball more and, on more responsive wickets, was able to get it to swing sometimes quite prodigiously. It was the thought of Garner and Daniel coming back which provided the spur, because I had realised from the moment the Packer dispute was settled there would be no prizes for coming second best. There were times at the end of that season when my biggest rivals were not the opposition but the other bowlers in the Barbados team. Ironically there was only one occasion when all four of us were in harness at the same time, against Trinidad, and they hardly appeared intimidated by our presence. They rattled up a formidable 541 - which soon put us in our place.

About 70 per cent of my victims that season were caught behind, either by David Murray or at slip. No wonder my respect for Murray is so complete. Agile, sharp and thoroughly reliable, I rated him among the best four keepers in the world and it was unerring how he scooped up just about every edge which came his way at a time when I badly needed every chance to go to hand. I should stress the rivalry between us as fast bowlers was always very friendly but it existed nevertheless and the Barbadian selectors must have been delighted it did. Fresh back from India I was now totally committed to a career in cricket and as my reward for having reached Test status, Banks decided I should get out and meet the people as a new 'celebrity'. I was elevated to a promotions manager, a job which had me out on the road, speaking to customers and filling in questionnaires. It gave me the chance to talk cricket all day and bask in my new position as a Test cricketer. This was a way of life I rapidly grew to like and there was no way now I would give it up without a fight.

I had no great expectations of ever doing much in my capacity with Banks because of a sudden twist in my still embryonic career. Hampshire, having lost Andy Roberts midway through the 1978 season, were on the look-out for a fast bowler. Charles Knott, chairman of Hampshire's cricket committee, got in touch with the Barbados president, Peter Short, three weeks even before I was due to go on tour and simply asked if there was anyone who fitted the bill. After conferring with Wes Hall, they came up with my name. I was summoned to Mr Short's office where, in the company of Hall and Vanburn Holder, I was asked if I fancied a career in county cricket. I was staggered to be even considered, particularly as I had only played once at that stage for Barbados. Without even discussing the salary offer of about £3,500, I agreed in a flash and set off for India with the West Indies. It really was happening so quickly. The English county results were always summarised in the Barbadian papers and I read them avidly, if only to see how the West Indian players were faring. Rather like following a racehorse because you like the name, I followed the career of a player by the name of Jesty. Little did I realise that Trevor Jesty and I were to become county colleagues.

I arrived in England in the spring of 1979 ready for my new career as a professional county player to find the English spring can be a cruel season for the likes of people like myself, used to endless days of sunshine. I was given a room in a pub just down the road from the County Ground at Southampton and for the first three weeks I sat, mostly alone, shivering and dreaming of my home in Barbados. It was not a happy introduction to life in England. Our first match was against Derbyshire and I hated every minute. For the first time in my 21 years I could not feel my fingers for sheer cold. I wore six sweaters and longed for the match to finish. Gordon Greenidge realised my plight and did his best to help me settle. Gordon was by now well established at Hampshire and, having been brought up in Berkshire, was the most Anglicised of the West Indian players. But he too had experienced loneliness as a teenager on the Hampshire groundstaff and he understood my predicament. For those miserable, cold three weeks I was overwhelmed by homesickness but I was determined to stick it out, although it would not have taken much for me to pack my bags and head home again. Hampshire were undergoing a rather transitional stage with Roberts and Barry Richards now gone and the wicket-keeper Bob Stephenson in charge of a team largely on the decline after some prosperous years in the mid-1970s. Stephenson had taken over as leader from Richard Gilliat and his captaincy methods caused me many problems as I struggled to settle in. Hampshire needed a ready-made world star. Instead they got me, a player still learning his trade like many others in the team. If they expected instant results from me, they did not get them and that led to conflict with my captain. It was not his fault the team was on the way down but at that time in my career I was in no position to halt the slide.

I was content, at first, to listen and learn, never saying much to the other players as I gradually found out about the sort of people the other players were and who held the reins. My first impressions were how negative county cricket could be. The big worry was the over-rate with the possibility of a collective fine if we failed to bowl a certain number per hour throughout the season. Winning a match was not a priority when I first started playing for Hampshire. Avoiding defeat and getting through the overs were the main items on the agenda and I suspect there were other counties with similar prime objectives. I am glad to say it has all changed now with Nick Pocock and Mark Nicholas far more positive in their approach, preparing to lose a match if it means they can also stand a chance of winning. Stephenson was a highly capable wicket-keeper, in fact one of the best I've seen standing up, but he was new to captaincy and patently not at ease in the job. He had a hard task with the players he had under his control but he did not make life easy for himself and we soon clashed. Call it sloppy if you will, but I prefer to wear a tracksuit when I am practising in the nets: My 'whites' are for matches and I don't like using them for training or preparation. Stephenson probably saw my refusal to wear 'whites' as a direct affront to his authority and he took me to Mr Knott, a father figure at Hampshire and a wise counsellor to many a captain, to sort it out. The outcome was that I was allowed to practice in my tracksuit and now most players do the same without ever denigrating our status as professional cricketers. It was not a good way to start my new job and, as a result, Stephenson and I never really made it up. I demanded attacking fields and rarely got them as the team started to lose rather more than we should have done. Our aim seemed to be to bat first, even on green wickets, and hope to get 300, a position from which we should at least be able to avoid defeat.

Perhaps we should have taken more chances that season and perhaps the captain could sense also that I was by no means a match-winner. That was not his fault. My record proved him right. I did not find English conditions to my liking as 47 wickets at 22.36 would appear to testify and, staggered by the amount of movement, my batting was little short of disastrous. I made 197 runs at the princely average of 8.56. I should have done better as a bowler but I tried to bowl too fast and ran into no-ball problems. Had Stephenson's field-placings been more aggressive I might also have achieved a little more but countless times the ball would come off the edge of the bat through a vacant slip cordon. It was very dispiriting at times but I resolved to persevere as my homesickness wore off and I came to enjoy the camaraderie of the Hampshire lads.

The World Cup interrupted my first season at Hampshire and in 1980, when Pocock took over, I was on tour with the West Indies, so it was 1981 before I had a full summer, by which time the Hampshire public must have been wondering if I was ever going to deliver the goods.

* Dilip Vegsarkar made a bad enemy in Marshall, as this chapter showed, and it was never clear if the rift was healed. The general belief is that it was not. Marshall was by no means a vindictive man but he had a great sense of justice and bore a grudge for years to come, though the talented Vengsarkar enjoyed a full and productive international career. Marshall liked captains with whom he could have a rapport. Clive Lloyd, Viv Richards and, for Hampshire, Mark Nicholas all played the game positively in his eyes and with them he could discuss tactics and field placings as a match developed. In his early career he encountered Alvin Kallicharran and Bob Stephenson as makeshift captains of inadequate or declining sides and he came to appreciate firmer hands on the tiller. As for umpires, maturity taught him that top class cricket did not necessarily ensure first class decisions. West Indian Test umpire Lloyd Barker said Marshall never disputed a decision against him, but his sheer speed represented a major challenge. "When he was bowling from the end where I was umpiring he had this ability to plant his right foot on the front crease at the same second the ball was arriving at the batsman. You had to choose between watching for a no-ball and the

batsman's end". Barker said Marshall was the most genial of the fast bowlers employed by the West Indies in the 80s and would wait until much later to discuss decisions. "He always engaged in friendly discussions and had something nice to say. He had a habit of making an umpire feel more relaxed in what he was doing." David Holford was also his first captain with Barbados and a team photograph from the 1979 Shell Shield final against Guyana shows that nine of 13 pictured players went on to play or were already playing for the West Indies: Desmond Haynes, Carlisle Best, Sylvester Clarke, Albert Padmore, Thelston Payne, Joel Garner, Holford, Marshall and Alvin Greenidge. The likes of Gordon Greenidge, Wayne Daniel,Hartley Alleyne,Ezra Moseley and Franklyn Stephenson would all have been eligible but were either not available or simply not chosen.

4.

A Brush with Boycott

MY DETERMINATION to become the world's premier fast bowler has occasionally got me into trouble, not least with my own friends and colleagues in the West Indian camp. My own petulance and a batsman by the name of Geoff Boycott almost contrived to finish me as a Test cricketer way back in 1980 when the West Indies were touring England. As a batsman, Boycott commanded the respect of every bowler in the world in his heyday and he was still very much in his prime when I faced him in the first Test at Trent Bridge early in June. Gower was not yet the player he is today, and indeed played in only one Test, while Botham was struggling to come to terms with the England captaincy. This meant there was only one formidable obstacle consistently in our path - and that was the Yorkshireman, even though only a few months short of his 40th birthday.

I was still the junior fast bowler in the party, eager for a chance to show I was worthy to be considered in the same breath as Roberts, Holding, Garner and Croft. As the rookie I realised that should an opportunity come my way I had to grab it with both hands because, as it would have been obvious to everyone, these four were at the height of their powers and, as a strike force, just about the best in the world. Imagine then my feelings when I learned on the eve of the first Test Croft had gone down with stomach trouble. I was called in immediately as first change after Roberts and Holding and as a number eight batsman.

That night Lloyd laid the plans for battle and the conversation never strayed far from Boycott. He was the key to the match and possibly to the series, as we saw it. Not surprisingly I all but dreamt of Boycott and his broad bat that night as the prospect of our confrontation drew nearer. He did not disappoint us. He made 36 in the first innings in which I took the wicket of Peter Willey at a personal cost of 52 and then made 20 myself as the West Indies scraped a narrow first innings lead of 45. With the distinct possibility the wicket might deteriorate it was crucial we quickly removed Boycott in the second and it was against this background that I almost blew my future away in one mad incident. Boycott had made about 30 when I hurled down a bouncer with as much venom as I could muster. Normally he ignores them or sways out of the way, but this one must have caught the great man by surprise because he fended at it and, to a man, we were convinced Deryck Murray completed a simple catch. I was ecstatic with delight for a few breathtaking seconds until I realised Boycott was standing his ground and, to my utter horror, the umpire, Don Oslear, making his Test debut, was not budging his finger either. 'Not out' was the verdict.

For another few seconds it was as much as I could do from restraining myself from taking some kind of physical action. How could they be so wrong? I was absolutely furious and it needed the calming influence of Holding in particular to get me to go back to my mark and carry on with the over. We had all appealed for the catch and it seemed a mere formality for the decision to be given in our favour and it was with a great deal of reluctance that I made my way back to my mark. Seething with anger and indignation, I tore in, unleashed another bouncer which soared high over the heads of Boycott, wicket-keeper Murray and bounced harmlessly down to the boundary for four wides. This only increased my blinding fury and, though I regret it now, I swore vehemently at Boycott and called him a cheat. He went on to make 75 important runs and was far and away England's leading scorer in a total of 252. I recovered my senses long enough to take the wickets of Willey again and Alan Knott but the damage had been done. Soon after we had completed a two-wicket win, my delight at victory was quickly tempered by the news that Oslear had reported me for my behaviour. I knew this meant trouble but I hoped it would all be brushed away as a rash outburst from an over-zealous novice.

The next Test, at Lord's, was a couple of weeks away and I spent much of that time wondering what my fate would be. It was not until the team meeting the night before that I discovered the full consequences of my ill-timed action, witnessed as it was by millions on television. Clive Lloyd is not a man to tolerate such aggressive and juvenile behaviour. He dropped me. As a direct contrast to the euphoria of selection for the first Test, it was left to the team manager, Clyde Walcott, to tell me this time my services would not be required. He did not mince words. 'You are being left out for disciplinary reasons,' he told me. 'Do yourself a favour and never behave like that again.' There was no point in protesting. Much as I felt I had been unfairly deprived of the one wicket which mattered, I knew also that I was wrong to display my sense of hurt so openly. It had reflected badly on me and, as Lloyd's summary dismissal of me from the team had shown, it had also reflected poorly on his team. I suffered in silence, withdrawing quietly to the bar of the Russell Hotel where we were staying and, just as unobtrusively, got paralytically drunk. Croft returned to the team and took nought for 77 and nought for 24 and the match was drawn.

On reflection - and it is my only consolation from a sorry episode - it was a very good match to miss and, my punishment duly served, I was brought back for the last three Tests of the series. Restored to my number eight batting position I made 18 at Old Trafford in another draw and, with figures of three for 36 and two for 116, did enough with the ball to warrant my retention. Curiously, in the light of my development since, I still regarded myself as foremost a batsman in 1980, often pleading with the tour management for more of a chance higher in the order for county games. I find batting is like riding a bike; the more you do it, the better you become. Batting at eight or nine in the West Indies side rarely provides for anything except a bit of hitting for declaration purposes.

It was against the counties that I enjoyed most of my success on this particular tour, with 34 wickets at 12.58 each and best figures of seven for 56. I only wish I had had greater luck in the Tests but I was no more proficient at the Oval in the fourth Test, which again ended in a rather tame conclusion. Two for 77 and nought for 47 did not represent the breakthrough I so desperately sought. The series went to the fifth Test at Headingley with the West Indies still leading by that solitary win at Trent Bridge. I failed to score a run thanks to a catch behind off Graham Dilley but I enjoyed my bowling, with two wickets in the first innings and three in the second as, yet again, the match was drawn without us even getting a second opportunity to bat. The series was duly won and since this was what we set out to do, then our achievement as a touring squad was complete. On the debit side was that awful incident at Trent Bridge and the failure to take Boycott's wicket in any of my four Tests. Fortunately, others did - and that is all that really matters. On the credit side my 15 Test wickets left me third in the averages and only Garner with 26 and Holding with 20 took more. As much to the point, Roberts managed only 11 wickets and Croft only nine in three matches at the rather costly rate of 34 each. As far as the West Indies were concerned they now had another fast bowler to complement the big four. As far as I was concerned I had proved myself at least the equal of the more experienced quick men and was now possibly ahead of two of them, if only because I could bat a bit.

There was time for me to return to Hampshire for the last five matches of what had been for them a traumatic and desperate season in which they were to finish last in the County Championship with only one solitary win. After my mediocre performance in my debut season the year before, they must have wondered if I was going to be much use but the advance I had made in those 12 months was apparent in making an unbeaten 72 against Northamptonshire and taking nine wickets in the match with Worcestershire, which was to prove our only victory of the summer. Hampshire were impressed enough to make me an offer of a new three-year contract with much improved terms. I duly accepted, though I made it abundantly clear that had the money not been better I would certainly have gone elsewhere, much as I wanted to stay with them. With the tour of Pakistan to look forward to, I returned to the Caribbean as a world-recognised Test player with a healthy contract under my belt. I had learned some valuable lessons in those 12 months, starting with the World Cup in 1979, interrupting as it did that somewhat disappointing first season with Hampshire.

The World Cup was an extraordinary experience for me in that I picked up a winner's medal without playing a single match. The Packer men were back en masse and it was a worrying time for those of us who had grafted away on the unyielding wickets of India. We wondered whether we would simply be forgotten or if the Packer men might be obliged to wait, as some people felt they ought. My success for Barbados ensured I would be among the party for the World Cup. When the squad was announced there were only four of us who had been in India and Sri Lanka with the official West Indian party. The others were Alvin Kallicharran, predictably, because he was very much part of the Lloyd entourage at the time, Faoud Bacchus, reward perhaps for his 250 at Kanpur, and Larry Gomes, called in more surprisingly maybe - but he had been just about our most consistent performer in India. The West Indies had thrillingly won the first World Cup four years before and were in no mood to surrender the trophy. The Packer men, now battle-hardened, were a formidable core built around Lloyd himself, Richards, Greenidge, Murray, Roberts, Garner, Holding and Croft. It was going to be hard breaking into a team of that quality but harder still to beat it, as the rest of the world were obliged to do. I was flattered to be chosen although after what I had done for Barbados, I would have been extremely disappointed had I missed out.

But, with the politics of the Packer rumpus still echoing around, it was difficult to gauge the attitude of the West Indian Board of Control or to guess whom they might pick. I did not expect to get in right away so I resolved to use the competition to glean valuable experience. Lloyd went out of his way immediately to welcome me to the squad and to make me feel at home. He was quick to realise that I may have felt like an outsider intruding on a private party or, as a 21-year-old, somehow out of my depth. He wanted me to consider myself part of the squad and a vital member at that. To a certain extent I was slightly overawed but I kept my mouth shut and listened to others. As I was told once or twice, if you break into the squad it's harder to get out of it, which was a pleasant sentiment bearing in mind that only injuries to others would give me the chance to show what I could do. Even though there were four of us from outside those who had played as a squad in Packer's World Series in Australia, there was no animosity towards us; Lloyd and Clyde Walcott, the manager, saw to that. Had I been two or three years further advanced I too would have pledged myself to Packer. The others signed because the money and the concept were correct and had I been a bigger name there is no doubt I would have signed. Packer's intrusion had, of course, helped me to get started, so although I never actually benefited directly from the World Series, my career might never have otherwise got started in the same spectacular fashion. For that, I owe Mr Packer my thanks.

Lloyd pointed out to those of us not playing that we still had an important role to perform as what he called 'watchers-on'. We were invited to criticise and comment on those who were actually on the field of play. It sounds easy enough but to a youngster like me with so little cricket behind me, it was asking a bit much. How could I dare pull apart Roberts, Holding and co. when they had achieved so much and I had achieved so little? More to the point, even if I did have a point or two to make, how would they take it from me? I resolved to keep quiet and watch the big men at work. I could only learn from being with such magnificent players. So for two blessed weeks I wandered around England in the wake of the superstars of West Indian cricket watching them analyse, dissect and clinically murder India, New Zealand, Pakistan and finally England by 92 runs at Lord's. Since medals are obviously not awarded for Test matches, the highest accolade a cricketer can receive is a World Cup winners' medal. Many great cricketers either never have or never will have one to carry with them into old age. I picked up my first just over a year after making my first-class debut and without ever having to earn it by playing. Can you wonder that I sometimes needed to catch my breath to believe it all? Less than a year before I had been a complete unknown and yet here I was sitting in the West Indies dressing room at the final of the World Cup. At times it was almost too much to take in.

Curiously enough I found the tension was far greater among those of us in the squad not playing than among those who were. Perhaps it was my rank inexperience showing through but while most of our major players were relaxed and disciplined, I was a victim of the great pressures which inevitably surround the game's major knockout tournament: Perhaps, also, it was because I had too much time to dwell on what was happening, but by the time the final had been won and lost I felt I had a right to my medal if only because of what it had done to my nervous system. I nearly got my chance when we were due to face Sri Lanka in a group match at the Oval but it rained solidly for three days and the match was never played, each side having to be content with two points, a situation which doubtlessly pleased our opponents more than it did us.

Since I never actually took Lloyd up on his suggestion that I sit back and comment on my fellow players, my medal came as the result of my stints as drinks waiter during those matches which were played. I soon learned though how harmonious was the West Indian dressing room. I had no idea what to expect when I first joined Lloyd's army, but I suppose I would not have been surprised if there had been a few personal tensions among so many important personalities and I was pleasantly impressed to discover there were none. If any criticism was made by the 'watchers-on' no one ever took it personally. The success of the team was all that mattered and, as the rest of the world have found out, we are successful. It was an education, the whole experience, and I matured more in those two weeks than I might have done in a year elsewhere.

While I sat biting my nails, so to speak, in the pavilion I watched as we began the defence of our title with the effortless demolition of India at Edgbaston with Holding taking four· wickets and Greenidge hitting a match-winning 106 not out to set up victory by nine wickets. After our struggles in India a few months before, that particular win was all the sweeter. Sri Lanka and New Zealand were also in our group, which gave us potentially an easier passage than Group B where England had Australia and the mercurial Pakistanis against whom to contest a place in the semi-finals. Picking up only two points from the Oval, rain not only delayed my World Cup debut it also meant we had to beat New Zealand to make sure of our place in the last four. We met the New Zealanders at Trent Bridge where Lloyd's unbeaten 73 and Greenidge's 65 paved the way for our 244 for seven from 60 overs. Roberts took three wickets as we restricted them to 212 for nine thereby ensuring victory by 32 runs.

In the other group, Australia, still shorn of their Packer men, had a disastrous time. Their only win was over Canada and they were heavily defeated by both Pakistan and England to leave us with a semi-final against Pakistan at the Oval. While England booked themselves a place in the final with a nine-run win over New Zealand, we knew we would have to bat to the best of our ability if we were to be certain of meeting England at Lord's. With Greenidge again excelling with an important 73 and Desmond Haynes making 65 in an opening partnership of 132 against Imran and Sarfraz our 293 looked to be enough, but Pakistan had great batting in depth as Imran's position in the order at number eight showed. Zaheer and Majid both made big scores as Pakistan responded as we feared they might. At one stage, with Majid and Zaheer in full flow, Pakistan were 176 for one before Viv Richards took three middle-order wickets, including Imran, to form the basis of our 43-run win. And so to the final itself.

We were, of course, red-hot favourites, but that was because of our reputation and simply failed to take proper consideration of the fact that England were playing at their headquarters in front of, mostly, their own crowd and in their conditions. At 99 for four we were in trouble. Then Richards and Collis King, that cheerful one-day specialist, put on 139 in 21 overs of which King's contribution was a spectacular 86. This gave us 286 for nine from 60 overs and now England needed a solid start. I watched intently from the balcony as Boycott and Brearley duly gave it to them with a brave but far-too-slow 129 for the first wicket. That put the onus on the middle-order batsmen to make up for lost time and instead, all they lost were wickets. From 183 for two, England slipped to 194 all out and a few hysterical moments later I was being presented, in a somewhat bewildered state, with my winner's medal. If this was World Cup cricket, I was looking forward to more.

I duly returned to Hampshire to complete the season with them and crossed my fingers that I had made enough of an impression to gain selection for the tour to Australia and New Zealand, hastily arranged as it was to coincide with a truce being called in the conflict involving World Series Cricket which had threatened to engulf the entire game. My performances with Hampshire had done little to suggest in that first summer that I was a potential world-beater and the World Cup had provided me with no chance to show of what I might have been capable. If they were going to take me to Australia it would, once again, be for my potential rather than because of anything I had already achieved. That was indeed the case. When the squad of 16 was named, I was in it. With only three Tests planned and the triangular one-day series also involving England, there was not going to be much chance for those of us classed as reserves - and so it proved. I sometimes went a fortnight without a game and played in only two first-class matches, taking seven wickets and scoring 39 runs. For the rest of the time it was a question of lapping up the delights of Australia and watching the masters at work, much as I had done during the World Cup.

Four years before the Australians had crushed us 5-1 and the memory left a bitter taste for nine of our squad who had been on the receiving end of that humiliation. I had seen the series on television at home and, with Lillee and Thomson still around and reinforced by Rodney Hogg, I was a little apprehensive at what sort of greeting we would get. I need not have worried. Australia was a wonderful and invigorating surprise. I had heard so much about the place; the cleanness, the freshness and the hard and fast wickets and I was not disappointed. The welcome could not have been warmer, particularly from their uninhibited young ladies. The girls in

Australia are less reserved and formal than they are in England or the West Indies. In Australia they don't wait to be asked out; they do the asking and for a shy young man on his first visit, it was all a bit of an eye-opener. There were always plenty of bikini-clad women at cricket matches in Australia and if they take a shine to you, they soon make themselves known when the opportunity arises. I could hardly believe the number of truly beautiful girls who would hang around the foyers of our hotels, all of them anxious to meet the players - and not just to collect autographs. If they fancied a player, they asked him out and, an even bigger surprise, were quite prepared to pay their way. I have never been a shrinking violet when it comes to women but this reversal of roles, as it were, and the sheer number of them, set me back a bit but, under the world-wise guidance of Richards and Garner, who had seen it all before, I was encouraged to take advantage of everything these lovely creatures had to offer. Aussie girls love West Indians and I, for one, was not rude enough to deny their eager hospitality.

Richards was the big target for the Aussie lovelies on my first tour. He waited; they came. Big Joel enjoyed himself to the full and, as my room-mate, he made sure I soon found my way around and got over my shyness. At times it was difficult to stop going over the top. The temptations were, and still are, always available in Australia - and in plenty of wonderful shapes. Incidentally, for those who wonder how Joel, all 6ft 8 inches of him, manages to sleep I can reveal he takes a double bed - and kips down diagonally.

The girls aside, there was much else to also admire about Australia. Sydney's fast, American-style way of life did not interest me as much as Melbourne, Perth and Brisbane where the beaches of Surfers' Paradise and the fantastic golf courses provided other diversions when there were no women to distract us. From the cricket point of view there was also much to learn. I was keen to meet this legendary figure, Kerry Packer, about whom so much was talked about by the other West Indian players. There was the chance additionally to bowl at the Chappell brothers, both of whom had loomed large among my childhood heroes and among our 'Test' matches under the Barbadian palms.

I played only against Western Australia and a Tasmanian Invitation XI on the Australian leg of the tour but did have one other claim to distinction. It was during the first Test at Brisbane when I was 12th man.

Desmond Haynes came off to give me the chance to enter the action. Bruce Laird, an obdurate opening batsman, was at the crease and, with 75 to his name, was standing in our way. Lloyd despatched me to backward point, not a position I would normally claim as my own. Off the very first ball, bowled by Garner, Laird got a nick and I plunged forward to hold the catch. It was my only positive contribution to the series which we won 2-0 and fully avenged the traumas of our own annihilation in 1975-76.

Australia, we found, were not the power they had been then. Brisbane, in fact, was the only place where the Aussies escaped defeat. We found Lillee no longer relied on extreme pace, but on cut and swing, Hogg was unable to reproduce the form he had shown against England and the injury-prone Thomson was only able to play in that first Test. The other Tests at Melbourne and Adelaide provided us with massive victories. At Melbourne they had no answer to our pacemen, Roberts, Croft, Garner and Holding, and lost to us by 10 wickets. At Adelaide the same four men did the damage and we won by the little matter of 408 runs. Revenge was sweet indeed. Much as I was pleased to see us win so comprehensively it was getting a bit frustrating just watching us being so successful. Patience is a virtue but mine was beginning to wear a bit thin as I despaired of a chance to break through. The others were bowling so well in the prime of their careers and there did not seem, barring injuries, much immediate hope of me nosing in among them. So, with Australia duly vanquished, we set off to New Zealand, new territory to most of us.

Some of our party probably wished they had never set foot in the place after what happened. To describe the tour as controversial would be an understatement. Fresh from our gigantic wins over Australia and victory in the limited overs triangular series against Australia and England, I suppose we might have been forgiven for taking life easy in New Zealand where we were not expecting as tough a contest. That was not taking into account the low, slow wickets and some umpiring decisions which seemed extraordinary to us. Once again my part in all this was very small. I took seven wickets in two first class matches and even when Roberts was injured at Dunedin before the start of the first Test, I still could not get in to the team. The spinner, Parry, was preferred instead for a pulsating match where seam bowling was the dominant factor and where, requiring 104 to win, the New Zealanders got home by one wicket.

After the match our manager, Willie Rodriguez, was not slow to criticise the standard of umpiring where the West Indies felt several important decisions went against them. If that match ended with tempers frayed, it was nothing compared with what happened at Christchurch in the second. It followed another defeat, by Wellington, on what we considered was an under-prepared wicket, and the party was not exactly in the best of moods when we reached Lancaster Park. We lost the toss, batted first, were all out for 228 and then it all boiled over on what the New Zealand Press termed 'Sensational Sunday'. At tea, with Geoff Howarth on 99, we held a team meeting in which it was decided that we would pack up and go home unless Fred Goodall, the umpire, was replaced. Rodriguez managed to persuade us to carry on for the time being and, to what must have been bafflement to everyone else that day, we resumed 12 minutes late with Goodall still officiating. That evening we cleared our dressing room because many of our players had no intention of coming back after the rest day. For some of us, the tour was over. Another team meeting followed and it needed all Rodriguez' tact to get us to change our minds. We felt the umpiring was so bad it was simply not worth our while continuing and if the New Zealanders wanted to win that badly then they could have the series on a plate. We duly returned but not because we wanted to.

Then came the next big incident. Colin Croft, coming in to bowl, had an appeal turned down by Goodall, and is alleged to have barged into the umpire. Goodall complained to Lloyd and afterwards Rodriguez said it was an accident. The match was drawn but the rows went on. The New Zealanders wanted us to punish Croft by dropping him, but we refused to agree. Instead we apologised for the incident in which he had been involved and the third Test got under way at Auckland. That too was drawn and the New Zealanders began their celebrations having beaten us one-nil. Rodriguez did not appear at the end of tour press conference and Lloyd wrapped up a miserable few weeks by criticising the umpires once more. After all that we were glad to be on our way home.

* Many players have Geoff Boycott stories. Boycott has one about him. After their early hostility they came to respect and like each other. In Marshall's Hampshire benefit brochure (1987) Boycott recounted how they would always greet each other in the same manner at the start of an innings.

As Boycott walked out to bat and Marshall prepared to bowl, Marshall would say: "Mornin', Boyks". Boycott responded: "Morning, Maco." Like two bowler-hatted City types greeting each other on a station platform. The formalities were now over and the next question came from Marshall. "You hookin' today, Boyks?" Like a man who had been offered something rather unpleasant by a passer-by on the street, Boycott affected disdain. "Not today, thank you Maco." With that, Marshall would bowl him a bouncer first ball and Boycott would sway out of the way. They would each smile and the real contest then began.

As for Australia, Colin Croft recalls how on his first arrival there, Marshall's small, slim figure baffled the waiting Aussie Press. "They did not believe he could possibly be a fast bowler. Next day in a Sydney paper Marshall, a then slender 5ft 10 inches, was pictured in the middle of an array of giants. There were Holding and Roberts at about 6ft 4 inches on the right side of him and flanking him on the left at more than 6ft 6 inches were Garner and Croft. He looked more like a wicket-keeper or jockey than a fast bowler. The caption read: 'Malcolm Marshall, West Indies new chum.' Every West Indian player laughed at that picture. How the Aussies and the rest of the world must have regretted their initial assessment of Maco."

5.

Behind Closed Doors

MANY CRICKET FOLLOWERS around the world must be convinced the West Indies have only to show up and play for five days to maintain our position at the top of the ladder. This is far from the case. I realise, of course, we have had the good fortune to possess the best international team for more than a decade. Other sides envy our ability to unearth a constant stream of top-class fast bowlers to add to our array of excellent strokemakers. But success and failure have a habit of running in cycles and it could be that we shall fall from our lofty place. For that reason alone we take nothing for granted. The West Indies squad consists of professional cricketers and it would be an insult to any of us to suggest that we expect our natural ability to see us through every match from Barbados to Bangalore to Brisbane and back again.

I cannot emphasise how much of a privilege it is to be part of the West Indies set-up. Some of our players, like Richards, Haynes, Greenidge and Holding, have been permanently ensconced for years but not even they would take it for granted that a place is guaranteed. We have to earn the right to be in the squad and we have to work to stay there. Once you have been at the top it is difficult to come to terms with anything less. Clive Lloyd always made sure there was never any complacency and for those who believed they had a divine right to a place, there was often a quiet word in the ear or, sometimes, instant oblivion. The recent history of our cricket is littered with such casualties and they have been examples to the rest of us. There was never any great fuss or drama. That was not Clive's way. The player concerned simply ceased to come into the reckoning.

Clive expected us to treat every match with the greatest importance and he also expected us to make sure our personal preparation was 100 per cent correct. It was not that he did not want us to enjoy our cricket, but he

67

wanted us to get ready with the utter professionalism he demanded of himself. Now, no matter who is captain or manager, we train diligently, practice hard and treat the opposition with the fullest respect. Over the years it has been instilled in us to underestimate no one, look down on none of our opponents and, above all, to work hard at our game in the sure knowledge that the next match might be our last for the West Indies. These days we have a set routine building up to Test matches. It is one which has come to suit us and to ensure our build-up is absolutely right. When the Lloyd nucleus were playing for World Series Cricket in Australia they came across Dennis Waight, a former Rugby League player, who for the first time underlined the importance of being in the peak of physical fitness. His argument was that all top sportsmen should be in top shape the whole time, even cricketers. It was a new concept to cricket and, although it may have caused a few raised eyebrows in certain quarters, one which was instantly welcomed by the West Indian players.

When World Series Cricket ended, Dennis was not forgotten and today he is very much part of our set-up in the West Indies camp. Wherever we go he comes with us and is as vital to us as any player. Dennis takes us for routine exercise but he also has individual sessions designed to help players overcome an injury problem or to strengthen weaknesses like my back. Our preparation for a Test match begins two days before the big day with Dennis, or 'Sluggo' as he is known, playing a key role. Usually he has an injury or two to massage and work on. Then he will take those of us not requiring specialist treatment on a rigorous set of warm-up exercises. Nobody goes into a Test match on behalf of the West Indies in anything less than the perfect condition, for which Dennis has been responsible. The exercises are followed by nets with everyone in the squad, including those who are unlikely to be in the team, taking part with both bat and ball.

With all the physical preparation taken care of, the build-up continues with the team meeting on the night before the Test. This usually takes place at about 6.30 before an evening meal. Here we discuss our tactics for the forthcoming game and the composition of the opposition. The captain will lead the discussion which is always attended by everybody. Our own team is often named at the team meeting, although injury might sometimes delay an announcement until the morning of the match after fitness tests have been carried out. Each of our players will be told what is expected of him and then we go into the strengths and weaknesses of our opponents. As a bowler I know, after years of constant involvement, what most recognised batsmen can and cannot do at both Test and county level. It is no great feat of memory; just part of my job. We talk of all the opposing players and every possible permutation of their potential batting order and about the bowlers they might use against us. Nothing is left to chance. Lloyd liked to have a set match plan and another up his sleeve in case the first started to go wrong. He called them, simply, Plan A and Plan B. If Plan A looked like failing he would say, 'Time for Plan B, fellas' and we all knew exactly what to do. Our team talks are never deadly serious. Desmond Haynes or Gus Logie make sure of that with a wisecrack or two, but the underlying message is always given and taken in a professional and responsible manner. When we break up after about two hours every player, including the reserves, knows precisely what is anticipated from him over the next five days. We may get beaten for a variety of reasons but lack of proper preparation will never now be one of them. We are mentally and physically in the right order by the time the two captains toss and the match gets under way. There may have been a time in years gone by when West Indies teams relied solely on superior natural ability. But not any more. No team could better our run-in to an important occasion.

After the meeting breaks up we go out for a meal. My own preference is for Chinese food but I am not fussy because so much depends on where in the world we are at the time. Sometimes, of course, it is not always easy or advisable to wander off into the streets in search of a restaurant, in which case we have no alternative but to eat in our hotel. No one tells us we must not drink alcohol on the eve of a Test match but we are old enough to know it is not advisable in great quantities, if at all. It is left to our discretion, although we are fully aware of the consequences if our performance was to suffer the next day. For most of us it is a question of relaxing before an important day. We have done the hard part of getting ready.

The tension is beginning to mount so we need to wind-down in order to wind-up. This is where the team's jokers come into their own; this is where they are most needed. Desmond is the court jester. Sometimes we just call him 'Comedian' because a joke or a laugh is never far from his lips. Little Gus from Trinidad is not far behind him when it comes to merrymaking. Some of our players can become a little uptight on the eve of a Test match but Desi and Gus make sure we relax and go to bed in the right frame of mind. On one occasion Desmond tied three knots in his tie so that it looked about three or four inches long. He had been going through a lean period as an opening batsman at the time but it had not destroyed his sense of humour. When we asked him why his tie had shrunk he told us it had got shorter because he was short of runs. Sounds trivial, I suppose, but as a way of destroying any anxiety it was brilliant.

On the morning of the match we rise early because we still have plenty of work to do before the game starts at 11 am. We get to the ground at least a couple of hours earlier when Dennis is vital again, having us run around the ground doing a series of exercises designed to loosen up every part of our body. Every member takes part in those exercises and the non-playing reserves also play a full part in the net practice which follows. Clive has been responsible for so much of the present success of the West Indians: one area he considered essential was team spirit. He did not want any jealousies to build up because of lack of involvement. That is why the reserve players are actively encouraged to share in all our last-minute preparations and for those not asked to do 12th man duties, there is compulsory net practice once the match itself has started. We are all squad members and, in every sense, all team members. As a result of this policy team spirit has always been exceptionally high and dressing-room rivalries reduced to a minimum.

Once the hard work of a Test match morning is over we await the result of the toss of the coin. What happens next is entirely dependant on whether or not Clive or Viv has struck lucky. If we are fielding first I feel I must be fuelled up in the right way. There is no point in attempting to bowl flat out at my pace for 15 or 20 overs a day if I have a bellyfull of heavy food or, worse still, I have no food at all. Fast bowlers expend plenty of effort and that requires the right sort of energy-giving material. Before we go out on to the field I drink plenty of liquid, usually fruit juice. Sometimes I knock back gallons of it and when we come in at the intervals I drink still more. I don't necessarily recommend it to every aspiring fast bowler but I do know it suits me because it provides the body with the vitamins it needs without over-burdening it with lumpy food which may be hard to digest. Sometimes I will augment this rather harsh, self-imposed abstinence with some fresh fruit but the result is the same. I never go into a long, hard day's bowling without plenty of liquid - and many of the West Indian fast bowlers have much the same beliefs when it comes to their diet during a big game. If we are batting, it is a slightly different story. The dressing room goes quiet while the opening batsmen get ready to take on the opposition and the new ball. For the first few overs everyone watches intently to soak up the atmosphere and to take in what the ball is doing, how the wicket is playing and to see what ploys our opponents might have devised. Once the pattern is established and the tension lessens the West Indian players settle down. Some continue to watch with avid interest, others, like me, find other things to occupy our time.

A favourite pastime among many cricketers is backgammon. Jeff Dujon taught me how to play the game and now he can't beat me! Gordon Greenidge and Joel Garner also learned at the same time and we have some rare tussles behind the closed doors of our dressing room while the rest of the cricketing world is riveted to what is happening outside. Sometimes our concentration is shattered by the uproar which accompanies the fall of a wicket and we rush to a window to find out the news for ourselves, or we congregate around a television set to see a replay of a dismissal. It is astonishing how often the learned tones of a commentator pontificating on a batsman's downfall conflict with the verdict of the player himself when he re-enters the sanctity of the dressing room. The flurry of such excitement soon subsides and we return to the backgammon as the other guys attempt to prevent me being the champion. At Hampshire we even held our own tournament with a £2 entry fee. Robin Smith organised it, put himself in the easiest of the two groups and was promptly knocked out in the first round. I was in the harder group, came from behind in all my matches and scooped the pool - one in the eye for Robin!

Cricket is renowned for its superstitions but among the West Indian players there are remarkably few quirks or individual preferences. I have only one minor one, which takes a bit of explaining and is not a real superstition, or so I ask you to believe. When I buy a new pair of pads, the feel of them has to be absolutely right. Some players prefer the pads' buckles to be on the outside, some on the inside. I simply discover which pad fits which leg the best and then make sure I always wear that particular pad on that leg by marking each 'left' and 'right'. I suppose it makes no real difference which pad is on which leg, but so much of cricket is psychological and any top player will tell you of the need to feel comfortable at the crease. Any distractions caused by the gear we wear will play on the mind at a time when one should be concentrating 100 per cent on the action. I have heard of some players who like to run out on to the field in a certain position in the pecking order behind the skipper. We have no such peculiarities, nor are there any in the dressing room itself. Greenidge, one of our quieter members, likes a corner if it is at all possible. Even he might be at a loss to explain the reason, but if it makes his preparation easier and makes for peace of mind, then no one will stop him.

The banter in the dressing room soon cuts any tension but for every Logie and Haynes, providing the chat and laughs, there are as many who prefer a calmer atmosphere. Larry Gomes and Winston Davis are the quietest without ever being morose or rude in any way. Of all our players they are the ones who prefer their own company and a little solitude as we get ready for a big match. But they will both join in any fun and I can honestly say there has never been a serious rift or clash of personalities among the West Indian players in all the time I have been connected with them. Occasionally a little quarrel will break out but in squads of 16 or 17 travelling to all parts of the world and living on top of one another, there is a refreshing lack of trouble and trouble-makers. We soon come to know who might be a little tetchy or potentially a little sensitive and so we never do anything which might cause a slight flare-up. Clive Lloyd, with his shrewd analysis of each player, saw to that and the legacy is a touring band of players all of whom tolerate each other's individuality and who are bound together with a team spirit second to none. I realise that some people outside the West Indies believe there must be some clash between the big names but I can assure them we have absolute harmony and this contributes to our success every bit as much as our natural ability to play cricket. We share a common ambition to be top of the world and there is not one ego which has ever been allowed to intrude in our shared aim. Not even Viv himself is bigger than the team, and he would be the first not only to acknowledge it but also to encourage the rest of us to look upon ourselves as equals.

If we had to hold a competition for the prize sleeper among our players certain finalists would be Richie Richardson, Winston Davis and Joel Garner. It is not uncommon for them to drop off on a bench in the dressing room or anywhere at any time. They seem to have a great capacity to close their eyes and switch off. I suppose it helps them relax from the rigours of touring or the demands of a big match, but I can assure you they are always wide awake when it really matters. Davis is among a big group of us who love our music. There is no greater fanatic of reggae, calypso and slow dance music than me but I have some serious rivals. Eldine Baptiste, Gomes and Dujon will also immerse themselves in the music of the Caribbean at the slightest opportunity. At home in Barbados I have a huge collection of records, mostly of reggae stars like Sparrow and Mighty Gabby, who are obviously not so well known outside their home islands, but who mean so much to those living there.

When the West Indies are travelling abroad we have to attend some social functions of a formal nature but one of the most pleasing factors about visiting countries more than once is the friends we make. As a result, we are asked to people's homes and parties and there is scarcely a city in the cricketing world in which I do not have someone I know. There are always other ways to relax and some of the West Indian players will take it easy, like me, by playing badminton, table-tennis, pool or darts. It takes the mind off the game for a little while and for a few precious moments it is possible to think of something else. I have just started to learn the vagaries of golf. Many of our players are top quality golfers so I figured it was about time I found out more about it. I had my first lesson at the Meon Valley club near Southampton and promptly lost five balls - I am prepared to concede I may need a few more lessons!

I have already emphasised our strength of team solidarity and I suppose my closest friends in the West Indian camp are Haynes and Garner. I guess this is because we are all from Barbados but no one should think we are deeply divided by whichever island we might come from. Joel and Desmond have been friends of mine ever since I was a youngster. Joel is a little older than Desmond and me but our careers have run parallel courses. Joel may be a demon on the field but he is much liked by the rest of the squad. He is an amiable giant and I sometimes wish he had a meaner streak when it came to playing cricket. Baptiste is another great mate of mine - on long tours you can never have too many friends. We need each other's company and I dread to think what life might be like if ever any ill-feeling developed or the party divided heavily into dissenting factions. The credit for our closeness is ultimately down to the management and, in my opinion, Clive Lloyd in particular. He has been a great influence on and off the field and we all have an individual debt to him.

When I first came into the international scene Alvin Kallicharran had been made captain virtually by default in that he was one of the few experienced players not to have been scooped up in Packer's net. The West Indies Board of Control turned to him in desperation and he did his best not to let them down. But though a brilliant batsman and an amiable man, he was indecisive and not firm enough when it mattered so I imagine the players were not the only ones pleased, not to say relieved, when peace was made between the game's ruling bodies and the Packer organisation. This meant Lloyd was freed to take over the helm once more and we were soon back on the right course. Clive is a powerful and influential personality without ever seeming to be the big boss man, cracking the whip to get us into line. By nature he is quiet, but there was never any questioning of his authority. He was the boss - and we all knew it.

Clive was slightly older than the majority of us and he had a formidable record already in Test cricket by the time most of us first broke into the squad. Indeed, he had been playing Test and county cricket while many of us were schoolboys. In the eyes of many of us he was a hero, yet now he was a colleague and team-mate. Many players treated him with respect bordering on awe but he never abused this slightly starry-eyed approach. He knew he had to keep producing the runs and to keep earning the respect of the rest of us. By the time he called a halt to his international career, he had done all of that. His record speaks for itself with 19 centuries and 7515 runs in 110 Tests. Can the West Indies have ever had such a magnificent servant? It was a pleasure to be part of his squad because he knew how to handle and get the best out of every player. No one was ever left out or left feeling neglected when Lloyd was in charge and in return he enjoyed our complete devotion and loyalty. Little wonder, then, that he was known affectionately as 'father' or 'father figure'. As with everything, he took it all in good part because very little disturbed his serene calm. He would smile at the nickname. It may have made him feel old but he knew it was meant affectionately and he took it all in his giant stride.

Clive was an outstanding and admired personality and it was a sad day for all of us connected with West Indian cricket when he decided to step down. I can safely say that without Clive, the West Indies would never have achieved what we have over the last 10 or 12 years while he was firmly at the controls.

Clive's deceptively amiable approach hid a fierce desire for success and a shrewd cricketing brain. No match was allowed to drift for long while Clive was in a position to influence its course. I know many followers of the game will believe he was a lucky captain to have so many fast bowlers at his disposal but he was wise enough to realise he needed more than luck to win crucial matches. Sometimes I believe he has not always been given the credit he deserves as a leader and as a tactician. I understand also how many other captains would have loved to have been in his position with so many top-class performers awaiting their chances to become match-winners. It would be easy for a West Indian captain in such circumstances to sit back and let outstanding talent overwhelm lesser ability. That was not Clive's way, although I concede that from the languid manner in which he loitered in the slips, it might have seemed like that. Clive's casual exterior concealed a remarkable ability to be aware of every ebb and flow in a day's play. Just when it seemed he was at his most disinterested and uninvolved he would make his move. He would approach me, if I was the bowler, and make a suggestion which, to be frank, I would not really understand. Sometimes I thought his ideas were downright ludicrous. I would say so if I thought that was the case and he would listen. That was his style of captaincy. But having heard my point of view, he would insist on his, usually a tactical change of some sort. I would do as he asked, bowling in a certain direction or in a certain way, often against my better judgement, and time and again he was right, probably in 90 per cent of the cases.

None of us argued with him because we came to trust his knowledge and expertise above our own. His greatest strength was to make things happen on the field and he had an uncanny knack of being correct. He was at his most dangerous when he appeared at his most casual. 'Father figure' will always be missed as far as I am concerned. That, of course, is in no way a criticism of his successor, Viv Richards. Viv never had to earn our respect in any way. We all knew him as the master batsman and as a capable stand-in as leader whenever Clive was missing. We knew also that whoever replaced Clive eventually would be faced with a desperately difficult task. How do you follow such an act? If we kept winning everyone would say Viv had inherited an outstanding team. If we started losing, questions about Viv's leadership would be asked. When Clive made it known he had reached the end of the road, there was not a dissenting voice when it was known Viv would be taking over. I suppose there were no other serious candidates but we wanted Viv as our leader and we were relieved when he got the job.

Viv is still learning as a captain of an international team and we are doing all we can to help him gain experience without the smooth running of our well-oiled machine enduring any interruptions. He has a style of leadership far removed from Clive's, outwardly far tougher and far more demanding. Viv has already proved himself to be something of a disciplinarian, clapping his hands and urging us to greater efforts. He has made it known he will not tolerate any slackness in the field and, in setting himself high standards, expects us to follow them. No one intends to let him down.   A captain is such an important part of a cricket team, probably more so than in most sports. That is why we West Indians were all shocked by the way the authority of Kim Hughes was undermined and eventually destroyed when we played in Australia in 1984-85. We had a comparatively easy series against such a deeply divided and troubled opposition. I got to know Kim and I liked him very much. We all did. If he had a fault as a captain it was that he could be a little headstrong but his every error, big or small, real or imagined, was blown up out of all proportion by the Aussie press, most of whose writers were former Test players themselves. They never gave poor Kim a moment's rest, vilifying his failures and denigrating the few successes which came his way. The entire country seemed to be against him and his own dressing room was, at best, divided in its support for him.

I found Kim to be the most approachable and, indeed, the nicest of the Aussies. We could not understand why so many people, particularly those who should have known better, were so vehemently against him. He must have been under almost intolerable pressure and there was not a West Indian player who did not feel deep and genuine sympathy for him. When his critics finally got their way, Kim bowed out with dignity and the good nature which had characterised his career. There may have been plenty of celebrations in Australia when Allan Border deposed him but, as his opponents, we were to a man sorry to see him go. As Border discovered in England in 1985, there is no easy way to the top and I hope for his sake the many ex-Australian players, who think they have a greater knowledge, do not turn on him in the same vicious and campaigning way. One thing is for certain, whatever happens to Viv in the years to come, he will never have to face so many outside pressures. He will make his mistakes in peace, safe to know that if he has made any at all they will be pointed out to him privately and not in every newspaper around the globe. I, for one, wish Kim all the best.

Viv may be captain but to me he will always be known as 'Sickest' as the outcome of some private banter over the years. To everyone else he is 'Smokey', after his look-alike, Smokin' Joe Frazier, the boxer. Whenever Viv caught me looking at or chatting to a girl, he would call, in whispered tones, 'Sick'. I would respond with a taunt of 'Sicker' and now it has reached the stage where I know him as 'Sickest'. Sounds a little childish but that's the way most nicknames are forged. There is no logic to them. Indeed we have a fine array of nicknames within the West Indian squad. Lloyd, as I revealed, was 'Father' while Wes Hall, our manager on many occasions, is always known as 'Chief', partly in deference to his status as a Barbadian senator and partly because, for many years, he was the outstanding West Indian fast bowler. Haynes is 'Desi' or 'Comedian' and Greenidge, for the way he so publicly carries his wounds and mortal injuries, will never be known by anything other than 'Hopalong'. Andy Roberts' love for soft drinks and juices earned him the title 'Fruity' and I have always been called 'Maco', as a derivation of Malcolm. Davis became known as 'Uncle Jed' on a tour of Zimbabwe and it has stuck with him, while poor old Croft was landed with 'Goofy' throughout his time in our camp. Garner is prone to all kinds of nicknames. We know him as 'Doc' and the great Michael Holding is 'Mr T' to the rest of us. Gomes is 'LG' according to his initials, or 'Portugee', according to his ancestry. Walsh is 'Caddy', Logie is 'Gus' or 'Mr F'. I cannot give any reasons why or how they picked up these epithets but they will never escape them now. All nicknames are used in jest and the players accept them with good humour. They make for good team spirit and, as I was saying earlier, that is every bit as important as natural ability. Good old 'Father'!

* Marshall's pride in the inner strength and unshakeable team spirit of the great West Indian sides under Lloyd and Richards is obvious from this

chapter and is all the more ironic considering how as coach and manager, Marshall and Lloyd were seemingly unable to instil the same sense of common purpose and togetherness in the West Indian sides of the modern era. They lamented how few present-day players had the same dedication or determination to work on their game, eradicating faults and attempting to improve. According to his friend, Dr Rudi Webster, three days before he died, Marshall told him that he wished the West Indian players would listen more and be prepared to learn about the art and technique of cricket. As for golf, Marshall became proficient and a devotee. He played 18 holes, carrying his own bag, at Hampshire's new course alongside the ground they were building at West End, Southampton only a few weeks before he died, making his sudden decline all the more harrowing.

6.

Racial Taunts

HEADINGLEY, the home of Yorkshire cricket, is the only ground in the world where I have experienced any form of racial prejudice. I admit the occasional drunk might have staggered to his feet in Australia to mouth off his contempt for my colour, but in Yorkshire it is different. At Headingley, where they pride themselves on their deep knowledge and understanding of the game, there is always a hint of malice from certain sections of the crowd.

Of course not all Yorkshire supporters are racists. The vast majority are probably decent, fair-minded people but there is a hard core among them who are never slow to voice their hatred for the West Indian players in particular. I don't know why this should be. I don't really care. But every time I go there I am the victim of obscenities from some of those who call themselves cricket fans. I'm not the only West Indian who has been the victim of racial abuse from the Yorkshire crowd. Richards, Garner, Daniel, John Shepherd in the past and recently David Lawrence, an Englishman of West Indian descent, have all felt the cruel whip of the racist's tongue. Perhaps it is because Yorkshire's rules forbid the importation of anyone from outside their boundaries and they somehow feel disadvantaged when black players they would regard as mercenaries come north to take on what has been one of the weaker counties while I have been playing in England. I have no grudge against any of the Yorkshire players in that respect. Most of them, I hope, are embarrassed by the ignorant behaviour of some of their followers.

If these people seek to intimidate us then I have news for them. In common with other West Indian players in county cricket, I always pull out that little bit extra against Yorkshire precisely because of the treatment their supporters are only too ready to hand out to us. For every bit of abuse I get from them, I redouble my efforts against their players. There was even a rumour going around that I was about to become Yorkshire's first overseas signing. Heaven knows how it started but in the context of what I had experienced at Headingley, it was absolutely laughable. For a start I was half way through a contract with Hampshire where I have always been happy and, secondly, I doubt if I could play for a club where racism among sections of their supporters appears to be so rife. Nowhere else in England or in any other cricket-playing country have I ever encountered any trouble to that extent. On the contrary, as West Indian cricketers our welcome has always been encouragingly warm and kind wherever we have been. People have been glad to see us the world over and we, as a group, have always responded by attempting to play cricket to the very best of our ability. Barbados has almost always been free of racial tension and I have always mixed easily with players of every hue. Only once has there been anything like trouble on the field of play.

The West Indies were playing Australia at Jamaica's Sabina Park in 1984 and it was the one occasion in my entire career when a racist outburst threatened to interrupt play. The Australians were being annihilated. This was the fifth Test and they had lost the previous two in Barbados and Antigua by 10 wickets and an innings and 36 runs respectively. Here in Jamaica they were a dispirited outfit, already well beaten and in danger of being humiliated once more. Recovered from injury, I was enjoying myself at their expense and in all I took eight wickets in the match. Only one man stood in our way as he had defiantly done throughout a very one-sided series. Allan Border was in no mood to surrender though all about him were. Perhaps he was at the end of his tether after what must have been something of an ordeal for him and his players in the Caribbean. Joel Garner bowled a bouncer at the beleaguered Australian captain and he must have picked it up late because he only took evasive action at the last split second. Border's temper spilled over. 'You black ———', he shouted, using a four-letter word to round off his outburst.

For a moment we were all too stunned to react. Had we heard him properly? Joel stood in the middle of the wicket with his arms on his hips rigid with disbelief. I was angered by what I had heard. I could not credit that a man in his position would use such a blatantly antagonistic phrase, least of all surrounded, as he was, by 11 black opponents. No amount of pressure could surely excuse such an unpleasant and outrageous statement. Had it been aimed at anyone other than the gentle Garner retribution would have been swift. Had he hurled his obscenity at me I would have charged in very fast indeed next ball and who knows what I would have unleashed. Garner, though, took it in his massive stride and in almost total silence went back to his mark and continued his over as if nothing had happened. We asked Joel what he was going to do about such an incident; especially as Border showed no signs of apologising. I don't know if he ever did, but Joel, hurt though he obviously was, nobly decided against any avenging action and the incident died quietly amid a sense of fury among his team-mates.

In Test cricket you have no friends among the opposition. It lacks the camaraderie of, say, county cricket. As Border had so emphatically proved, it is often fuelled instead by desperate aggression. Australia duly lost by 10 wickets for the second time in the series and, even though Border was top scorer in both innings, there was no sympathy for him in defeat. Border is a fiercely competitive player and admired by me as a highly skilled batsman, but in common with my colleagues I don't suppose we shall ever forgive him such an unnecessary and racist outburst. Why he said it, we shall never know. I can only reiterate that he was lucky it was Garner who was bowling to him. Sometimes he is too soft for his own good.

Garner was an important part of the team when the West Indies flew to Pakistan for four Tests in November and December 1980. After establishing myself in the series in England earlier in the year, I had expected to be part of the squad and, with my reputation beginning to blossom, I was eager to take my place on the plane. My enthusiasm was increased by the knowledge that Roberts was not going - this meant a vacancy for a front-line bowler, although the call-up of Sylvester Clarke was a reminder of our ability to produce from our ranks a top quality replacement when the need arose. Michael Holding, though chosen, was not to have a happy tour. A shoulder injury restricted him to three first-class matches and a limited-overs international. That, naturally, worked in my favour because it provided me with more opportunity and, in effect, cleared the path of two of my greatest rivals. I would hate, incidentally, to give the impression of any animosity between any of us. As in Barbados, the sparring is friendly. Andy and Michael are men I rank as friends and in the early stages of my time in the West Indies squad, both went out of their way to help and encourage me.

So we set off for Pakistan with five fast bowlers in Holding, Croft, Garner, Clarke and myself, but if India had been a cultural shock, Pakistan was ten times worse. It was largely dirty, unhygienic and very smelly. Bacchus went down with food poisoning immediately and Gomes and myself paid the penalty for eating unwashed grapes. Luckily the hotels in Karachi and Lahore were of high quality even if much of what we saw outside them in terms of sheer squalor and poverty assailed the senses.

It did not take us long to realise how, amid the shambles, Imran Khan was revered almost as a god in his home country. His haughty film star looks shone down from advertising hoardings and on television he extolled the virtues of Coca-Cola. He was a national hero to end all heroes and on his willing shoulders the hopes of Pakistan clearly rested. Imran and I have always enjoyed a mutual respect and admiration. He takes the game seriously, fully aware of the enormous responsibility he carries with him in Pakistan and, on his day, is one of the great match-winners in Test cricket. I am sorry he was injured at the peak of his career because he was out of the game at a time when he may even have rewritten the history books, and certainly provided in that respect a close rival as an all-rounder to Ian Botham. I would see them very much as equals though Botham's phenomenal record speaks for itself. There may never be a player like him again and for sheer strength and aggression there is not now. Imran is a different sort of cricketer and who knows what he might have achieved had that leg stress-fracture not intruded. In 1980, though, he was very much in his prime and we knew from the outset he was not going to make it easy for us and, with so much batting strength, we were in for a tough time in hostile conditions.

We soon discovered how slow the Pakistani wickets were as they attempted to negate our pace attack. But in trying to take the sting from our bowling they created some dangerous batting tracks instead. The tops soon went and batting, designed by their groundsmen to be easy, became a lottery instead against any type of bowling. It was at Lahore, his home city, that we were first alerted to Imran's massive presence. They call him 'tiger' in Pakistan and apparently there can be no greater compliment. Roared on by huge crowds, he came in at number seven and brushed us aside with a typically masterful 123 in the Pakistan first innings of 369. Clarke and Croft took the new ball, I was first change with Joel Garner next in line and at 95 for five we had them in trouble. It was then that Imran took over and, although I took some pride in eventually dismissing him leg before, the damage had been done. The giant-sized pictures of Imran, which many of the crowd seemed to bring with them, were waved and wafted from every direction as the great man rose to the occasion, responding like a true champion to his country's hour of need. Our chance lost, the match was drawn.

At Faisalabad in the second Test, Garner did not play because the match was going to be won, if at all, by spinners. Batting was always difficult and it needed two disciplined innings from our own batting champion, Viv Richards, of 72 and 67 to set up a situation whereby we could hope to win on a rapidly deteriorating surface. With our main spinner, the Trinidadian policeman Ranji Nanan, dismissing Imran without scoring, I played my part with four wickets for 25 to finish off the match and to give us victory by 156 runs. This put the onus on Pakistan to win at least one of the last two Tests, at Karachi and Multan, to prevent us winning the series. Imran tried his hardest, with four for 66 at Karachi and five for 62 at Multan, but there was nothing he could do to force us to lose our grip. Both matches were drawn and we returned home triumphant, glad to have overcome a strong batting side on their own grounds and to have got the better of a living legend.

Pakistan ought to have achieved so much more over the years, though their internal strife has been well documented. Imran, I believe, is technically better than Botham but he has suffered from not having the bowling support he so desperately needs. That said, I don't think Sarfraz Nawaz ever got the recognition he deserved. A volatile character who did not always see eye-to-eye with his country's selectors, I found him to be a highly competent performer who was underrated, bearing in mind how the slow Pakistani wickets can have done nothing for him. Javed Miandad was at his peak during that tour and I have the utmost respect for such a gutsy and competitive batsman. Like Sadiq, he was a fighter and against those two, I always felt I had a battle on my hands to earn their wickets. In contrast I did not rate Zaheer on the same high plane. I found him to be scared of genuine pace, a failing I was not slow to exploit, and I suspect the basis of his reputation was made on the comfortable batting surfaces at Bristol for his adopted Gloucestershire. Certainly he achieved nothing against us on this particular tour.

For all their batting strength, Pakistan have always appeared to rely heavily on Imran for inspiration in much the same way England look to Botham. Of the world's all-rounders I would put Imran marginally in front on technique alone. Kapil Dev is probably not as good a bowler as his record might indicate. I believe, in contrast, he is a better batsman and may even establish himself as a high class middle-order batsman in due course. Hadlee is very much a bowling all-rounder for whom conditions have to be right for him to be an effective batsman. Coming in at number seven, he can be a volatile hitter but he is a far more dangerous bowler. Clive Rice is a genuine all-rounder and he might have become one of his generation's outstanding exponents in other circumstances.

For my own part, I still like to think of myself as an all-rounder and in weaker batting teams than the West Indies, and indeed Hampshire, I might have developed more rapidly in that direction by now. It still rankles slightly that I have not done better as a batsman, but I believe there is plenty of time for me to make my mark as a Test-class batsman. In less talented teams I feel certain I would have already done so. Unfortunately there was nothing about my batting performances in Pakistan to have suggested I was about to develop as an all-rounder. My 13 wickets in four Tests at 24.53 each was not a bad haul in view of the type of pitches we played on, but 13 runs at an average of 2.60 hardly supported my desire for a position higher in the order.

At the conclusion of the series in Pakistan my Test record was moderate. In 11 Tests I had taken only 31 wickets but allowing also for my inexperience, there are mitigating circumstances. I was being brought along slowly by the West Indian selectors. They were letting me learn about all types of wickets and conditions in the hope that I would blossom sooner or later into the sort of player I am today. At most I was only getting two spells of bowling per innings because there were always older and wiser players ahead of me in the queue. I don't believe I was bowling particularly poorly; it was simply that my chances were limited even when I was fortunate enough to break into the team. With four or sometimes more fast bowlers to call upon, the captain can afford to be choosy. That is why, I would suggest, no West Indian is ever likely to head the list of international wicket-takers for long. We are forced to share our wickets, in contrast to other countries for whom there might only be one outstanding bowler. Look at Botham and Kapil Dev. They have run through teams; picking up five, six or seven wickets at a time. They have often had to because the support is not there. In the West Indies team, it is rare for one bowler to be so dominant at the expense of the others, so it is much harder to collect a big tally of wickets from one innings or one match. Garner is proof of my theory. In reaching 200 Test wickets, he only took five wickets in an innings six times, which is not a great record for a great bowler. Had he come from another country he might have doubled that. In the West Indies line-up, we pass our wickets around.

I had my heart set on playing against England in the Caribbean in 1981 and, after returning from Pakistan, went back to Shell Shield cricket with a certain gusto. I sensed there were real opportunities for me to make a decisive breakthrough into the team so what I needed more than anything was a successful domestic season. I needed wickets by the bucketful - and I got them. Only Andy Roberts with 25 took more than my 17 for Barbados at 18.11 each and I had every reason to believe my big leap forward would be rewarded with a Test place. My most outstanding performance was against Jamaica where I took six for 75 and then hit 49 not out to confirm my own belief that I was making progress as a genuine all-rounder.

The West Indies selectors obviously failed to agree with my assessment when the team for the first Test was announced and to say I was disappointed by my omission would be a severe understatement. Instead the selectors went back to the old firm of Roberts, Holding, Garner and Croft and, while I readily concede their individual and collective excellence, I felt I ought to be in there somewhere because I was at least their equal as a bowler now and a better batsman than them all. The infamous Robin Jackman affair, when he was banned from Guyana because of his South African connections, reduced the series to four Tests and that hardly helped my personal cause. I was left to sulk at home in Barbados as England were swamped by an innings and 79 runs at Port-of-Spain, Trinidad. It is a curious situation a sportsman in a team game finds himself on such occasions. On the one hand I wanted the West Indies to win and for each team member to do well, but on the other hand I needed someone to fail in order to reclaim my place. There must have been, over the years, many players with similar emotions. In this instance, I believe I should have been in from the start because, apart from the first Test, Roberts struggled to justify his position. Unfortunately from my point of view Roberts enjoyed his only real success of the series in Trinidad, contributing an unbeaten 50 in our first innings total of 426 for nine declared and taking five wickets for 82 as England capitulated with scores of 178 and 169. This meant, of course, that the decision to go into the match with our four recognised top pace bowlers, on a pitch where spin invariably predominates, was completely vindicated. If there had been any doubts in their minds about my own inclusion, they were surely vanquished as England were so ruthlessly swept aside. I wondered if I would ever get my chance now that the West Indies had taken such a crucially early lead. There was no need to change a winning side - and I knew it. Even so I was summoned from my fretful exile to Guyana for what should have been the second Test.

All the players in the West Indian camp knew about Jackman's South African links. They were hardly state secrets. Our own attitude was straightforward enough. We wanted to play against England, no matter who was in their team. We were in Guyana to play cricket and that's all we were interested in. Politics has a habit of intruding into sport as it is bound to. On this occasion, we hoped that President Forbes Burnham would overlook Jackman's past connections with South Africa and allow us to get down to the business of beating England at cricket. As I point out elsewhere in this book, I have no time for apartheid or for any government which discriminates on the basis of colour. But in this case, Jackman was not a South African. He was there as an Englishman to play cricket against us and, as players, we were ready to accept him to a man. It was with a sense of disappointment, then, that it all collapsed in front of us and England were obliged to leave Guyana, the series now soured by the incident. Barbados thus became the venue for the second Test, a day or two short of a full month since the first match in Trinidad.

I'm not sure what all this did for England's morale but even reinforced by Jackman's fierce commitment and enthusiasm, they did not cause us too many problems at the Kensington Oval. I was called up once again to the squad but without any realistic expectations of playing. From the pavilion I watched as 12th man as Jackman took three for 65 to restrict us to a modest total of 265 of which Lloyd's patient 100 was a vital contribution. If this was by no means an exceptional total, it soon began to look likely to win us the match as England folded under a barrage of pace from our big four. It was with mixed feelings that I saw Roberts take two, Holding three, Croft four and Garner the other wicket as England plunged to 122 all out in less than 50 overs. This took the pressure off us and Viv Richards was at his imperious best in making 182 not out of our second innings total of 379 for seven before Lloyd declared leaving England the little matter of 523 to win. It was way beyond them and it became merely a question of how long it would take us to roll them over a second time. Richards took a couple of wickets with his off spin but it was our fast men who split the rest between them, with Croft making it a personal seven in the match with three for 65.

In my opinion England were patently shell-shocked against our quickies and, pleased as I was to see the West Indies win so decisively, I only wished I could have been out there to take part in the sharing of the spoils. Graham Gooch was the only batsman to stand in our way, battling against all-comers in a brave and defiant 116. I had another reason for wanting to be in the team. Our 12th men only pick up half the salary of the others during a Test match. I admit it's easy money for such a simple and undemanding job but one can get used to the fat, post-Packer pay cheques of full-blown Test cricketers.

So it was for the third Test at St Johns, Antigua, home of Roberts and Richards, that once more I was destined to watch and wait as 12th man to a very powerful team with two Tests already under its belt and scenting a whitewash. Poor Roberts was desperate to succeed in front of his own people in Antigua's first ever Test match, but with figures of nought for 59 and nought for 39 he was beginning to struggle as the West Indies number one bowler, a position he had held for the best part of seven years. Peter Willey, a player whose stubbornness and determination against the most ferocious of fast bowling I have long admired, hit 102 not out batting at number seven, but the England score of 271 never looked likely to be enough to put them into a position whereby they could think in terms of winning, which of course they had to do. Their plight was worsened as Richards, responding to the massive adulation of his home island, brought the place to a frenzy of hysteria with a magnificent 114. At 468 all out, the

West Indies were all but 200 ahead and the best England could hope to do was survive another large, morale-crushing defeat. With Roberts unable to make any inroads, and Croft unable to repeat his commendable first innings six for 74, Boycott grafted to a century and Gooch made 83 in a first wicket stand of 144. England duly got away with a draw at 234 for three, leaving Antigua with their pride partially restored.

I left Antigua convinced that I might be due a match after the failure - for the first time - of our pace attack to force a victory. I was especially keen to play in the fourth Test because Kingston in Jamaica is just about my favourite ground. I love the Jamaicans' attitude to the game and I love playing there. I know Barbados has the reputation for producing a steady stream of top-quality players, particularly in recent years, but I have always found the Jamaican crowd to be knowledgeable, appreciative and fun-loving. They like good cricketers no matter where they come from or whom they represent. As a Barbadian player I have always done well against them at Sabina Park in the Shell Shield but they have never resented it. On the contrary, they have always warmed to me. I would go so far as to say in fact that I am regarded as something of a hero in Jamaica, more so possibly than in my native island. The crowds are vociferous, as they nearly all are in the Caribbean, and they lap it up when I joke back at them. I try to stir them up and to amuse them and they are never slow to join in. They have an uncanny ability to spot and respond to my many moods on the field, breaking the tension with a wisecrack or two or lifting me when they sense I'm on a high and feeling ready for a wicket or two. We have a mutual admiration in Jamaica and if it was at all possible I would take their crowd around with me as personal assistants en masse.

Sure enough I was drafted in as replacement for the tiring Roberts and there was not a happier man in the Caribbean when I learned of my selection. Here was the chance to get in and stay in and I meant to take it. I had waited around too long to get in on a permanent basis and I made up my mind that my time had come. As far as I was concerned, Jamaica was the perfect venue.

I shall always remember this Test. Gooch scored 153 in the England first innings total of 285 after I had opened the bowling with Holding. Michael was playing in front of his home crowd at Sabina Park and they were baying for him to run riot through the England batting. At his best, with that lyrical, rhythmic run of his, he could be exceptionally fast and, with the adrenaline flowing, he was very quick. I felt obliged to compete with him for pace and soon paid the price. I tore muscles in my stomach trying to emulate him and spent most of the match nursing my pain and trying to make an impression all at the same time. I took the wickets of Willey and Botham in the first innings for 49 while, even on an unresponsive wicket, Holding's sheer aggression was responsible for his altogether healthier five for 56. Greenidge, Haynes, Lloyd and Gomes each got more than 50 as we built a big total in reply of 442, big enough to give us the chance of winning again. Our hopes were raised when I had Gooch caught at slip for three and Boycott and Athey soon followed. This left England 32 for three but, with Willey for company, Gower showed the class I had first spotted in him as a youth with a fine innings of 154 not out which saved the match for England. We hardly helped our own cause over the space of the five days. I reckon we must have dropped eight or nine catches which no side, least of all at international level, can afford to do. My own match figures of three for 64 would have been far more impressive had some of those catches been accepted. England did all that could be expected of them by their supporters in staving off defeat but we knew we should have won.

The match however represented something of a landmark in my career. It was here in Jamaica that I bowled as fast as I have ever bowled in my life for the first time. For too long I had been regarded as a fast-medium bowler with pretensions as an all-rounder. Now I was ready to slip myself and to be classified as a genuinely fast bowler. I found I could sustain my pace and still be able to control the movement of the ball, which many out-and-out fast bowlers cannot always succeed in doing. In short I could use pace as my main weapon - though I liked to think there was more to my game than pace alone. As I saw it, Roberts - as his eight wickets in three Tests had shown - was no longer a fast bowler; Garner was never very fast and Holding was only ever going to let rip when injuries and occasions like this Test allowed.

I believed, at a couple of days short of my 23rd birthday, I was now the West Indies number one fast bowler; I would trace it all back to that one particular match. As for my old adversary, Graham Gooch, he was a much straighter player in those days. In recent years he has picked up a habit of playing across the line. He can get away with that on slower wickets but not in the Caribbean. I was looking forward to many more tussles with him in my new capacity as a fast bowler, fit to be ranked with the quickest around.

* Marshall spent much of his playing career trying to convince others that he should be regarded as an all-rounder, and in particular a batting all-rounder. A career total in excess of 11,000 runs and seven first class centuries says he was right. He always lamented a lack of batting opportunities whether with the West Indies or with Hampshire. There he had the Smith brothers, Greenidge, Paul Terry and Nicholas all batting ahead of him when he was in his bowling prime in the 80s. He had been hired to bowl fast and his job was to get the opposition out. Later, when he did get chances higher in the order, he did not always take them. As for that day at Sabina Park when he realised he was now the West Indies' number one fast bowler, it was a defining moment in his career and he bore the mantle jealously until he knew time would inevitably catch up with him. It was strongly rumoured that Yorkshire were keen on signing Marshall late in his career but nothing developed and he held no grudge against them. Richie Richardson from Antigua became one of their first overseas players but he was, on his own admission, not a great success.

7.

Captains - Positive and Negative

TOO MANY COUNTY CAPTAINS are negative in their approach to what is after all a game and a spectator sport. I realise it is a source of some mystification how 17 counties can survive with fully professional staffs year after year without going out of business.

When I first came to England and surveyed the empty grounds each day I wondered who was paying my wages. It simply did not seem feasible that professional cricket could continue on that scale when on some days the players outnumbered the paying customers. Were it not for the massive hand-out from the Test and County Cricket Board to the counties from Test match receipts, I'm sure some counties would go to the wall, even though many have become conscious in recent years that they must generate revenue off the field.

This is where county captains play such an important part in the future of English cricket. They must lure people through the turnstiles by producing attractive performances from their team, irrespective of results. I believe a disappointingly large percentage of the 17 skippers have a sort of soccer mentality whereby they equate success with the number of times they escape defeat. Looking around the counties, I can think of no more than half who are prepared to lose in order that they may also stand a chance of winning. Everyone wants to win, naturally, but there is an unfortunate tendency among some of these trustees of the English domestic game. Their next priority is not to lose under any circumstances and they are just as prepared to kill off any hopes of a positive verdict if they think they are in danger of going under. It's a depressing attitude and one which players from overseas always find difficult to understand. Players from Australia, New Zealand and the West Indies have come to recognise it as the 'English way' of playing the game and it does not always reflect well on those who are genuinely attempting to entertain their clients - the paying spectators who, these days, can just as easily find alternative ways of spending their money and their leisure time.

Lack of positive cricket was never something of which you could accuse a team captained by Clive Lloyd, the best skipper I have ever come across - and I always compare other captains with him. He made things happen by setting fields to make batsmen make mistakes, as did the deep-thinking Mike Brearley. Brearley may not have been a truly Test-class batsman but his captaincy left a lasting impression on me and the players he actually lead. His record speaks for itself as an international leader. He is the one England skipper to have got the best out of Botham, as that memorable series against the Australians in 1981 so conclusively proved. Middlesex were always a powerful and well balanced team when he was in control and, with him at the helm, they were successful as well.

Of course it is always easier to lead a strong team; easier to dictate how a match should be played when you have players for all wickets and eventualities. Yet some counties never get the best out of what talent is at their disposal because their captains are not ready to take risks and chances. Keith Fletcher is one of the best leaders I have come across in my time in county cricket, shrewd and calculating but happy to keep his opposition interested if he thinks they may be shutting up shop. Mark Nicholas at Hampshire is a positive captain, following in the tradition of Nick Pocock in keeping matches open and never simply trying to avoid defeat. I'm not even sure I would want to continue county cricket if I thought our captain was not interested in taking chances. I would certainly not show the enthusiasm I do now. Nicholas's attitude has been recognised at Lord's and his leadership of MCC and England B are due reward. Mike Gatting is a good skipper in my view, as are Clive Rice, Chris Cowdrey and David Graveney at Gloucestershire.

I must also record my appreciation of Botham as a captain. After his failure as England's skipper, many people wrote him off, believing his prodigious talents were best left in the hands of those who knew how to get the best out of them, like Brearley. His term of captaincy at Somerset was equally short-lived but for different reasons. His county obviously felt his continued absence on Test duty impaired his ability to lead the team properly. Whenever we played him while he was Somerset's captain we always found him enterprising and adventurous and both Richards and Garner spoke approvingly of his style of captaincy. Perhaps in time he will regain the leadership of both Somerset and England and the cricket world will come to recognise that Botham's massive talent also includes leadership. Unfortunately it is easy to get the impression that for all his ability as the world's most successful all-rounder, he may have upset some prominent people within the England set-up and the opportunity to lead his country again may never be forthcoming. That, I do not know. All I can say is that I was impressed by the manner he led Somerset and there is no way he would ever play negatively.

I regret to say there are many others in county cricket about whom the same cannot be said. These guys have the future of the game at professional level in their hands. It is no good using weak teams as a legitimate excuse because weak counties with strong, imaginative leaders can still engineer unlikely victories. In my experience cricket followers in England want to see a good game and to be entertained. They like to see their team win but this is not a priority.

I would love the opportunity to lead the West Indies and I believe I have the credentials to do so. Viv Richards has plenty of years on his side and will captain us for as long as he desires. When he goes there will be one or two of us vying for the chance to lead the best team in the world. There does not seem to be any obvious long-term candidate. Greenidge, Gomes, Garner and Holding are of similar vintage to Richards, and Holding keeps talking of retirement. Jeff Dujon has his followers in Jamaica and Roger Harper will receive support from those in Guyana who reckon he has the temperament and skill to become captain of the West Indies regional team. Time will tell. I like to think I read a game as well as any of them and that I'm tactically aware. I realise that, like them, I lack experience of captaincy at first-class level and perhaps in time I will get the chance to lead Barbados in the Shell Shield now that I've been made West Indies' vice-captain as the first step towards the ultimate prize. I am not naive enough to think that leading the West Indies side would be a doddle. Even the finest engines will grind to a halt if they are not looked after properly, particularly now that so many of our opponents regard it as a moral victory if they simply avoid defeat against us. Even with an array of great fast bowlers available, it is not always a simple task breaking down teams whose sole objects are not to get out and to last five days.

It is possible I will never get a chance while I am able to produce the goods on the field. I have struck a rich vein of wickets and I'm at last showing people I can bat responsibly and successfully. With Botham as the obvious example, the powers-that-be are possibly reluctant to let me lead a team in case my form dries up as suddenly as Botham's. For that reason if I felt the captaincy would hamper my performances with bat and ball or in any way detract from the team, I would turn down any offers to lead the West Indies. I would have to be certain in my own mind that I was ready for the job and able to do it without ruining my own game. Too many players, in my view, should never be captains because, although they may be excellent players, they are not necessarily tactically the best judges. Some would say Botham fits into that category. I have already said why I disagree with that verdict. A good captain may have qualities which are not always apparent. Cricket is, after all, probably the only major sport where captaincy is such a vital part in any team performance. There is no point in having a team laden with great talent and outstanding players if the captain does not know how to get the best out of them. My own big hope is that since being given the vice-captaincy the West Indies selectors will be looking at me as a future leader, partly because I feel I could do the job and partly because, from a purely selfish point of view, it would be the high spot of my career.

Captaincy was far from my mind when I returned to England for the 1981 season with Hampshire. I had played in only five matches for them the previous year and they were obviously as anxious as I was to give a full summer's service, particularly as they had finished bottom of the championship in 1980. With the team being rebuilt, I realised they were expecting great things from Gordon Greenidge and myself. Gordon, as reliable as ever, responded with nearly 1500 runs at an average-of 49.72 to provide the solid starts Hampshire had so sorely missed previously. Gordon is sometimes taken for granted, I feel, because he goes about his job as opener with minimum fuss and maximum dedication but his true worth is readily acknowledged in the dressing-rooms of Hampshire, Barbados and the West Indies. They all know what a fantastic player he is. When I first came to Hampshire I felt they relied on him too heavily. If he failed the team invariably struggled and he must have carried a huge burden on his broad shoulders. It was a little the same in 1981 and Gordon did not let them down.

That season Hampshire had every right to expect something special from me. In 1979 I was a novice and I had played very little the following year because of my involvement in the tour of England by the West Indies. As a measure of my progress in 1981 I took 68 wickets at 19.42 each, but I missed seven of the 24 first-class fixtures primarily through a groin injury which at times prevented me bowling as fast as I would have liked. The atmosphere among the players was much better than when I first came over and under Pocock's buccaneering leadership, we enjoyed our cricket. I love playing the game and I have yet to look upon the constant travelling involved in county cricket as a tiresome slog. Of course it takes some getting used to, but then, as now, I relished every moment.

Hampshire had been told when they signed me unseen that I was an all-rounder and I was determined to develop into one. At this stage of my career, I was watching Botham, Kapil Dev and Imran perform heroic feats with both bat and ball for their countries and I began to think I should be getting close to doing something similar for the West Indies, even allowing for the fact that there was a far greater spread of talent among the West Indian players. To this end I set about attempting to become a more prolific batsman. Hampshire knew I could bat and they knew about my ambition to become a better batsman - but they wanted me for my fast bowling and consequently were reluctant to let me go higher in the order than number eight where my chances to build a big innings were invariably restricted. The result was a far-from-outstanding 425 runs at 21.25, not bad for a number eight but not as many as I would have liked.

The highlight of the whole season for me was my performance against Essex at Southampton. In rising to seventh place in the table, we won six of our matches in a much-improved showing and I like to think I accounted for Essex virtually on my own. It was the first time in my career at the top level in which I was able to dominate a match both as a bowler and as a batsman. I have no wish to detract from the great success Essex have enjoyed over recent years, particularly under Keith Fletcher's leadership, on slender resources. Their list of trophies is testimony enough to their achievements, but sometimes I have wondered how they have managed it! For various unknown reasons I have recorded some of my own finest achievements against them. I get the impression several of their players have a distinct dislike for fast bowling, judging by the way some have faced up to me and, as a county, we have always done better than most against them. They have always been a well balanced side and in John Lever, Graham Gooch and Ken McEwan they have had players of the highest calibre - yet I have never really seen why they have dominated English domestic cricket. So it was at Southampton in August when we beat them by 136 runs, though Gooch's absence admittedly helped our cause. I hit my then best-ever score of 75 not out batting at eight and then took four for 67 and four for 39 in two of the fastest spells of bowling I had produced for Hampshire. Essex did not show much of a stomach for battle as they slumped to 105 all out in the second innings and, as an all-rounder, I felt I was on my way. Unfortunately the groin strain intruded and I played only three more first class matches, but I ended the season having taken four or more wickets in an innings 10 times with best figures of six for 57 against Leicestershire early in the summer. My aim was still 100 wickets in a county season and obviously I was well short, though I was pleased to have gathered the 68 I did take fairly cheaply.

It was not until the following year that I was able to realise my ambition and break the 100-wicket barrier. I found the pressure, both physical and mental, to be very tough and demanding. The mental effort, in fact, was greater than the sheer physical grind of bowling over after over. Richard Hadlee did remarkably well to do the double of 100 wickets and 1,000 runs in a season and, for all my all-round pretensions, I know I will never be able to do the same. In the limited time left to me in county cricket I would love to score 1,000 first class runs in a season but there again I acknowledge it could be difficult from my position in the batting order, way down at seven or eight. I think if I was to get 1,000 in a season I would be delighted even though 1,000 is a decidedly moderate target for the average county batsman. Indeed there are some very ordinary cricketers getting 1,500 or more in a summer from prime positions in the batting order. Lack of quality bowling and flat wickets can enable batsmen to flatter themselves and start being talked about as Test players. I can tell within a few overs if a batsman has the quality, skill and temperament to reach the top. Too many are scared to get in line to a fast bowler and will plunder runs, instead, off medium-pacers or the slow bowlers.

When it comes to county cricket I'm not particularly conscious of records, either my own or anyone else's. My job is to bowl fast for Hampshire and if I can score runs also then I feel I have earned my wages. I admit to looking at the averages in the papers as the season goes on but I have won awards for such things as Bowler of the Month from various organisations without being aware necessarily that I had done better than others. I hope that does not sound ungrateful because it is not meant to be. The busy months of the English season tend to merge and it's a job to keep a track of who is doing what to whom, though it is always nice to be surprised by winning an award or two.

When it comes to Test cricket it is a totally different matter. I'm aware of every run and every wicket and how they affect me in the record books. Having passed 200 Test wickets there are only about 20 players above me now and by the end of my career I would like to be top of that list of Test wicket-takers. My last 100 came in a month short of two years and while I concede I may not be able to sustain that sort of strike-rate, it would be nice to think I could overhaul Ian Botham before too long. Those same record books show that Holding, Garner, Gary Sobers and Lance Gibbs with 309 are the only West Indians ahead of me and with Holding and Garner approaching the end of productive careers, time is on my side. All this is assuming I can stay clear of injury and illness over the next four or five years and that is not as easy as it sounds. Roberts and Holding and, of course, Lillee learned to use the ball more skilfully as they got older but lost something of their extreme pace. I may have to learn something similar if I want to extend my life as a Test cricketer because it's obviously difficult to maintain your speed much beyond the age of 30. My view is that there are plenty of young fast bowlers emerging in the West Indies - look at the way Patrick Patterson came from nowhere - and once I show signs of losing my venom and hostility the selectors will simply find someone else to replace me. It is the same at Hampshire. Once I'm no longer able to blast out the opposition they will look elsewhere for another young fast bowler on whom to spend their money. I have a limited time at my disposal to make a living and to dictate terms. I realise and fully accept this.

Once I became established in first-class cricket I set my heart on reaching 1,000 wickets and I'm pleased to discover that they have come regularly enough for me in recent years to start thinking in terms of 1,500 or maybe even more before I have finished. I got seven more towards my target when I was selected for the first ever tour of the newly-named Zimbabwe by the West Indies Under-26 squad. It was the first time a West Indian team had set foot in Africa but, with Robert Mugabe now in power, it was felt by the Zimbabwe Cricket Union that a visit from us might fire the imagination of blacks and get them to start playing the game in greater numbers. The Zimbabweans insisted they would choose their teams on merit and would not under any circumstances pick black players as token gestures. The result was we never played against a single black African in nine matches. At least the Zimbabweans were attempting to make changes but it was clear to us they were going to take time and patience. We did our bit in helping to spread the message by taking part in coaching sessions for young Africans and we can only hope that our visit and those made subsequently by ourselves and other countries will speed the process.

On this tour our welcome from all quarters could not have been more friendly or more genuine. The whites were pleased to see us and to test the strength of their cricket, now that they were members of the ICC, against representatives of the game's strongest nation. It was difficult for our selectors to gauge how good the Zimbabweans were, bearing in mind that the white population numbered only about 250,000 and that two of their best-known cricketing sons had gone elsewhere. Brian Davison was coaching in Tasmania and Paddy Clift, the Leicestershire all-rounder, was playing in South Africa.

Faoud Bacchus, the only player older than 26, was our captain on the tour and Desmond Haynes was his deputy in what was a mixture of untried raw talent and proven ability. Later that year there was a full West Indian tour of Australia and of the squad in Zimbabwe, Bacchus, Haynes, Gus Logie, Jeff Dujon, Harold Joseph, the 25-year-old spin bowler from Trinidad and myself joined it. Of the rest of the 14 tourists, Wayne Daniel, Everton Mattis and Winston Davis had either played Test cricket or were to do so later in their careers. Marlon Tucker of Jamaica, the Guyanese opening batsman Timur Mohammed, Ignatius Cadette, a wicket-keeper from the Windward Islands, Mark Neita from Jamaica and my old friend, Hartley Alleyne, made up the party. Hartley, by now playing for Worcestershire, earned his selection after playing only three matches for Barbados, the strength of his home island had left him largely out in the cold, but he certainly had enough talent. In that particular season, 1981, Barbados had Daniel, myself, Sylvester Clarke, Joel Garner and Alleyne from which to choose three or four fast bowlers. They were spoiled for choice.

In Zimbabwe we were surprised how good our opponents were, the high standards of the grounds in Harare and Bulawayo and the warmth of our reception. The crowds were usually large and appreciative and although, to my regret, I never did get to see the Victoria Falls, I did come away from the three-week tour with one permanent memento, my first century. After winning the first three-day match in Harare by seven wickets, my moment of glory came in the next match, which was drawn. Batting at number seven I hit 109 against a side containing Kevin Curran, now at Gloucestershire, and the veteran spin bowler John Traicos, who had appeared for South Africa in Test matches before their ban. My maiden century came in the second innings which we had begun with a deficit of 64 - I was absolutely ecstatic when I reached the magic three-figures. I was eventually caught behind but by that stage we were on our way to a sizeable total. I had been playing first class cricket for three-and-a-half years by now and I was in need of a ton to underline my own belief that I was an all-rounder who needed to be treated seriously. My previous best score had been that 75 not out against Essex a couple of months earlier and my century came at a time when I was beginning to despair of breaking the barrier. My chances of building a big innings had been severely limited by my position in the batting orders for Hampshire, Barbados and the West Indies but here in Bulawayo, of all places, I had been able to take my time without being under pressure to score quickly for the sake of the team. Zimbabwe showed tremendous ability as fielders so I was made to work for my runs. Now I knew I could score centuries and the West Indian selectors must have been as pleased as I was, even allowing for the moderate reputation of our opponents. The selectors had always hoped I would develop as an all-rounder - and now I had proved it.

The third three-day match was also drawn, leaving me reigning supreme at the top of the tour averages with 175 runs at an average of 43.75, ahead even of my pal, Desmond Haynes. Alleyne, Daniel and Tucker finished ahead of me in the bowling averages, though, my seven wickets coming at 27.42 each. So after an enjoyable and productive little break on the African continent it was off to Australia for what we knew was going to be another rough and tough series. Little did I realise how close I was going to come to ending my career there, the victim of the worst injury I have ever suffered.

* There is no doubt that Marshall would have liked an extended run as a captain in his own right, not as someone else's deputy, and he always believed that being a fast bowler mitigated against him in this respect. Captains tended to be batsmen. His theory that he was an all-rounder and therefore the perfect choice was not always shared by others, but he relished the chances he did get. The West Indian players enjoyed playing against each other in county or regional domestic cricket and their rivalry was real enough. Viv Richards memorably took Marshall apart for Glamorgan at Southampton late in their careers. Talk of Hartley Alleyne prompted Kevin Emery, a house-mate of Marshall's for a summer or two, to recall one clash between the Bajans when Alleyne was playing for Worcestershire. He told the Evening Advertiser, Swindon: "The West Indians would raise their games whenever their paths crossed. Alleyne was batting at Worcester and Malcolm got him out. As Malcolm carried on with his follow-through, he did not stop and ran all the way to the pavilion and opened the gate to allow Hartley to leave the field. It was a magic moment."

8.

Injury Trauma

AUSTRALIA 1981-82 should have provided my career with the springboard it needed. Instead I returned from a bitter, pain-filled tour a virtual invalid on a desperate search for a cure for a severe back injury. At 23 and with several other tours under my belt as a junior member, I was now ready to play a much fuller part in the destiny of West Indian cricket. I had been to Australia a couple of years before as part of the listening and learning process the West Indian selectors had outlined for me since I had first emerged from nowhere at the age of 20. Fresh from my success in Zimbabwe, I was looking forward to taking on the Aussies in the three-Test series and in the one-day internationals against Pakistan and Australia. Roberts, Holding, Croft, Garner and Sylvester Clarke were potential rivals for my place but our squad had a very strong look about it with Greenidge, Richards, Gomes and Lloyd forming the basis of the batting. No wonder I was so eager to get involved. Three months later I was little more than a cripple, gripped by agonising muscular spasms around my spine. As I lurched from specialist to specialist in Australia and England and the West Indies, I seriously doubted if I would ever play again and, in gloomier moments, I pondered also on the possibility that the injury might even be permanent.

It all began smoothly enough for me and I felt in top form while making 66 against South Australia in a big win at Adelaide in the middle of November soon after our arrival. A month later I bowled as well as I had ever bowled at Brisbane in another crushing victory, this time against a depleted Queensland side. It proved to be my last first class match of the tour. I didn't even get a bat as we amassed 539 for seven before Lloyd declared, but I played my part by snapping up five for 31 in 18 very fast overs to have Queensland all out for 165. We duly won by an innings and

92 runs. It was around this time that I first became troubled by what at first I thought was little more than a pulled muscle. The one-day internationals were running simultaneously and it was against Pakistan in Perth that I was suddenly shaken by a sharp twinge which seemed to burn through my entire body. I took no real notice because the pain, searing though it was, wore off and I was able to play out the rest of the match without further discomfort. At the end of the match I did not even draw attention to it to our physiotherapist, Dennis Waight, though I could feel it was still there. Instead I resorted to putting ice on my back to ease what I figured was a little inflammation. To be honest I had no real idea what it was but it did not seem too bad. I could live with it and the last thing I wanted was to rule myself out of contention because of a minor problem with my back. There was simply too much at stake to drop out; too many people ready to take my place.

I had never been injured before; I had never known what it was like to endure the misery of extreme pain and as the tour progressed my back worsened. It got to the stage where I found sleeping not only difficult but also fraught with agony. Our physio arranged for me to see doctors and no fewer than three different specialists in a bid to find some relief and even a cure. They all told me the same: the muscles in my back were weak and bowling fast was putting pressure on them. Cricket was my life, my living and now, for the first time, I could see it was all under threat. I attempted to put such negative thoughts out of my head while I was given a series of injections which did at least enable me to perform in a majority of the internationals up to the finals. My last match was against the Australians in a day-night match in Sydney on 19 January where, although we lost on a slower scoring rate after a rain stoppage, we still managed to get through to the series of four finals of the Benson and Hedges World Series Cup. I was in no shape to carry on. The injury had got the better of me and I was destined to sit out the finals - which we won 3-1 - and all three Tests.

The back was painful enough; it was made all the worse for having to watch others take my place and succeed. The Tests ended 1-1 by virtue of a thrilling, Clive Lloyd-inspired win at Adelaide in the third Test, but by then I was little more than a passenger, mystified and worried by my back and genuinely fearful for the future. Could this be my last tour? What would I do for a living if this was the end? These sort of questions plagued me in the loneliness of my capacity as non-playing reserve. Others, including Lloyd, tried to reassure me that it was only a temporary scare. No professional sportsman, he said, went through a career without encountering some sort of injury, sometimes bad ones. He had had trouble enough with his knees but operations had helped him continue through more than 20 years at the top. A back injury was different, I contended. There was no way I could bowl fast without it being fully mended. Hampshire had hired me to bowl fast and although I could bat without undue difficulty, there was no chance of them keeping me on as a batsman alone. I was a regular visitor to a specialist in Sydney and he was able to relieve the pain a little - but it soon returned, sometimes more excruciatingly than ever.

The rest of the squad flew home in jubilant mood. We had retained the Sir Frank Worrell Trophy, thanks to that win at Adelaide, and we had won the Benson and Hedges World Series Cup. Our mission had been accomplished, but while others celebrated, I alone had little to get excited about. This might well have been my last trip to Australia, a country I had grown to love, and the end of me as a Test player. Being part of Lloyd's army was a privilege I was not keen to surrender. What's more I had grown used to the money. It was an unhappy journey home.

On my way back from Australia I called in at Southampton in a vain bid to get myself sorted out. They gave me massage, some treatment, a tablet or two and plenty of sympathy, but when I boarded the plane from Heathrow to Barbados I knew I had not been cured nor was my back even showing slight signs of improvement. It would have been nice to have got home basking in the light of our triumph in Australia. Instead I made my way home a deeply troubled and worried man.

Barbados were holding their trials in preparation for the impending Shell Shield. Naturally I wanted to be part of the team, my national team. I had played every year for them since 1978 when I made my debut and, with so much competition around, I was in no position to take my place for granted. Besides, the Barbados team was filled with my friends, some of whom I had known since childhood days, and we had grown used to monopolising the Shield. No one could match our success when it came to winning the trophy and it was a source of great national pride when we did so. Cricket means so much to the people of Barbados and to be seen to have the best team in the Caribbean has the same effect on its people as winning the soccer World Cup would to the average Englishman. Rivalry between the islands is always intense, particularly when it comes to cricket, and more so than people outside the Caribbean would understand. Barbados is my national team; the West Indies is the regional team. It is as though the EEC, for instance, inaugurated a combined soccer side, choosing players from all the Common Market countries. The West Indies cricket squad is the equivalent of that. Our first loyalty is to our home countries and then to the federation.

A few days rest at home eased the pain and I began to feel a little more optimistic but the real test was going to occur when I started to bowl again; when the strain and stress on my back would either disappear for ever or come back in the form of that terrifying shooting pain. I approached that net practice as nervously as I would have done had I been called up for the first time. My whole future depended on the reaction. Other players were laughing and wise-cracking as the session got under way. I was not among them. I was moody and silent, fully aware of the implications of what was for everyone else nothing more than a warm-up in front of the selectors. I tried to build up to my fastest, taking my time and not putting pressure on my back until I felt ready. I bowled three overs off my short run, one off my long run and another off my short one again. To my horror, the pain was still there and as crippling as ever. As others carried on, I turned and headed for the showers, deeply distressed and close to tears. What the hell was I going to do next? I was now at my lowest ebb. There was no chance of me playing in the Shell Shield and the new county season was less than two months away. I might be able to bat with some difficulty but there was simply no way I could bowl.

I had nowhere to turn and I was bereft of ideas about how I could rid myself of this curse which threatened to ruin me just as my career was about to take off. It was then, literally when I had all but given up hope, that I got to hear about Edmund Sealey, physiotherapist to the Barbados athletics squad. It was something of a last resort when I called him and arranged for him to have a look. I had to explore all avenues and this was yet another. But I kept asking myself what he could do for me that highly-qualified specialists in Australia and Britain had been unable to do. If they were unable to help, what could this man do?

Sealey was a muscular man in his forties and came to Barbados from his home island of St. Vincent. He operated from his base in River Road and it was there that I went, praying he might sort me out. Sealey was friendly and business-like. He gave me the once over, felt the troubled area and seemed to know immediately what to do. He told me, as I had heard before, that my back muscles were weak and they needed building up with constant exercises. For a whole month he massaged my aching and ailing back, easing the pain and at the same time breathing new life into my whole spirit.

As the treatment began to look as if it might be proving beneficial, Sealey prescribed for me a task of doing 100 sit-up exercises each day to strengthen the muscles at the base of the spine. It does not sound a lot but I can assure you 100 is hard work and I could feel the effects almost immediately. There were other exercises also and for the whole month I sweated and laboured in the knowledge that this was very much make or break time. Sealey told me exactly what to do. At the end of the month my back was much better and I began smiling again for the first time in four months; even sleep was easier. Sealey was as pleased as I was - but then came the warning. Unless I did at least 50 sit-up exercises every day for the rest of the season there would be a real danger that it could flare up all over again. It was a salutary lesson. Now, before the start of every day's cricket I play, no matter where it is or whatever the competition, I bend and arch my back and run through my list of exercises. I will never take my fitness for granted again. I realise now the strain a fast bowler puts upon his back. Lillee, for one, knows all about that. So do Imran and Graham Dilley. I realise also that if I want to keep playing at the highest level for a few more years then I must work at staying fit. My back could go again at any time. It ought not to, thanks to the expertise of my Vincentian friend, but it might - and I will never take a chance. I have no hesitation in saying he saved my career and for that he will always have my profound gratitude. The history of the game is littered with the names of players who might have achieved so much but were cut down in their prime by injury. I was nearly one of them. If I subsequently go on and take, for instance, more wickets than any other Test cricketer, the first man I shall thank publicly is Edmund Sealey. The prize will be his.

Edmund and I are today good friends and we find plenty to laugh about now, though laughter was noticeably absent when I first went to see him. I was a desperate man. Every time I'm home in Barbados I go to see him for further treatment, a massage or two and for a progress check. Because of the exercises, my back no longer troubles me but the fear that I might break down remains with me. His reassurance has much to do with my mental well-being and enables me to go about my business as a fast bowler with complete confidence. His treatment came to an end just as I was due to report to Hampshire for the 1982 season. They had been aware obviously that I had a back injury problem but were probably not aware of its extent. I felt fit, the back felt better but as I returned to England, the question was would it stand up to a long and rigorous county season? To say I looked upon the new English season with trepidation would be an understatement. I might break down again in my first over or I might be restricted to bowling medium pace, which would have pleased nobody. Only time was going to tell and my pre-season preparations were decidedly gentle. As it turned out, I was about to enjoy my most successful season ever in county cricket.

I gave no indications of what was to come, however, as I took my first tentative steps back into first class cricket. With Andy Roberts playing for the opposition, I managed the somewhat unimpressive figures of two for 56 and nought for 44 against Leicestershire at Southampton in the first match of the season and in my next, at Nottingham, fared little better with three for 53 and one for 52 in a 272-run defeat after which Clive Rice, the Nottinghamshire skipper, accused us of lack of spine when we were shot out for 56 in the second innings. In my case it was a slightly ironic accusation.

I found I was able to take wickets without having to slip into top gear. To be honest I was very reticent about doing so in case my back failed me again. That attitude changed with one heated moment at Southampton. We were playing Worcestershire and the Pakistani batsman, Younis Ahmed, was in our way. I bowled him a good length ball and, to my astonishment, he began to square up to me as if he wanted a fight. I laughed at him, which only intensified his anger and we exchanged a few four-letter words in the middle of the wicket. He accused me of trying to maim him, as I remember, and that made me livid. By now I was angry as well and I figured that if he thought that delivery was fast, it was time I really gave him something to think about. I told him so and he must have wondered what he had let himself in for as I paced out my full run for the first time for the best part of six months. I ran in, fired by anger and determination. Younis duly hit the ball into the hands of mid-wicket and retired to the pavilion. It suddenly dawned on me that I had bowled flat out and my back was still intact. I never looked back. I started to bowl off my full run regularly and I went from strength to strength.

When I consider the background to the 1982 season in England, my phenomenal success is all the more difficult to understand. Even now I wonder how I managed to achieve so much. When I reported for pre-season training the most I hoped for was about 50 wickets - provided my back improved enough for me to bowl at full strength towards the end of the season. I had envisaged, instead, I might be more use to Hampshire as a batsman. Yet once I realised Edmund Sealey's magic cure had worked and I could bowl without physical discomfort, I could do no wrong. I don't believe I shall ever be able to emulate my achievements of that particular year. In the previous three seasons with Hampshire, the record books show I took a total of 132 wickets, though in 1980, of course, I had been limited to just five matches by the West Indian tour. In 1982 I was to more than double my tally of wickets for the county. Those same record books remind me that I finished with 134 at an average of 15.73 each in first-class matches, another 20 in the John Player League and six more in the Benson and Hedges Cup. For some unaccountable reason I didn't manage one in the Nat West Bank Trophy even though we reached the quarter-finals. That apart, I simply ripped through county after county with an ease I could never have expected in a million years.

I suppose there were several causes for my huge bag of wickets. My back has ceased to trouble me; I had learned through experience how to bowl in English conditions; I was coming in faster than ever before; many wickets around the country were helping me and, as a team, Hampshire had improved. Many edges, previously unaccepted by our fielders, were this time going to hand. Bob Parks, our young wicket-keeper, didn't miss much behind the stumps. Scorers around the country were able to write the line, caught Parks, bowled Marshall time and again. At least it made life a little simpler for our own scorer, Vic Isaacs. Parks ended as the country's most successful wicket-keeper in terms of victims with 76 to his credit, 25 of them off my bowling. Our slips were also useful allies and did not miss much, even allowing for the speed at which the ball was reaching them.

There is nothing worse for a fast bowler than to do the hard part by getting a batsman to touch a delivery towards where the fielders are stationed and then watch the chance go down. Slip catches are never easy - and I have dropped my share - but it is surprising how many matches are won and lost in the slip cordon.

I was the only bowler in the country to reach 100 wickets for the season but I had to work hard to get as many as 134. I had to bowl 822 overs which, at my pace, is a hell of a lot of overs. Only Nick Cook of Leicestershire bowled more than I did and as a left-arm spinner he was coming in off a few paces, not 30 or so yards like me. I didn't mind having to bowl so much even though Nick Pocock was anxious not to bowl me into the ground. He had remembered how Andy Roberts had walked out on Hampshire in the middle of the 1978 season complaining he had been over-bowled and abused and did not want the same to happen to me.

Pocock was in a difficult position in that I was his prime bowling asset; his match winner. If I had reached the stage, like Roberts, when I felt I was shouldering too big a burden, Pocock would have killed his golden goose, so to speak. Luckily for him, I was more than happy to bowl whenever he asked and sometimes even when he didn't! As long as I felt fit, willing and able I was prepared to keep coming in and the number of overs I got through is testimony not only to my stamina but also to my desire. I have always been a fierce competitor and I was as keen as I have ever been about anything in my life.

I will admit the ambition to top 100 wickets, preferably ahead of everyone else, was a great spur initially and then a new record loomed up for me to chase. I discovered that since the County Championship had been reduced to 22 matches to make way for the one-day competitions, the highest number of wickets taken in one season was 131 and it was held by a West Indian - the great spin bowler, Lance Gibbs, had set the record when he was playing for Warwickshire. There is a great feeling of one-upmanship among West Indian players. We always want to better our team-mates and come out on top in individual clashes. I would have been keen to have beaten this record no matter who held it but the fact that it was held by another West Indian fuelled my determination still further.

I reached target number one, 100 wickets, on 25 August at Dean Park, Bournemouth when Barry Dudleston of Gloucestershire was leg before, one of 37 lbw's that season. I should add that Barry, their assistant coach, had by then scored 111. To celebrate, I took two more wickets in my next five deliveries and I was on my way to target number two. There were only four matches left but I was in such form that I knew, injuries permitting, it was not beyond me. I took eight wickets in that match, eight more in the second match of Bournemouth Week, against Yorkshire, six at Derby, seven at Uxbridge against Middlesex and so it was all down to the last match of the season at Southampton where Warwickshire were the visitors.

Bob Willis's county were bottom of the table while we needed only bonus points to ensure third place. I was now on 128, three behind the legendary Guyanese spinner who had long since gone into retirement. I soon removed Andy Lloyd and David Smith, the Warwickshire openers, had Dennis Amiss leg before to equal Gibbs and then bowled Asif Din to go one better. It was a marvellous moment, the culmination of a season's hard graft and, as far as I was concerned, a happy ending to beat all happy endings. Gibbs had set his record in 1971. It was as gratifying to learn that my 134 wickets was the best in a season since 1966 and although I know mine can be beaten, as Fred Trueman said about his 300th Test wicket, whoever does it is going to be a very tired man when he does. My one tangible reward was the Daily Telegraph's Swanton Trophy for being the first to 100 but the knowledge of my achievement had much to do with the belief I now held that I was the equal of any fast bowler in the world, and I had the facts to prove my theory was not conceit.

My best individual performance that season came at Southampton against Worcestershire when I took eight for 71 in a match we lost by one wicket off the penultimate ball, despatched for six over long on by last man Steve Perryman. It was one of 12 occasions in which I took five or more wickets and the Worcestershire match was one of four in which I nabbed 10 or more. So much for the facts. It is only when I look at them again I realise how well I had played. It is a pity we could only finish third behind Leicestershire and the champions, Middlesex, but their better balance pushed them above us, though eight wins in 22 matches was no mean achievement for a team which had been lodged at the bottom only a couple of years before. I suppose my efforts are put into perspective when I tell you that I took slightly more than a third of the county's first class wickets and my 822 overs represented a quarter of the team's entire output. Now you know why I say it was a summer to remember.

Much to my own satisfaction, my batting continued to make progress with 633 runs and a batting average of 22.60 going in mostly at number seven in the order. The highlight was an innings of 116 not out against Lancashire at Southampton. Lancashire had Clive Lloyd, whom I was always keen to impress, and Colin Croft in their line-up and I was anxious not to miss the opportunity to score a few points at their expense. Lancashire made 210 in the first innings and my five for 48 included the wicket of Lloyd. At 98 for four at the close of the first day, we were not in a good position ourselves to expose Lancashire's moderate total. Pocock was the man who changed all that. He only scored two centuries in his entire career but his 164 was of the highest class once he had overcome a streaky start. The wicket was in perfect shape and I never felt I was going to get out when I came in at 261 for five. Croft tried hard enough but his final figures of two for 102 reflect our dominance. I attacked anything loose and just under two hours later had safely recorded my first county century. It was a sweet moment in a sweet season and helped pave the way for a pulsating finish. We required 112 to win in 18 overs and we did it, thanks to some big hitting by Greenidge and John Rice, with eight balls to spare.

One of the lighter moments of the season occurred during that undefeated century against Lancashire. When I came in to bat Pocock said to me 'Take your time.' I told him since I was batting at number seven there was no time. 'I'm going to enjoy myself,' I told him. I duly lofted David Hughes' left-arm spin out of the ground and never looked back. Lloyd spotted I was not wearing a helmet and remarked on it. When I laughed, he shouted: 'Come on Crofty, he's not frightened of you.' Momentarily my smile disappeared but on a good wicket there was nothing even someone of Colin's pace could do. I have discovered many fast bowlers don't like being on the receiving end of bouncers and, although I'm not scared of them, I could never say I like facing them. As I said to Clive, 'I ain't no hero' as I called for my helmet.

Unfortunately I only managed one other score of 50 or more in 30 starts, which was a little disappointing for my own taste, but since I was doing so much bowling it would have been churlish to have expected better. Hampshire wound up the season by coming equal fifth in the John Player

League and we were able to reflect on our collective improvement. Certainly it had all been far more than I had dared hope five months earlier. I had gone from being a virtual cripple, for a professional athlete, to the top of my profession in one short English summer. I knew now I could match the best and it was a slight setback that, for once, the West Indies had no tour ahead on which I could confirm my big leap forward. I went instead to Australia in a far better frame of mind than when I had last left it, freed from pain and ready to advance my claims to being the world's best fast bowler.

* The English season of 1982 was something of a watershed: He knew he was now the best in the business. Healing physiotherapist Edmund Sealey remained a close friend and soon after Marshall's death told Barbados' "Best and Mason" radio show how Marshall returned from England at the end of the 1982 county season to thank him for saving his career. "He had already paid me for my services and said he did not have much money with him at the time and promptly gave me 100 pounds." Marshall's delight in beating Lance Gibbs' record of wickets for a county season was typical of the competition among West Indians. Colin Croft also remembers: "Invariably when playing for Barbados against Guyana in the national competitions he would greet me as he came into bat with 'Crofty boy, you are bowling fast today. I'm going to lash you and that pace around the boundaries'. He would then smile disarmingly."

9.

Million-Dollar Man

AFTER GRAHAM GOOCH and the English rebels had limped home to a three-year ban it became apparent that South Africa was back in business and prepared to spend any kind of money to lure the best players their way. The South Africans had been in cricketing exile for more than 10 years and it was obvious to us all that they were thirsting for international competition. Gooch's tour was a test case for them. The players came, the crowds came and from the easy way in which the rebels were beaten, the South Africans were quick to deduce that they were still an international power.

Having had a taste of combat with players from outside their own borders, it was inevitable they would want more. How could they improve on a tour by the Englishmen? A rebel team of Australians, perhaps? Then the rumours started to fly in England during the county season. The South Africans wanted to take on the West Indies. They were only rumours but they set us all thinking. I found it difficult to comprehend that the South Africans could even consider such a proposition would work. I found it just as difficult to believe that West Indian players would do anything other than dismiss such a notion with the contempt it deserved. How could any West Indian go to South Africa and expect to be treated as an equal when people of their race were blatantly and cruelly discriminated against for no other reason than that they were black and the minority in power were white?

I should say here that I am not highly motivated politically - indeed not many cricketers are. The many I know want to be left alone to make their living where and when they choose without political interference. I held absolutely no grudge against those of my white county colleagues who spent the winters coaching in South Africa, some of whom coached black and coloured players anyway. Cricketers have a limited time available to them to make what they can before age inevitably catches up. If this meant spending the English winter in South Africa, then in common with other West Indians in county cricket I fully supported their right to do so. At Hampshire two of my best friends are Chris and Robin Smith, both born and bred in South Africa. It never occurred to me in any way to ignore them simply because they were the sons of a regime abhorred by the rest of the world. They were my friends and if they chose to go home for the close season, then so be it. But it was another matter altogether for black players to consider offers to head for the land of apartheid; of separate development for the races and where black people could never be regarded on a par. Surely the unthinkable was not about to happen?

Dressing-room talk around the county circuit is always laced with rumours and while nothing was ever said directly, I soon realised that a West Indian tour of South Africa was far more than pie in the sky. It was a distinct possibility. I would occasionally broach the subject to other West Indians playing for the counties. Some were emphatically against the idea, some were prepared to be open-minded about it. I was surprised any of them would so much as give a second thought to an offer, no matter how large and tempting it might be. At this stage, though, money had not entered the proceedings and to my knowledge the rumours had only been mischievous whispers. Nothing more concrete than that. Instead the South Africans produced as their next coup a group of Sri Lankans who, new to Test cricket, were hopelessly overwhelmed by a far stronger and more determined team. The financial backers lost money, the public was disappointed and the rumours about a West Indian rebel squad started flying again.

By playing the West Indies, the South Africans could discover exactly how good they really were. We were the best and they knew it. Also a tour by a team of black players would have the double effect of showing to the rest of the world that cricket could break down the barriers of apartheid. It was a sort of propaganda trap and it staggered me that some West Indian players were prepared to walk straight into it. I thought no more about it. I had received no offer and I did not honestly believe such a tour would ever get started, if only because I reckoned too many West Indian players would reject the idea instantly on the grounds of principle alone. How wrong I was.

After the end of the English county season in 1982 a rare and welcome gap appeared in the hectic schedule of West Indian cricket. Since I had been first privileged to have become part of Clive Lloyd's touring circus there had not been many prolonged opportunities for rest or to find other things to do. At that stage of my career, though, in 1982 I was not a rich man and I was open to offers. India were due in the Caribbean after Christmas but from the middle of September I had the best part of four months available to me. While many of my Hampshire colleagues flew off to South Africa on coaching assignments, I accepted an engagement with Moorabbin in the Melbourne Sub-Districts League. Desmond Haynes would be playing in the same competition for Dandenong and Hartley Alleyne, the third Barbadian, joined us for some gentle practice, some coaching and a bit of relaxation in one of my favourite cities before returning to take on India.

Moorabbin finished fifth in their group that season and while I was there I took 25 wickets without exerting myself unduly. Desmond, Hartley and myself were all in 'digs' and we enjoyed ourselves as we prepared for the more rigorous cricket ahead. One day, totally out of the blue, I got a phone call at the place where I was staying. It was Dr Ali Bacher, a former South African Test player in the days before they were thrown out of the ICC, and now a powerful influence on the South African Union Board of Control. I thought it was a joke at first. How did he get my number? In very cryptic, hush-hush tones Dr Bacher told me a tour of rebel West Indians was imminent and he wanted me to be part of it. I was staggered, rendered almost speechless by the suddenness of it all. It was all in the strictest secrecy, he emphasised. No one should know negotiations between his board of control and myself were taking place. The offer was straightforward enough. I would receive 200,000 Rand, about £50,000 in those days, for a two-year contract. Airline tickets from Melbourne to Johannesburg were prepared and waiting for me in the city centre.

I could hardly believe my own words when I told him I was intrigued and a little flattered by his offer. I would give it my fullest consideration. I put the phone down dazed by our long-distance and rather one-sided conversation. The money was good; very good for someone like me still on the fringes of the West Indian team, unsure of a regular place and with no certainty of being part of the squad much longer. As Wayne Daniel had learned, no one could take it for granted that they had a job for life in Lloyd's army. I could contain myself no longer and got in touch with Desmond and Hartley, both of whom were staying nearby. They were close friends so I knew I could confide in them and even ask their advice on my dilemma. Then came more surprises. They too had received similar temptation from Dr Bacher. They, too, had been sworn to secrecy. Like me they had been told tickets were ready for them. All they had to do was board the plane and sign the contract on arrival. We were all still reeling from the shock when we made an alarming discovery. We had each been made offers which differed widely from one another. This put suspicion in our already confused minds. From this discovery, and from Dr Bacher's manner on the phone, I became a little worried by the whole episode. I formed the view that I might not be able to trust him. He must have known we would talk about it among ourselves. He must have known also that we would discuss the size of our contracts.

We pieced together our conversations with Dr Bacher. From what he had told us, Lawrence Rowe had been lined up as captain and, among many others, David Murray and Colin Croft had already signed away their birthright for a fistful of Rand. I was astonished players of that calibre had agreed to go to South Africa and I can only imagine it must have been made worth their while. I was particularly perplexed by Croft's decision. I knew he was having trouble with his back but here was a fast bowler in his prime, feared the world over for his snarling aggression and for his sheer success. He was barely 30 with 125 wickets already under his belt and as part of the Holding-Roberts-Garner-Croft pace attack seemingly assured of at least another two or three years at the top.

Now there was something to think about: while they were in harness I was still a reserve and, much as I wanted the West Indies to be successful, I also wanted a regular Test place. But with Croft out of the reckoning I figured there would be a chance for me to break through and, as I thought to myself, once you are in the West Indies team it is almost as difficult to get out of it, providing you are supplying the goods. I must admit it was the thought that Croft had defected which helped influence my decision not to go to South Africa. The South Africans had done their homework. They knew I was vulnerable to an offer because until 1982, as a fast bowling reserve, I had played in only 12 Tests for a moderate haul of 34 wickets. I had been around for the best part of four years and had not been able to clinch a regular place in the international team, and there was always the fear that an unknown might emerge from one of the islands as suddenly as I had or that I might be injured, in which case I would be discarded as just another player who nearly made the grade. The money would be enough for me to set up a business at home in Barbados and I could continue in county cricket if I wanted.

But Desmond, Hartley and myself also knew the consequences. There would be no wishy-washy half measures like a three-year ban. Our players would be out of cricket for life and, at 24 years of age, this was something I was not prepared to contemplate or accept as an inevitable by-product of my defection. In short, after a good deal of lonely soul-searching and collective discussion we all resolved to leave Dr Bacher's offer on the table. Once made, we were all the happier for our decision, though it wasn't easy to wave goodbye to £50,000!

Most of all it was my love of Barbados which prevented me taking up the South African bait. At the back of my mind I was plagued by the idea that I could become an outcast among my own people for helping add succour to a political system which openly denigrated blacks and, indeed, anyone who was not white. I wondered how I would be accepted. Would I be shunned in the streets of my home territory? Would family, friends and neighbours refuse to talk to me? Would I be forced to take my ill-gotten gains and go into exile to some place which I knew would never be home? These sort of questions played on my mind and I considered what to do.

Having declined the offer and feeling better for it, we went about our business in Melbourne, hoping that we had heard the last of Dr Bacher. Unfortunately this was not the case. Word got out that a West Indies tour was going ahead almost immediately and every name under the Caribbean sun was being bandied about as a possible candidate. Then the speculation became more specific. One morning I picked up a copy of the Melbourne paper, The Age - a paper I like and respect - and discovered I was in Johannesburg ready to join the rebels. Since I was coaching at the time on the peninsula about 15 miles from Melbourne city centre, this came as quite a surprise! Desmond and Hartley were also supposed to be in Johannesburg but they were with me at the time. Obviously someone had told The Age that the South Africans had made us an offer which they thought we would be unable to refuse. It must have come as a shock to all concerned with the rebel tour that we had apparently snubbed them. Anyway, our time and contracts in Melbourne were up and instead of going to Johannesburg to infamy and fortune, we turned instead to Barbados and peace of mind.

As the plane circled over the palm-fringed island of Barbados, little did we realise what sort of reception would be waiting for us when we stepped on to the tarmac of the little Grantley Adams Airport. There to meet us among cheers and tears of welcome was a government minister, Senator David Simmons, chairman of the National Sports Council. 'I am so glad you boys have had the good sense to turn down the offer and to come home to your own people,' he told us. 'You will not regret this. You will be able to live with yourselves which may not be the case for some of your countrymen.' I think we were all slightly embarrassed by the intensity of our reception but it was all rather emotional after such a long flight home. Perhaps Mr Simmons and his welcoming committee had not realised how close we had come to saying 'yes' to Dr Bacher. For a few heady minutes, though, we were heroes in our homeland and delighted by it.

Mr Simmons and the Barbados government might have been glad that the three of us had decided to stay legitimate but they had to come to terms with the news that nine Barbadians, including Albert Padmore, the manager, and Gregory Armstrong, the liaison officer, had not. In Lawrence Rowe's rebel squad were some close friends of mine, all of whom had accepted the repercussions of an inevitable life ban and decided to take the massive offers from South Africa. I, for one, did not blame any of them. Joining Padmore and Armstrong were Alvin Greenidge, Sylvester Clarke, Franklyn Stephenson, Ezra Moseley, Emmerson Trotman, Collis King and David Murray. Alvin had played a few Tests when Kerry Packer creamed off most of our best players, and of the others only Murray and Clarke were still candidates for a Test place: Murray is the best keeper I have bowled to but even he was now being pressed for a place by Jeff Dujon.

Only Murray, Clarke and Colin Croft were on the last official West Indies tour of Australia in 1981-82 so the rebel party had the look of a fringe squad. Within the Barbados contingent there were many close links which may have accounted for their mass acceptance. Greenidge and Trotman, for instance, were cousins, while Padmore and Stephenson were brought up in the same district of St James. Clarke, Moseley and King were also friends from their boyhood days. Alvin Kallicharran and Lawrence Rowe were, of course, exceptional players but neither had any realistic chance at this stage of their careers of getting back into Test cricket.

By a twist of fate the rebel tour had now opened the door to me to hold down a regular Test place. Croft had been in my way and Clarke, with his pace, bounce and strength, was never far from the thoughts of the West Indian selectors. Now they were both out of the reckoning by their own choice and my path was nicely smoothed by their absence. I think Sylvester, who never says much, had probably come to the conclusion that he was always going to be, at best, a handy reserve but I was surprised at Croft. He had taken up residence in Miami, Florida and had ambitions outside cricket, but I am sure he would have been given preference over me at Test level even then. I often wonder what might have happened had I joined the rebels. Like the others, I suspect I would have been forgotten quickly, taking with me memories of the few Tests I had played in and the countries cricket had enabled me to visit. The South Africans may have been delighted with their coup and the Caribbean governments had cause for their sense of concern and outrage, but from a purely cricketing point of view, the West Indian rebel 16 hardly represented the best from the islands and the strength of the official team was not going to be impaired for long, if at all.

Those players who headed for Johannesburg knew they would never play any kind of cricket in the Caribbean again, not even club cricket with their friends. They were isolated in a cricketing sense for the rest of their careers. Like me, they must have wondered if they had made the right decision. After all, a life ban and the wrath of family and friends are not the sort of things anyone can take in their stride. The life ban was soon implemented but to their surprise and delight, the hatred from their countrymen never materialised. Obviously politicians declared their opposition in no uncertain terms but the ordinary people, particularly in Barbados, were right behind the players; not for going to South Africa but simply for taking a brave decision to make the very best of their ability and the limited time available to them in which to do it: I never heard of any rebel being ostracised. Indeed the support they received must have stunned them. My own attitude, and it's one mirrored by other West Indian players, is that they made their choice and they deserved the best of luck. I did not condone their decisions but I knew what sort of agonies they must have gone through before agreeing to the tour. There was a lot of money involved and since many of those who went did not have regular employment, it would have been hard to reject the terms on political opposition alone.

Some of these guys were to receive money they could only have dreamt about. Some of them could envisage being set up for life; their futures and those of their families secure for ever more. Can you imagine the torment they must have gone through? I was confident that at that stage of my career I had made the right decision, for I was not married and had no commitments. What's more, I was a member of the West Indies squad with a long future in the game stretching in front of me. Compared with many others, my choice was an easy one. For the vast majority of the players who eventually made up the rebels the temptation must have been incredible. It would have been far harder to have turned down the South Africans. With that in mind, they all - to my knowledge - were backed fully by those close to them and by the cricket-loving public in their native islands. Certainly in Barbados the view among all those I spoke to about the subject was that these men were professional cricketers who had made a professional decision to take their expertise where it was most wanted. Unfortunately that place was South Africa and its despised regime of racial discrimination.

I had heard so much about South Africa and seen at close quarters the high calibre of their players performing with and against me in county cricket. Many white cricketers in the county game went to South Africa in the close season and came back with tales of its beauty and the wealthy life-style they enjoyed out there. The fact that it may have been enjoyed at the expense of 24 million blacks did not occur to many of them. In fairness, they had not taken an openly political decision to go there. Like the rebels, they had received offers as professional cricketers from the South Africans and, in the absence of viable alternatives, had accepted it. But it was always noticeable how names like Soweto and Crossroads did not crop up in county dressing-room conversations. Why should it? Nor did Handsworth or Brixton. We are cricketers not politicians.

Even so, I was anxious to find out from black cricketers what they thought of South Africa when they returned from the first, highly-successful tour. The reaction was mixed but the sentiments were the same. In short most of the rebels had lapped up the experience without feeling at ease there. The whites could not have been more hospitable or welcoming. The crowds were large and appreciative. The country was indeed beautiful and the lifestyle for those with whom they came into contact, that's to say the white sponsors, was pampered and expensive. I formed the impression the black rebels were well received as a team; a squad of bold pioneers.

But as individuals, it was a different matter. There was not the same open-armed acceptance. The well-documented story of Croft getting into a whites-only train carriage in Cape Town is a case in point. As a group who had defied their own governments and who at a single blow had ripped down political barriers, the rebels were greeted like men who had rescued shipwrecked survivors on a desert island. As private citizens, the welcome was not quite so gushing. David Murray told me how much he had enjoyed the cricket but Kallicharran said he missed the atmosphere of official Test cricket. Others knew they had only been shown the best of South Africa. They had stayed at the best hotels and travelled in style. They had gone to all the glittering receptions and had enjoyed the adulation of a cricket-mad public starved of international competition. In the first year, the tour was over before many of the players had had a chance to form lasting impressions of the place. At the conclusion of the second year, most of the rebels said it had all been novel and exhilarating for a time but as individuals, they would never contemplate returning. Admittedly King, Kallicharran and one or two others have gone back on club and provincial contracts but with a life-ban hanging over them, it was often a question of doing that or doing nothing back home in the Caribbean.

I thought my part in the South African business was dead and buried. The tour of 1983 had already taken place and the tour for the following year by the West Indian rebels was well beyond the planning stage. After the visit of India to the Caribbean early in 1983 I returned to England to play for Hampshire in the County Championship and take part in the World Cup. As far as I was concerned, these were my immediate and only objectives. But the South Africans would not leave me alone. They had obviously sensed how much I had wavered in Melbourne before declining their offer and they seemed convinced I could be bought off. At the end of the 1983 tour they had come to the conclusion that the West Indian rebels needed bolstering with a couple of big names, and from what I have since discovered, I was on a hit-list of four. Dr Bacher was sent to England with

Malcolm Marshall at the height of his powers

Marshall the dynamic bowler...

...and batsman

Marshall the Coach

Marshall with Shaun Pollock and Barry Richards at Robin Smith's Benefit match in 1996

Connie Marshall and son Mali seated
at the Memorial Service in Southampton.

Tributes were paid to Marshall at the memorial service in Southampton by (right) former Hampshire captain Mark Nicholas...

...and (left) mentor and fellow Barbados and West Indies fast bowler, Rev. Wes Hall...

...and (right) current Hampshire captain and close friend, Robin Smith.

Cricket played with a smile

MALCOLM DENZIL MARSHALL 1958 - 1999

an open cheque book to sign me, Gordon Greenidge, Viv Richards and Joel Garner. The South Africans had told Richard Austin, Herbert Chang and the Jamaican fast bowler Ray Wynter they would not be required for the second tour. Austin had played in two Tests, Chang in only one and Wynter none at all. They were not the sort of names who were going to bring crowds through the turnstiles of The Wanderers or Newlands and, duly paid off, they were expendable. If Dr Bacher could persuade one or all of us to go to South Africa in 1984 it would represent another coup for them and give the second leg a massive boost.

Dr Bacher is a persuasive man but I thought I had heard the last of him the previous year. Far from it. He got in touch, told me about his plans and informed me that he could now talk really big money, if that was what interested me. No cricketer can afford to reject an offer without careful consideration and once more I was plunged into a maelstrom of doubts and contrasting thoughts. All the mixed emotions I had encountered in Melbourne and which I had so happily cast aside flooded back. The least I could do was meet Dr Bacher and talk through my problem with him. We arranged to get together at Portsmouth, where Hampshire were playing a county match, and he slipped into the ground anonymously, watched some of the game and fixed a meeting at a seafood restaurant in Southsea. We talked about the state of cricket, the West Indies, South Africa, county cricket and lots more besides. I was anxious to hear every word about the prospects for the next rebel tour. Was I interested? he asked. I told him I was but only tentatively. I needed to know more before I was able to give him a final and definite answer. As we left the restaurant he promised to come up with a financial offer and we arranged another meeting.

Our next liaison was straight out of a James Bond movie, except the location was hardly of the exotic variety. I cannot imagine Bond at work in a Wimpy Bar but this was where Dr Bacher and I had our next, and last, meeting. Dr Bacher was anxious to keep his mission as secret as possible and, to my knowledge, no one knew he had been conferring with the four of us at different venues around England in his attempt to persuade us to defect to his side of cricket's iron curtain. Certainly there was not much chance of us being spotted at breakfast time at the Wimpy Bar in Southampton's London Road. Among little groups of dock-workers heading home from nightshift and early morning commuters we sat down to talk terms. Like two boxers sparring, the conversation went in short, sharp bursts but neither of us was very happy in such strange circumstances.

Eventually it came down to the bottom line. 'How much?', I asked him. The Doctor paused. He wanted me to play for Transvaal as part of the deal. 'How much?', I asked again. He could contain himself no longer. 'One million United States dollars,' he said, leaning across the greasy table. It was my turn to pause. I thought I was dreaming. Had he really said one million dollars? 'That's our offer,' reiterated Dr Bacher with the look of a card-player who had just pulled out a string of aces. I gulped as I tried to take in the sheer enormity of the proposition. One million dollars for one, three-month tour and a contract with Transvaal. Fleetingly, I tried to imagine what I could do with such a vast amount of money. I looked him straight in the eye. 'No thanks,' I told him. Now it was his turn to be staggered. He spilled his coffee down his shirt-front in his shock! Recovering his poise and wiping down his shirt, he could scarcely contain his disbelief at my audacity. 'Malcolm Marshall', he said. 'You are a very good cricketer but a foolish young man.' With that he excused himself and we left the dock-workers to their breakfasts.

I heard no more from the Doctor. The affair was over once and for all, or at least my role in it. I discovered subsequently that Viv had rejected an offer of 1.5 million US dollars. I have no idea the size of the carrots dangled in front of Gordon and Joel. In the end all Dr Bacher had to show for his visits were the contracts of Monte Lynch of Surrey, Faoud Bacchus and my old friend, Hartley Alleyne. Bacchus had played for the West Indies in the World Cup in 1983 and was probably still a contender for a Test place. He comes from a wealthy background and was living in Canada when he made his decision. As for Hartley, I could see why he had made up his mind to join the rebels. He had been in outstanding form for Barbados in the 1983 Shell Shield season but had been called for throwing in Jamaica and Trinidad. I know Hartley is not a 'chucker' but it is difficult to shake off such a reputation once it has been formed. Hartley also had his problems at Worcestershire during the English season of 1983 and I think he must have realised it would be wise, at a low ebb in his career, to take the South African money. He was a success on the tour and has subsequently returned to play for Natal. For my own part I have never had cause to have any doubts about my decision not to go. Not for one moment have I regretted my stand. I know I was right and what has happened in my career since then has confirmed my belief. I am only glad the decision was not forced upon me by circumstances. I was in a powerful position to refuse and I am glad I did.

If South Africa was ever readmitted to the Test arena I would have no hesitation in going there to see it for myself but I cannot see any way in which this is ever likely to happen. South Africa has no chance of rejoining the ICC during my career span and so that is the end of the matter. There is no way I would ever jeopardise my Test place now, not even for a million dollars.

* South Africa was still the cricketing demon when Marshall's career was at its peak. Dr Ali Bacher persuaded many of his contemporaries to join the rebel tours but it was never a serious consideration for Marshall nor, he claimed, the other major names. None of the rebels returned to official international cricket but some, like Sylvester Clarke, were able to continue simultaneously in English and South African domestic cricket. Clarke played for Surrey and Transvaal where Marshall, of course, was offered the job before him. Eventually, post-Apartheid, Marshall did go to play provincial cricket for Natal.

Robin Smith, born in South Africa, went on to have a full career in England's Test team and became a close friend. Smith remembers his debut against Marshall at Leeds in 1988. "It was the fourth Test and the West Indies won it comfortably by ten wickets to take a 3-0 lead. I remember the very first ball he bowled to me in Test cricket. We had joked in the Hampshire dressing room about what would happen if we ever had to face each other. He always said that if he had to bowl me my first ball in Test cricket it would be a half volley. To my astonishment he was as good as his word. I was so nervous I failed to hit it properly. When I got down to his end I asked him to bowl me another but he just laughed. 'You have had your chance,' he said. That was Malcolm for you. For all his desire to win he was a nice and decent man underneath. He knew I would be petrified and wanted to give me one off the mark. Can you imagine anyone else doing that?"

10.

Fast Bowlers' Union

FAST BOWLERS HAVE a curious alliance, I have discovered over the years. Bowlers win matches, as the West Indies can readily testify, and good bowling sides are more likely to be successful than sides depending on their batsmen. That's why I thought the top bowlers would somehow be kept under wraps away from too much fraternisation with the enemy. Yet one of my greatest influences has been Dennis Lillee, a man never slow to talk about his craft, analyse his wickets and pass on tips and information - even to rivals like me.

Lillee gives credit to the Englishman John Snow for teaching him how to bowl the leg-cutter. He taught the trick to me and I have since passed it on to Imran Khan. I suppose you could say the information has gone from Sussex around the world and back to Sussex again but, if nothing else, it shows how friendly most fast bowlers are towards each other and how much we are aware of problems encountered by people who should be at our throats. That's not to say we take it easy against other fast bowlers when we play against them. Far from it. There is a sort of kudos to be had from getting out another fast bowler. On the field there is plenty of rivalry. Off it we tend to be pals, united by a common aim - to destroy the opposition by pace and cunning. When Lillee was in his prime he could go through any batting order by speed alone but as he got older and injuries took their toll, he learned to modify his game and to claim wickets as much by stealth as by raw pace. At my age, I can get wickets through speed but I like to think I use my head already in the knowledge that, like Lillee, I must learn to adapt when age creeps on.

I have never been scared to approach other fast bowlers to talk tactics and technique, indeed I did so regularly when I was serving my apprenticeship with the West Indians, surrounded as I was by some of the greatest exponents of the art, and I have done so since with both friend and foe. Lillee was always easy to talk to and I went to him when I noticed every now and then how he would roll his wrists, almost like a spinner. I wondered what he was doing and what he was attempting to achieve. Lillee admitted it was the leg-cutter he had been taught by Snow and how it had become one of his most effective weapons. Much depended on the type of surface on which he was bowling but he felt batsmen struggled to recognise the delivery and were not always adequately prepared to cope with it. As he neared the end of his career he used it more and more and, as we all know, he was still picking up wickets as regularly at the end as he was at the beginning. Lillee was only too keen to pass on the 'secret' and now it has become a vital part of my armoury.

I have a lot of time for Lillee. I didn't see much of him in his prime in the early 1970s yet in my opinion he was surely the best of all fast bowlers. Even at the end when he was tired and reaching the finale of a long and successful career, he was always trying, always pumping those arms of his like pistons. I shall never be able to thank him enough for passing on the tip about leg-cutting - after all, he didn't have to! I have since lost count of the number of times that particular delivery has got me a wicket. I began to use it during the English summer of 1982 for Hampshire and a fair proportion of my 134 wickets were the result of my perfecting it on all types of surfaces, though only after plenty of practice and trial and error in the Southampton nets. Dennis, among many others, made me realise how essential hard work was to any type of success, but once I had literally come to grips with the leg-cutter I knew I now had something other than great speed at my disposal and, with the thought that my back could go again at any time, this was a great comfort.

I have admitted how some of the wickets up and down England in 1982 helped me but there was a strange irony involved. Once my reputation started to get around and I started taking wickets by the bucketful, county captains not unnaturally conspired with their groundsmen in a bid to deaden my effectiveness when I came to their neck of the woods. I would go out before the start of play on the first morning of an away match and notice how the groundsmen had obviously done everything possible to make sure I would get no help whatsoever from the pitch. They would even tell me it would be better suited to spinners, little realising they were playing into my hands. The leg-cutter is - or can be - like a 90 mph spinner and those same groundsmen who had worked so diligently to reduce my capacity to run through the home side were in fact doing me a favour. By close of play there were, more than once, accusing glances aimed in the direction of groundsmen who thought they had done their best for their skippers only to prepare instead a pitch absolutely to my liking. Imran Khan must have noticed I was using something different when I was bowling and after watching me carefully he asked me how to bowl the leg-cutter one day at Hove. Imran was a little worried that he was becoming predictable with his in-swing to the right-hander and needed some variation. It gave us both cause for a smile when I told him how I had learned the trick from Dennis Lillee, who in turn had been told about it by John Snow. Snowy and Imran had even been team-mates at Sussex for a short time in 1977 I have since found out, though Imran had only recently moved there from Worcestershire and Snow was just ending an illustrious career.

Of present players outside the West Indies, I admire Imran as a bowler above all others. He has been a magnificent performer for his country and he is just as likely to get batsmen out at Sydney as he is in Lahore. Like all great bowlers, Imran has a fierce pride in his professionalism and a determination to give value for money. Looking at his record of nearly 300 Test wickets, I often wonder how he might have got on in stronger bowling teams, but he has never complained and has been a magnificent example to all of us in the game about how to conduct ourselves and how to play every game with 100 per cent effort. He is now nearing the veteran stage for a bowler but his powers show no sign of abating and he remains as dangerous today as he did in his prime. It is precisely because he knows how to vary his pace and deliveries that he has been able to extend his career in spite of the day-to-day wear of five months of county cricket and Tests at home and abroad. I hope I can do the same because there are some fast bowlers who refused to acknowledge the passing of the years and were still trying to do in their early 30s what they were doing 10 years before.

Jeff Thomson was the most feared fast bowler in world cricket in the mid-70s and was still making a living out of the game at 35 thanks to his great strength and his ability even at that age to trouble batsmen with that famous action of his. Yet, on the evidence of the Australian tour to England in 1985, unlike his great partner Lillee, he never learned to vary and alter his game - at least not to the same extent. This may seem a strange statement to make about someone who took 200 wickets in 51 Tests but it ought to have been many, many more. Geoff Lawson looked at one time as if he might be a world-class successor to Lillee and Thomson but the record books confirm my view that his greatest moments have been on home soil. In young Craig McDermott, the Aussies have a potentially outstanding young fast bowler and time is on his side, but I suspect the Australians will have been a little disappointed in recent years not to have unearthed a new pair of Lillee and Thomsons. These things tend to run in cycles. When Clive Lloyd's team were being beaten 5-1 in 1975-76 in Australia, the Aussies had an embarrassing quantity of quick bowling talent at their disposal. Ten years later, after Packer and the South African rebels, there is a dearth of genuine class and the memory of Lillee, even struggling with injuries in his last days, remains fresh in the memory of a hungry public.

McDermott will learn there is more to fast bowling than bowling fast. It is a craft which requires constant work to perfect and hone into shape and I have no doubts he can reach the top and stay there. To the outsider it looks a simple job, just running up to a certain mark and bowling at a set of stumps at the other end 22 yards away. The history of the game, though, has famous examples of players who either did reach the top or nearly did and then disappeared as quickly as they arrived. Before my time, Bob Massie of Australia is an obvious candidate for the title of Nearly Man. At Lord's in 1972 he took 16 for 137 in the Test against England but within a year or two his powers had mysteriously vanished and he was not even able to get into his state team.

No one connected with Hampshire will ever forget the case of poor Kevin Emery, a tall young fast bowler who came to us from Minor Counties cricket and in his first season, 1982, took 83 wickets, showing enough to earn selection for England B against Pakistan. I knew Kevin better than most; he even lived at my house for a summer or two and there is no logical reason why he could not now be England's number one - I believe Kevin was as good a player as I have seen from England since I have been over here. Yet, all of a sudden, he lost direction and self-belief. A foot injury did not help but he never again achieved the same success and after two exasperating years, Hampshire were forced to release him. Kevin has since tried to force his way back via other counties and on ability alone, he has few equals. His story is a sad one and a lesson in its way to all of us. We must treat our job seriously but there is a thin dividing line between that and becoming over obsessed with the theory of our craft: sadly in Kevin's case his loss was also England's.

No one thought more about the game and his part in it than Andy Roberts, the man I succeeded at Hampshire and in the West Indies team. Andy was a deep thinker about most subjects and particularly when it came to cricket. He could think-out a batsman by varying every ball and he was never slow to take me under his wing and to offer me advice. Andy had made his reputation, like Lillee, as an out-and-out fast bowler, but he knew he could not expect to surprise batsmen by pace for the rest of his career if he hoped to continue after the age of 30 or so. Holding and Garner were also always ready to help a rookie and if I now analyse what in essence they all told me it was this: never bowl the same ball twice in succession - variation is the key to success. I pride myself on being a good learner but it took me some time to realise what good sense they were aiming in my direction. I was getting wickets by sheer speed and I could see no logical reason at first why I should modify the whole approach to my work. I now know why and I will always be grateful for their advice, tolerance and understanding. They helped make me the cricketer I am today.

I was lucky, of course. Not many other cricketers can claim to have had coaches with more than 200 Test wickets each to their name. They became my friends as well as my mentors and, although in time I became faster than all of them, I never ceased to marvel at their particular individual skills. Roberts faded from the scene at about the time I was reaching maturity so I have to admit it was my advent which finished him as a Test player. He would be the last to hold it against me. There is a limit to the number of fast bowlers any team can field - even the West Indies - and one day I too shall be replaced, quite possibly by someone I helped to teach. In their own right, Roberts, Holding and Garner are or were great bowlers, and now that I have also passed the 200 mark in terms of weight of wickets, we must be the most successful pace attack of all time.

When it comes to batsmen I have no hesitation in saying Lawrence Rowe is the best I have ever seen. I loved the way he played, his feel for the game, the grace of his shots and his consummate artistry. Lawrence is my favourite player of all time, apart from Sobers, and probably a more orthodox player than even the great man. I only wish the statistics of his career did him full justice, but sadly I fear he will be remembered principally for the endless succession of injuries which marred his progress rather than for what he actually achieved. In praising Lawrence so highly I take into account how I have been a colleague of Viv Richards for the best part of a decade. Viv is a fantastic cricketer, I'm the first to concede, and will go down in the game's history as one of its great exponents; yet in my opinion, Lawrence was a better conventional batsman. Viv will have the record to prove his greatness when he retires and it is a shame Lawrence will never be considered by historians as at least an equal. Lawrence never possessed Viv's awesome power, or his ability to brutalise an attack, but for technique and timing I have never found anyone to match him. Fielding to him was always a tantalising experience. He used to place his shots measured to the last inch just out of reach of a fielder. I can only describe it as like trying to catch a butterfly; just when you thought you were going to cut off the shot it would elude your grasp and run away to the boundary.

I first saw Lawrence in action at my home ground in Bridgetown in 1974 in the third Test against England. England supporters will not need reminding how Rowe enjoyed his finest moment, scoring 302 and inviting comparisons with George Headley and Donald Bradman. From my vantage point in the big crowd at Kensington Oval it was magical stuff. Like everyone else privileged to witness it, I was enchanted and mesmerised by the Jamaican's command over the bowling. Without ever assuming any of the sort of domination we have come to expect from Richards or Gordon Greenidge, Lawrence stroked his way to 302, the first 40 or so I remember coming in boundaries. It was a superb exhibition. I went home, an impressionable 15-year-old, convinced I had seen a new star born; a player fit to hold the centre stage of world cricket for the next 10 years at least. He was utterly correct in every movement, as elegant as any player I have ever seen, though he was never slow to punish a bad ball. I thought him the complete batsman and for a few brief weeks he even replaced Sobers as the focal point of my idolatry.

Unfortunately for himself and, I would venture, the game in general he was never able to fulfil his massive potential. It is not necessarily rare for a cricketer to have to return from an overseas tour because of injury - it nearly happened to me in Australia in 1981-82 - but it is rare for a player to have to go home three times from tours. That's what happened to Lawrence and that's why I suppose he was unable to milk the full benefit of his great talent. We called him a 'softie' because most of his ailments seemed so trivial and it must have crossed the minds of various managements that he was something of a hypochondriac. Twice followers in England were denied all but glimpses of his rare skills in 1973 and 1980 when he was forced out of tours through injuries comparatively minor in retrospect.

In fairness it was a different story in 1974-75 when problems with his eyes curtailed the tour of India, Pakistan and Sri Lanka when he was being billed as the star batsman. Jamaicans worshipped Lawrence and I saw enough of him later to realise why they felt he was the closest batsman yet to perfection. From his debut in 1972, when he scored 214 and 100 not out against New Zealand, he only played in another 29 Tests, finishing his career with just over 2,000 runs at an average of 43.55. In my view this fails to reflect the outstanding qualities of a man I shall always look upon as the batsman I most enjoyed watching. Even before he lead the rebel West Indians to South Africa in 1983 and thereby ended his first-class career, I, among many others, hoped he would somehow shrug off all his injuries to bask once more in the world spotlight. By then, of course, Viv had become the overlord of the West Indian middle order and Lawrence was well down the queue for a vacancy. He last played for an authentic West Indian team in 1980 when he was 31, at an age when he should have matured into an all-time great.

I suppose Lawrence's story, not that I need reminding, shows all professional sportsmen how injuries - or lack of them - can play such a crucial part. Who knows what he might have achieved if he had stayed clear of trouble and allowed his unmatched natural ability to flow as it should have done. As it is, tales of Lawrence's 302 will be overshadowed by the deeds performed instead by Viv in particular, Clive and Gordon. I will always rate Lawrence higher than Viv but that is in no way intended as a slight on a player who, unlike Rowe, has gone on to prove himself the best in the world. Viv is the master batsman and I'm the first to acknowledge that mastery and to applaud his stupendous achievements all around the world. It has been a pleasure to play with him and a pain to bowl to him. If he is in the mood there is simply no way to stop him.

To those who don't know him well, Viv comes across as a shy, rather quietly spoken sort of man with his deep faith in God and impeccable good manners. To those of us who see him at close quarters within the West Indies dressing-room he is supremely confident and a very tough character. We can tell when he is in the right frame of mind to want to go out and hammer the opposition, and it needs either an exceptional ball or the onset of boredom to remove him from the crease. He is the most dominant cricketer I have ever seen and one who relishes his acknowledged accolade as the world's number one batsman.

One of the reasons why Viv has already achieved what Lawrence should have done is, I suppose, the sheer strength of his personality. He dominates the West Indies dressing-room as much as he does the opposition's bowling, not by bawling and shouting louder than everyone else, or by baying orders at the rest of us; his mere presence is enough. He is the same sort of man on the field as he is off it, arrogant and disdainful at times and always the centre of attention. It is fantastic to watch the way he imposes himself on a game and not much fun if you are bowling at him. Attacking fields change immediately when Viv swaggers to the wicket, even before he has faced a ball. He expects to score runs and he usually does and, most importantly, he succeeds on all types of wickets and on all types of occasions. That is the hallmark of a truly great batsman and to that he owes not only his incredible talent but also his unshakeable self-belief, a strong ego and a fierce pride in his performance.

Not every player, even with world-class talents, shares those qualities of character. There are many other cricketers with similar ability but who will never be able to destroy bowlers by force of will as Viv does. With Ian Botham in the same team Somerset have been fortunate to have two such formidable men who are not just ordinary cricketing talents. Most teams have outstanding players whom the opposition respect and worry about but Botham and Richards have been genuinely feared internationally and around the county circuit. I love nothing better when playing for Hampshire than to dismiss Richards, because of this great but friendly rivalry which exists among West Indians. We chide each other on tour about what we are going to do to each other when the next county season comes around. Viv is always telling me how he is going to take me apart and I'm always telling him how I'm going to destroy a legend and how I know all his weaknesses. As a result every meeting has a bit extra to goad us on and I suppose over the years we have come out about equal.

Roger Harper, the Guyanese all-rounder who plays for Northamptonshire, is another with whom I have a verbal joust in the off season or English winter and then a more physical battle in the County Championship. These guys often boast about how they will smash me to all parts of the ground and I never forget even if the comments are made in jest. They know I will be ready for them when they take on Hampshire, though everything is always said in fun and never meant to be taken too seriously. Even so, the rivalry does add a little spice to our clashes since many counties employ West Indians and this means most matches contain some kind of personal duel. If nothing else, and it must all seem a little trivial to those not involved, it shows the competitive spirit among West Indian players.

At one time, with some justification, the West Indies were accused of being something of a soft touch; highly skilled but often liable to crumble under pressure. Clive Lloyd changed all that and now we have the instinct for a challenge to match any nation. That is why England are so lucky to have Botham when he stays out of trouble. Among all his great qualities is this love of a battle - as he proved so fabulously against the Australians in 1981. I always pull out my best when I play against him, no matter what sort of match it is. Like my little confrontations with Richards, the same sort of intensity is stirred up when I take on 'Beefy'. I relish the challenge and so does he. Like Viv he is prepared to try something new the whole time, something others would not dare and more often than not, they both get away with their audacity - which is very disheartening for their opponents. I have had my fair share of success against Botham over the years, rather more than he has had against me, but I always know I must be at my best against him if he is bowling or batting.

It's lucky for me that neither Botham nor Richards are left-handed, because if I have a blind spot, then it is bowling to left-handers: I hate them. I struggle to get my angles right and since so many of them look so awkward, it really irritates me when they start scoring runs off me. Of all the batsmen I have ever played against in 10 years or more of top cricket, the South African-born Australian opening batsman Kepler Wessels was the one I least enjoyed bowling to. I mean no great disrespect when I say Wessels hardly looked a Test player, but with those nudges, flicks and pushes, he wore me down and was probably as successful against me as any batsman. His record of 1761 runs in 24 Tests showed others had problems with him too.

A final word, talking of players I love and hate to play against: I can always sense when a batsman is apprehensive and among those I'm convinced has no stomach for the fast stuff is Derek Randall. Yet he is such a clown I cannot be sure he is not trying to con me. For a man who might not relish the truly fast he has certainly piled up some runs over the years. I should also like to place on record my admiration for the former England wicket-keeper, Bob Taylor. I have already said David Murray is the man who has kept best to me, but there has been no one to touch Taylor for technical excellence in my estimation. For me he was the master of his trade.

---

* Ian Botham called Marshall a 'skinny wimp' in jest but there was no hiding their mutual admiration. Roger Harper, a national teammate and county adversary, and later to replace him as West Indies coach, recounted in the Guyana Chronicle how Marshall was capable of getting wickets in any conditions and developed different strategies for different countries. "When we were playing in Pakistan on very flat tracks, he would request only one slip but would have a ring of fielders on both sides of the wicket. The aim was to get the batsmen out bowled or lbw while not giving away easy runs. As he always said, 'You have to do what is necessary to get the job done'."

At the time of Marshall's death, Kepler Wessels was a South African national team selector. "The duels with Marshall will always be one of the highlights of my career. As the spearhead of the West Indian attack, he was very aggressive with a lethal bouncer. There was no malice in his approach. He just played the game hard. Respect was the key when one played the West Indies at that time. It was a tough task to win their respect but once a batsman did so they admired him for his skill and courage. So it was with Malcolm and I. We were both fierce competitors who came hard at each other but there was always respect. I will treasure those battles. They were hostile and intense but somehow one feels a more complete person for having gone through all that."

Kevin Emery, remembered here by Marshall and now captain of Swindon Cricket Club, recalls an incident of a batsman less brave than Wessels: "We were playing Surrey and you could almost smell the fear of Grahame Clinton and Alan Butcher as they faced Marshall at his fastest. I was at silly point to Butcher and Malcolm was coming in very fast. Malcolm bowled a snorter to Butcher that passed him by the throat, clipped him on the shoulder and went through to our wicket-keeper Bobby Parks. There was a muted appeal from Malcolm and Bobby. The umpire was unmoved but Butcher still walked off. I knew the ball had come off the batsman's shoulder and confronted him in the bar afterwards. 'No I didn't touch it,' he told me. 'But at least I'm alive, aren't I?' That said it all."

11.

Vengsarkar Vengeance

DILIP VENGSARKAR is one of the finest batsmen in contemporary cricket and proof of his quality came in 1986 when he became the first overseas player to score three Test centuries at Lords: not even Bradman could match that. Yet, while I readily acknowledge his fine achievement, I could not bring myself to get very enthusiastic about it. He is the one cricketer I have ever disliked and the only one I have felt consistently hostile towards. It all stems from my Test debut at Bangalore in 1978 when his constant appealing in my short innings, I believe, was responsible for me being given out unfairly. It was the day I cried my way back to the pavilion and the day I was humiliated in public. I will never forget the taunts and the disgrace and, possibly unfairly also, I saw Vengsarkar as the main culprit. I vowed revenge and in 1982-83, four long years later, I got it.

My anger had largely subsided by then and my broken pride repaired: I felt my main job was to help the West Indies win the series when the Indians arrived on their fifth tour of the Caribbean. Vengsarkar was just another fine batsman in a strong Indian batting line-up. Mohinder Amarnath and the durable Sunil Gavaskar were more likely to get in our way and any team with Kapil Dev in its ranks had to be taken seriously. Amarnath, in fact, emerged as the Man of the Series with 598 runs at an average of 66.44, but it scarcely mattered as far as we were concerned because we won the series 2-0 with India hanging on for draws in two of the other three matches. By now I was bowling as fast as at any point in my career and I was determined that in helping the West Indies win I would also let India pay the price for my misery four years earlier.

Although we played well within ourselves, it was a tour not without its acrimony. Indeed, the Indian manager, and former captain, Hanumant Singh felt obliged to lodge a complaint about what he felt was intimidatory short-pitched bowling by the West Indies and by me in particular. This was because of their much-vaunted batting, only Amarnath finding it comfortable to cope with our pace and our tactics. He scored centuries in the Tests at Trinidad and Antigua, Gavaskar managed only one, in Guyana, and Vengsarkar none at all. He did, however, come close to getting one in Antigua and it was then that I pulled out everything to prevent him having the satisfaction of reaching three figures. By way of a new strategy I was now bowling more and more around the wicket which meant the batsmen, mostly right-handers, were getting the ball angled across them and, moreover, because I was coming from behind the umpire, they had less time to pick up the flight. Vengsarkar had done nothing in the previous four Tests to make me feel any better disposed to him. As he had done in India, he appealed time and again unnecessarily - though he found the umpires rather less responsive. He had gone four Tests without a century and I was not going to let him get one now.

The St John's wicket could not have been more benign. It had absolutely nothing in it for the likes of me, Andy Roberts, playing on his home ground, or Winston Davis from St Vincent, making his Test debut in place of Joel Garner, who was in need of a rest after a long, hard season playing for South Australia in the Sheffield Shield competition. It was a wicket made for the Indian stroke-makers - and that meant Vengsarkar. Kapil Dev lost the toss, as he did in every match, and Clive Lloyd made India bat first with the series already safely won. Bowling around the wicket I soon had Gavaskar caught behind and with Gaekwad caught at slip by Richards off Roberts, to the delight of the Antiguan crowd, Vengsarkar arrived at the crease with Amarnath as his partner.

Until Amarnath left the field with leg cramps, they were hitting us all over the Recreation Ground, as it is called, and my feelings of intense dislike - not hate - for Vengsarkar were stirred again when he became involved in what I believe was blatant gamesmanship. Standing at the non-striker's end while I was bowling, I heard him repeatedly telling the umpire while I was in earshot that I was over-stepping the crease and bowling no-balls. If that was designed to upset and irritate me, then he certainly succeeded. I was furious and absolutely beside myself with anger as the memories of his performance at Bangalore flooded back. I have never felt like this about an opponent, either before or since, but I will admit now that I not only wanted to get him out, I didn't mind if I decapitated him in the process. I came in quicker than ever as he faced up to me, just 22 yards away, and I showered him with a hail of bouncers. He was aggressive from the start of his innings and as he raced to his 50 and beyond, my desperation grew more intense by the run. There was no way I was going to let him get his century after what he had been trying to do to me.

On he went, 60, 70 to 81 when our battle reached a new and crucial stage. Once more I let him have it with another bouncer which smacked into his helmet. That shook him but his response could not have been more positive. Realising now that I meant business, he took three boundaries from the remainder of my over in what I can only describe as risky shots. If I was desperate to get him out before he reached his hundred, he was becoming desperate to get there. This was war.

He was in the 90s now and within tantalising distance of his ton. Surely nothing could stop him, not even me bowling with fire in my belly. Once more I tore in and gave him yet another short-pitched delivery. On 94 there was no need for him to take any more risks, but Vengsarkar was rattled - I could tell that after hitting him on the helmet - and he was not behaving normally. He had been shifting nervously in his crease and he was patently not as in command as a man six short of his century should have been. I sensed my chance. He went for the hook, top-edged it and to my lasting delight, Davis held the catch on the long leg boundary. Another couple of yards and it would have been six runs - and his hundred.

I have never been more elated at a wicket nor so relieved at a dismissal and as he plodded dejectedly back to the dressing room, my fury subsided and my ill-feeling towards the Indians, and Vengsarkar in particular, disappeared. My ghost had been laid and now I regard him, almost, as just another opponent, though I suppose I shall never forgive him fully for what happened in Bangalore - or in Antigua. I went on to take four for 87 in the innings but India took full advantage of the easy paced wicket to amass 457 with Ravi Shastri, batting at six, hitting 102 before being stumped off Larry Gomes. Then Gordon Greenidge and Desmond Haynes each scored a century in putting on 296 for the first wicket on our way to a total of 550 of which my contribution, from number nine, was two. Jeff Dujon and Lloyd also made hundreds as the match drifted towards an inevitable draw, though the innings was marred by the illness of Gordon's daughter. He was batting brilliantly with 154 already to his credit when he had to retire in order to fly to her bedside in Barbados. She died two days after the match was completed from a kidney disorder.

With a lead of 93 to overcome there was little for India to do except bat out time, but not before I had one last dash at Vengsarkar to prove I was now his master. The match was in its last day and even the vociferous Antiguan crowd appeared bored, unaware I still had a point to prove. In the last over before tea I had Gaekwad, the opener, leg before for 72, thereby ending a patient innings of nearly four hours, and that brought Vengsarkar back to the crease. I was ready for him. In the same over, without a run to his name, I had him caught at the wicket. Game, set and match to Malcolm Marshall. Amarnath went on to score 116, the match duly died a death and Greenidge, enduring his bedside vigil, was named Man of the Match for a century made under what must have been intolerable mental pressure. For me, revenge had been sweet. The series was won and the exit of Vengsarkar for the second time in the match gave me a total of 21 wickets in the five Tests at an average of 23.57 each, not a bad haul in what was my first full series as an established bowler.

I might well not have been in the team had Colin Croft and Sylvester Clarke decided not to join the West Indian rebels in South Africa. I had been competing with them for four or five years and now, at a stroke, they were gone, richer but for ever. Such was the strength of West Indian bowling that there still remained Roberts, Holding, Garner and myself, with Davis emerging as a whippy alternative. For the first time I was under no pressure to produce the goods every time I took the field in a Test match. My place was secure and I felt better for that knowledge. I did not let the West Indies selectors down. Only Roberts, with 24 wickets at 22.70 each, topped me against India with Holding and Garner, for one reason or another, contributing only 21 between them.

In only one match, however, did I take five wickets in an innings - the second Test at Trinidad, a place normally expected to help spin bowlers. The rest were hard graft for the quickies, as they usually are in the West Indies in spite of our country's reputation for being beneficial for fast bowlers. In county cricket, for example, and in most Test-playing countries, wickets are prepared with the home bowlers in mind. That's natural and I'm not complaining about it. The problem for we West Indians is that most of our major venues, even the Test grounds, are over-used and it is enough simply for the groundsmen just to come up with a track which will last five days. The wickets are bound to be hard in the main because of the constant sunshine, but we do not always get the type of wickets in the Caribbean which get the best out of our pace attack. I know we have not lost a home Test match since a defeat by Pakistan in 1977 and we have crushed New Zealand, Australia and England in successive series in the West Indies but psychological factors come into play as much as the type of wickets. It is the uncertainty about our wickets which undoes so many opposing batsmen, not necessarily the pace. On West Indian grounds, the outfields are always poor, the result of soccer, athletics and hockey being played on the same surface and never being repaired properly. We suffer from lack of sponsorship in the West Indies which means that many grounds are not looked after with the most modern equipment. For all that a home series is always the highlight of my year.

I have said how much I love playing in Jamaica and Barbados, where the people are so knowledgeable and appreciative of good play no matter from what source. Trinidad is a curious place to play cricket. The ground, under the shadow of the mountains, is one of the most beautiful in the world even if it is a graveyard for fast bowlers, hence my surprise and delight at taking five for 37 against India. I have found, also, how difficult the Queens Park Oval crowds are to please. They can be critical and sarcastic if the run of play is not going exactly to plan, though I can think of no real reason to bear a grudge against them because I have always done well there.

Sabina Park, Jamaica, in contrast a venue for the real cricket-lover, was the scene of the first Test against India and it provided a tense and exciting finish as Jeff Dujon, with me as his partner, hit the winning runs off the second ball of the last over to give us victory by four wickets. The match was seemingly drifting towards a draw when India were 167 for six at tea on the last day. That all changed with a highly skilled and devastating spell of bowling by Roberts, who took the last four wickets for one run in 20 balls. This left us, somewhat unexpectedly, a target of 172 to win in 26 overs, a rate of 6.6 an over, and although that may not seem unreasonable in the John Player League, in Test cricket it is a very different and much more exacting proposition. As I remember, we needed five runs off the last over, bowled by Amarnath, and I might have gone to the first delivery had the bowler not broken the stumps before gathering a return from midwicket as we attempted to scamper a single. Then Dujon hit the winning runs next ball and an astonishing victory had been achieved when we had all but given up hope. India had matched us all the way for five days literally until the last session when, thanks to Roberts, they blew it. It was an important win for us at the outset of the series and I doubt if the Indians fully recovered from the impact on their collective nerve and morale.

We might well have won the second Test as well, having established a huge first innings lead of 219 on a Trinidad wicket uncharacteristically green and helpful to the quicker bowlers. I am told it was the former West Indian opening batsman Joey Carew who supervised the pitch's preparation and Lloyd, with me, Holding, Roberts and Garner at his disposal, must have been delighted when he won the toss and unhesitatingly chose to field first. It was then that I produced my best bowling performance in my 14th Test, coming on first change after Roberts and Holding had had first use of the new ball. I took the wickets of Vengsarkar, Shastri, Kapil Dev, Sandhu and Maninder Singh in 19.1 overs and accounted for poor Yashpal Sharma, who had to retire with concussion after being hit on the helmet by one of my bouncers. Luckily, he was able to resume later, though not in time to prevent India being all out for 175. It was the first time I had taken five or more wickets in an innings at this level and it all contributed to the general feeling that I had somehow arrived at last as very much part of the West Indian pace battery. The grassy wicket might just as easily have been made to my specific orders. It helped the ball swing everywhere and I could well have taken even more than I did.

Sensing that we stood a real chance of winning the match, we made a disastrous response, losing Greenidge, Haynes and Richards with only one run on the board. Then Gomes and Lloyd put on 237 for the fourth wicket and each made centuries as the wicket eased and the Indians were unable to capitalise on their heady start. My part in a total of 394 was only 14, batting at number eight, but by then I was more than ready to have another go at the Indian batting. Unfortunately it never worked out that way. Amarnath made a brave and critically valuable 117, Kapil Dev launched a furious late assault during a two-hour century and I had absolutely nothing to show for more than 27 overs of unremitting effort. India duly saved the match and we all moved on to Bourda in Guyana for the next episode in what was already developing into an exciting and, from my point of view, highly promising series.

Guyana has a reputation for poor weather to rival Manchester's and two days, the second and the fourth, were lost to the effects of heavy rain. The match never really got going as the result of being deprived of so many hours and the easy paced wicket made life for quicker bowlers nearly impossible. Lloyd won the toss, Richards scored a century, Greenidge took nearly four hours over 70 and the captain himself, on his home ground, made 81 in a total of 470. The wicket itself, so dead and unhelpful, was right up Gavaskar's street when India replied and, when we were able to get on the field, he grafted his way to 147 not out in not much less than six hours to ensure the most meaningless of draws. My own contribution was 27 runs and the wicket of Amarnath for 39, but by the end of it all I began to dream of Barbados and the Kensington Oval where I knew the wicket would be full of pace and bounce; not much good for Gavaskar but just my sort of pitch. So it proved to be.

The wicket at Kensington had everything about it I could possibly have asked for and I reckon the Indians knew from the moment they first clapped eyes on it, they were not going to escape this time. They had lost three of their previous four matches at Kensington over the years and now I was ready to help made it four out of five. They lost the toss again, which did not do their cause the slightest good, and were obliged to defend with all the skill at their disposal as our four fast bowlers got to work. I continued to carry out my theory that they did not like short-pitched deliveries, and they liked them even less when I came in at them from around the wicket. The record books show how seven of their first innings wickets fell to catches close to the wicket off bouncers. Only the dogged and technically excellent Amarnath had the ability to stand up to this incessant barrage in making 91 out of 209. Take away his plucky contribution and there was little else to distinguish the Indian first innings. Quite simply they had no idea how to cope with so many quick bowlers using a wicket with so much pace in it.

It must have been an ordeal for them, as it was for those countries who followed them to the Caribbean in subsequent years, but I offer no apologies. I know there are many people in other parts of the world who say what we do is just not cricket. I tell them to look at the rules. There is nothing there to stop us using such tactics as a legitimate part of our strategy and even though I was the subject of that complaint by their tour management during the series, I cannot honestly believe the Indians thought I would somehow, seized by a fit of conscience, alter my methods.

In this case Andy Roberts took eight wickets and the scene was set for our batting stars to carry out the second part of our destruction by making a huge score as the pitch began to ease. This is precisely what they did. Greenidge, Haynes and Richards all made over 50 and little Gus Logie, taking advantage of an unbelievable missed slip catch, made 130, the highest score of his brief Test career. We were all out for 486 and now the Indians had to score 277 just to make us bat again. From the start it didn't look as if they had the stomach for the battle. Once more only Amarnath - later Man of the Match for the second time in the series - stood in our way, even coming back to defy us after being forced to retire when one of my bouncers struck him in the mouth. They were all out for exactly 277 and we won by 10 wickets when the only ball of our second innings, tossed up by the wicket-keeper Kirmani, was adjudged a no-ball. I took two wickets in each innings and was well pleased to have been part of a team which won a Test so convincingly on my home ground: thus, to our great satisfaction, the series was won.

By now as a team we had come to believe we were invincible. Lloyd knew otherwise. He had been part of West Indian teams which had tasted defeat, but there were many others, by now integral parts of the team, who had never experienced the misery of failure. I had never been a member of a West Indian team which had lost a series - apart from that in New Zealand, which we tended to discount on the basis that we had been on the end of some very poor umpiring, and my very first series in India when we had been considerably under-strength because of the defection of the Packer players - and it was unthinkable as far as I and some others were concerned that we could ever lose anything important. Sure enough, we expected to lose the odd one-day international, even possibly the occasional Test, but never a whole series, and it was in this frame of mind that we moved on to England for the 1983 World Cup.

We had won the previous two competitions in 1975 and 1979 and after beating India in the Caribbean there was a decidedly complacent air about us. It is history now that India beat us in the final against all the odds, inflicting on us the greatest humiliation I have ever known. I was sure we were going to win the World Cup. In fact I was so positive about the outcome that I had even ordered a new BMW car on the misguided belief that I could pay for it out of my winnings. What utter folly! I cannot now comprehend my arrogance and stupidity. Perhaps some of the more experienced players in our squad should have whispered in our ears the dangers of taking too much for granted. Cricket has a nasty habit of punishing those who come to believe in their infallibility, and so it was at Lord's on 25 June 1983 that we paid the ultimate price for an act of complacency of which we shall never again be guilty. We should have realised in the group matches that it was not going to be as easy as I, for one, felt it was bound to be.

India, Australia and Zimbabwe, the winners of the ICC Trophy, were in our group and we qualified for the semi-finals as group winners. With Viv Richards scoring 80 not out and Larry Gomes undefeated on 50, we hardly broke sweat in beating Pakistan in our semi-final and we were doubly delighted when India upset the form book by beating England, the team we most feared, in the other game at Old Trafford. We should have learned our lesson from the group match defeat by India, but we felt that on the big occasion, a World Cup final at Lord's, there was no way they could beat us a second time. We were the world champions and there was no chance of them depriving us of our title.

If we have a failing in one-day matches, I would say we are not always at our best in chasing the smaller totals and this was a case very much in point. India batted first and as far as we were concerned it all went according to plan. Gavaskar, the Indian danger man, was caught behind off Andy Roberts for two and even though Amarnath and Srikkanth were largely responsible for them reaching 90 for two at one stage, they soon fell away. We bowled tightly, fielded sharply and India subsided to 183 all out in 54.4 overs. Roberts took three for 32, while Gomes, Holding and myself each finished with two in what we viewed was a competent team performance. We duly sat back in the dressing-room and waited, as tail-enders, for our batsmen to finish off the job, as they usually did.

To say I was in a relaxed mood would be an understatement. I could just visualise myself sitting behind the wheel of that flashy sports car and I hardly paid much attention to the cricket when we went out to get those

184 runs in the 60 overs available to us. Other players were in a similar state of mind; there was no way we could fail. Listed at number eight in the order I honestly believed I would not be required to bat so I simply prepared myself for the inevitable. I had already won a World Cup winner's medal in 1979 as a squad member without, you will remember, actually taking part in any of the matches apart from the occasional sortie as a fielding substitute. I was now expecting another.

At 50 for one and Viv Richards beginning to give full rein to that irrepressible arrogant streak of his, our confidence seemed well founded. Then wickets began to fall with a disconcerting, rather than alarming, regularity. Suddenly there was a new interest in the game from the West Indian dressing room. Greenidge, Haynes, Richards, Lloyd, Gomes and Bacchus, all of them quality batsmen, had come and gone, diddled out by the gentle medium pace of Sandhu, Madan Lal, Binny and Amarnath, not one of whom, with the best will in the world, could be described as a great destructive force. Kapil Dev was different, of course. We knew he would cause us trouble but we could not see where his support was going to come from. Now, however, we knew.

Scarcely had I time to gather my wits and take in the enormity of what was happening than I was out in the middle with Jeff Dujon, fully aware that at 76 for six, a major repair job was badly needed. Dujon, a free-hitting number seven, had already been obliged to dig himself in. I was going to have to do the same. He met me on my way to the crease, greeted as I was by a mounting crescendo of noise from the massed ranks of Indian supporters crammed into Lord's that day. 'This,' said Jeff with masterly understatement, 'is going to be tough'. Faced by an Indian attack wearing us down with their accuracy and a little bit of movement we put on 43 precarious runs for the seventh wicket before, not for the first time in the tournament, I was out chasing a wide delivery, caught at slip. Jeff, with 25, went soon afterwards and the next thing we knew, we were all out for 140 in 52 overs, giving India a totally unexpected victory by 43 runs. Our supporters were stunned into premature silence; the rest of the cricket world rejoiced.

I heard it said at the time that our defeat by India was good for the game in that it broke the West Indian monopoly. It is obviously not a theory to which I can subscribe. The scene in the West Indian dressing-room afterwards I never want to see repeated. There was a strange, eerie quiet about the place as if a death of a close friend had just been announced. There was indeed a sense of mourning for the passing of a close friend, the World Cup. As the champagne corks popped in the Indian section of that famous pavilion we conducted our own morbid inquest. What had gone wrong? The shock turned to anger, the disbelief to fury. The feeling of humiliation was already beginning to set in. The world was laughing at us, or so it seemed.

Clive Lloyd saw it as a clear indication that a new hand was required on the tiller, that at nearly 39 it was time for him to go. After mulling over the full implications of the disaster, he told a stunned audience of head-bowed cricketers that he was resigning. 'I have had enough,' he said. 'Somebody else can take over.' It was his way of saying he was retiring from the international scene and it left us still further dumbfounded that 'Father' was going to desert his children in their hour of need. One or two of the players muttered something about not being hasty. Another had the courage to say he should not be making such a momentous decision in the heat of a rare nasty moment. Gradually we pulled ourselves around, got changed, congratulated the Indians - because, after all, they had won it as much as we had lost it - and headed for the bar. As we stared into our glasses we all came to the same conclusion. Clive would have to reconsider and return to lead us back to the straight and narrow. In time, he duly did and gave us a year or two more valuable service before handing over to Richards, but when we trooped off back to our counties we had no real inkling he would change his mind. It was only a communal gut feeling, but the double blow of losing so ignominiously in the final and losing our guide and mentor made it a very unhappy journey home. I went back to Hampshire a chastened man, determined to put behind me the humbling experience of Lord's.

Within a couple of weeks I had atoned in my own mind with a century in less than two hours against Surrey at Southampton and another against Kent at Bournemouth in August during an eight-wicket win. For once Derek Underwood was not able to get the better of us as he invariably does. I ended the county season with a batting average of 46.91 from 563 runs and 80 wickets at 16.58 each. After the debacle of the World Cup it was a real pleasure to be back among my mates at Hampshire in the lesser demands of county cricket. Along the way I was named the Mail on Sunday's bowler of the month for July as Hampshire showed their rehabilitation in reaching third place in the County Championship behind Essex and Middlesex. After the rigours of the World Cup and the subsequent anguish, it was nice to be on the road again... though not, of course, in a BMW!

* Marshall did eventually get his BMW, a red one, and had it shipped to Barbados where at the time it had a rarity value; there was no BMW dealership on the island and spare parts had to be shipped in from Trinidad or even further afield when required. The distinctive MM numberplate meant he could not drive anywhere in Barbados without flashing lights and honked horns greeting him and there were waves and smiles from well-wishers along every road. He loved the recognition.

The one bouncer an over edict, introduced later by the ICC, irritated him and all fast bowlers who felt that yet again legislation had been brought in loaded heavily in favour of the batsman. The element of surprise, and fear, had been removed. Mike Selvey, cricket correspondent of The Guardian, remembered in his obituary how Marshall took on Gavaskar and Vengsarkar in 1989 when playing for the MCC against the Rest of the World in the MCC bicentenary game on a slow, flat, unresponsive Lord's pitch. "Marshall wanted to be not just good but demonstrably the best. He raised his game to a level above any other fast bowler - Imran, Hadlee, Kapil Dev, Clive Rice and Walsh - in the match. Had it been anything but a festival occasion, Sunil Gavaskar would have been given out lbw to Marshall's first legitimate delivery, and it irked the bowler that the great opener was able to go on to make 188. In the second innings, with the game dead, Marshall nonetheless tore in and bowled him without scoring. Most telling, though, was the encounter with Vengsarkar for whom Marshall had an antipathy. Coming in round the wicket, the bowler flogged life, pace and bounce from the pitch, and almost knocked the bat from the batsman's hands as he fended a catch to gully. Showpiece match it may have been but this was vengeance chillingly executed. The man was awesome."

12.

Taking the New Ball

ONE CRUCIAL COMMENT by Michael Holding, a friend, mentor and in his prime the most perfect of fast bowlers, made me realise I had become, in 1983, the West Indies number one quickie. I had of course been pushing for such recognition for the previous three years although I had only been sure of my place in the team for about two of them. We went to India for six Tests with a formidable array of fast bowlers. Holding and his old partner Andy Roberts were still in harness but, even without the massive presence of Joel Garner, there was still myself, the resurrected Wayne Daniel and Winston Davis. Andy was now 32 and not as fast as he had been seven or eight years earlier and both Daniel and Davis were very much on trial. It was obvious now that the West Indies were going to have to rely on me more and more and I relished the prospect. This was what I had been working towards all my career and the confirmation came at Kanpur in October of that year at the start of the first Test, a match I shall always remember for another reason altogether.

Andy had been unlucky enough to fall ill before the game, which persuaded Lloyd and the tour management to go into the match with me, Holding and Davis as his main strike bowlers and Eldine Baptiste as the medium-pace support. We were still not sure who was going to do what when Lloyd lead us out to field. He turned to Holding and myself. 'Who is going to have first use of the new ball?' he enquired. Holding did not need long to consider a reply, possibly sensing my reluctance to appear pushy. 'Let Malcolm have it,' he said without hesitation, 'He's the fastest now'. It was the finest compliment ever paid to me. Here was one of the great bowlers of all time conceding that in terms of consistent pace, I was now his peer. It was a proud moment as memories of five years hard graft; of my apprenticeship around the world and the tribulations of being a reserve came racing back. I was top dog - and that's the way I liked it. Never before had I been entrusted with bowling the first over of a Test match and I lapped up the importance of the responsibility.

I was by no means nervous about the occasion. There was no need to be. I had served that apprenticeship and worked my way up the bowling order, as it were, until now I had put myself in a position to supersede men who had been my heroes. Needless to say, I grabbed the opportunity with both hands and throughout the six-Test series it was I who bowled the first over, it was I who took the new ball. This, I'm afraid, signalled the end for Andy. I had so much to thank him for through the years; for his patience, his help and his understanding. Yet my elevation to all intents and purposes brought a close to his most distinguished first class career: He actually made a comeback, shrugging off his illness and injuries to play in the fifth and sixth Tests, bowling as fast as I have ever seen him bowl, probably aware that his livelihood was on the line.

Andy poured himself into his task and I think we all knew he was under pressure to succeed. Perhaps he was trying to prove a point to me about speed but the harder he tried the less he achieved: In the last Test I bowled 26 overs and took five for 72 and Andy, for all his huffing and puffing, ended with only one for 81 from 28 overs of real menace on a lifeless Madras wicket, and even suffered the anguish of seeing Gavaskar dropped at the wicket by Dujon off a mis-hook. Poor Andy. We were all willing him on, hoping he would get his share of the spoils. It was, however; to be his last Test match. After 47 games and 202 wickets Andy was finished.

The squad was moving, on to Australia from India to take part in the one-day internationals and there were going to be changes. Garner was fit to come back and Greenidge needed to return home. But it was not a question of a straight swap. Milton Pydanna, the reserve wicket-keeper, was no longer required and nor, to our collective disappointment and regret, was Andy. Richard Gabriel, an experienced opening batsman from Trinidad, was drafted in for a surprise first taste of international action and, as it turned out, found the transition altogether too much for him. I would go as far as to say we were all genuinely shocked by Andy's omission. He was a likeable man, a shrewd and calculating cricketer and a reliable and calming influence in a multitude of West Indian squads. It was somehow unthinkable he was no longer going to be part of us. Daniel and Davis, both of whom might have been candidates for the same treatment, came with us instead to Australia and played competent roles in the winning of the World Series Cup.

Andy had served us so well and for so long. He was a dejected figure as he headed back to the Caribbean knowing that he probably had a year or two left in him, but that he would not get the chance to prove it. Before he left he told us he would give it one last shot and if he failed to regain his place he would retire, albeit prematurely. The Australians were due in the West Indies for a full series of Test matches and Andy believed he could force his way back if he performed successfully for the Leeward Islands in the Shell Shield competition. With that great determination which was his hallmark, Andy became the Leewards' leading wicket-taker and he waited for the call to return to Test cricket. It never came and, although he went back for one more summer with Leicestershire, he bowed to the inevitable and brought an end to nine glorious years during which he had taken 889 wickets in the first-class game at a highly respectable 21.01 each. Had he been English or Australian he would most likely have still been an international player. Instead he gracefully stepped aside and, at 33, settled permanently in his native Antigua, to a new life as a deep-sea fisherman, where he is revered as much as Viv Richards, their other favourite son.

There is never an easy way to tell a player of his class and quality he is no longer needed. One day it will happen to me and I will be as hurt and as disappointed as he was. They say it is best to go out at the top but the temptation is always to continue; to squeeze another year or two out of ageing limbs. I hope I have the maturity to get out while I'm still at the height of my career, but who knows? I suppose, in an ironic sort of way, Andy was a victim of the success he himself had helped to create for the West Indies.

By 1983, the World Cup fiasco aside, Lloyd and the selectors had built a tremendous cricketing machine and I was now its spearhead. We were aware nevertheless that the Indians would be a much tougher proposition on their own grounds and with their own umpires than they had been a few months earlier in the Caribbean. Following the terrible humiliation of defeat at Lord's in the World Cup final there was a sense of urgency and strong desire for revenge when we kicked off at Kanpur. It should have been the scene of my first Test century yet I failed by eight runs and the disappointment of that failure lives with me today. I came in when the score was 309 for six to join my county colleague, Greenidge, and we went on to set a new seventh wicket record for Tests between the two countries of 130. I survived an early lbw appeal and was never in any trouble after that until Greenidge, after nearly 10 hours at the crease, was caught behind off a tired shot. Then suddenly, when I was well set, we lost three quick wickets and for the first time I could see my chances of reaching my goal were going to be ruined by lack of partners. I panicked a bit, swinging my bat irrationally for three lots of two runs. Winston Davis, our last man, was now at the crease and I resolved to smash every ball bowled at me. Kapil Dev came in, I hit the ball perfectly and, to my horror and astonishment, he held a sharp return catch. The ball could have gone anywhere and I would have been four runs nearer the magic figure. I was a very dejected man as I made my way back to the pavilion, the West Indies all out for 454, because I knew I had lost a wonderful opportunity. When you bat seven or eight, as I do, there are not many chances to build a big innings of this sort and through my own folly I had wasted it.

I made up for my self-punishment by taking four wickets for five runs in 27 balls as the prelude to a comprehensive win by an innings and 83 runs. I finished with eight wickets in the match, Holding six, Davis five and Baptiste the other. The unfortunate Roberts was hardly missed. With that result under our belts India knew they would struggle to pull it back. The second Test at Delhi was much closer even though we were reinforced by a fourth fast bowler when Daniel was preferred to Baptiste, thereby playing his first Test for seven years. Wayne celebrated by taking six wickets, three in each innings, while the Indians were making 464 and 233. He certainly upstaged me because all I could manage was one for 105 in the first innings when Gavaskar and Vengsarkar were making good centuries, and a much-improved three for 52 in the second. Needing 314 to win, we ran out of time at 120 for two and the match was drawn.

As a measure of my importance to the West Indies I was being rested and saved for the Test matches, something which had never happened to me before and which confirmed my belief that I was now number one. I suppose I should reiterate also that I actually still preferred the old ball to bowl with though it was the prestige of the new one which really mattered

- and continues to matter every time I take the field in West Indian colours. In fact I played in only one other first-class match, as a warm-up to the first Test, so that all my energies were being channelled into what I could achieve in the Tests. With a gap of roughly two weeks between them I was fit and well prepared for each match, as I was when the series moved on to Ahmedabad.

What we saw there caused apoplexy among us. Clive called the pitch the poorest on which he had played Test cricket and the umpiring the worst he had come across in his playing career. I could only agree. We batted first, somehow making 281 thanks to Dujon's 98, and established a 40-run first innings lead, not through any efforts of mine (one for 66) but because Daniel cleaned up with five for 39. Kapil Dev, taking advantage of the wicket and the umpires, then recorded a magnificent nine for 83 to have us all out a second time for 201, and with figures like those he might have expected greater reward than defeat by 138 runs. Requiring 242 to win the wicket just broke up and once Holding had removed Gavaskar, India slumped to 103 all out. There was a draw at Bombay where we were set 244 to win and ended at 104 for four - which left India needing to win the last two Tests to level the series.

By now I was bowling faster than I had ever bowled before, possibly to justify my new position while Roberts was forced to watch from the sidelines, and possibly because I was getting the rest I felt I warranted between the Tests. I would go so far as to say I have never bowled as consistently fast in one completed series as I did in India. I was at my peak and it was up to me to maintain it. As a result I dominated the fifth Test at Calcutta, which we won by an innings and 46 runs to confirm our overwhelming superiority. By getting rid of Gavaskar, Gaekwad and Amarnath with only 13 on the board, I was able to finish with three for 65 as India were all out for 241. Then, for the second time, I saw the prospects of scoring a century snatched away, though I remain proud of the way I played in making 54. I came in at 88 for five to join Lloyd and we put on 87 important runs just as the Indians sensed an opportunity. I was obliged to graft against good quality spinners but it was Roberts, scoring 68 in his penultimate Test innings, who enabled us to take a 136-run advantage in the first innings. India had no stomach for a fight after that and in 15 of the fastest overs I have ever bowled in one Test innings I ran through the opposition to end with six for 37. India were all out for 90 and suddenly I was being hailed as a hero back in the West Indies. I can tell you I loved every minute of the new adulation.

As the West Indies opening bowler it became increasingly important to me, as a matter of pride I suppose, to scalp the opposition's opening batsmen and in this case it meant getting rid of the redoubtable Gavaskar. He has worn down and seen off more accomplished bowlers than me, as his formidable Test record would appear to indicate. Much as we also had to respect the records of Vengsarkar, Amarnath and Kapil Dev, Gavaskar was the batsman we most feared. It was impressed on me from the start that my job was to get him out - and as quickly as possible. I relished the challenge and the competition with the world's heaviest scorer in Test cricket partly because I knew that if I was to establish some kind of dominance over him then we would have a great chance of winning the series and partly because, as contests go, I could scarcely have chosen a more exacting examination of my new status within the West Indian set-up.

By the time we reached Madras for the sixth and last Test in Christmas 1983, I had taken his wicket in five of his 10 innings and I like to think I had the upper hand. He still managed 121 at Delhi and 90 at Ahmedabad but overall he struggled to impose himself on the proceedings as he normally did. His record against me justified my claim that I was on top. I got him twice at Kanpur for nought and seven, twice more on his home ground at Bombay for 12 and three and then once more for nought in the first innings at Calcutta. Perhaps the Indians had come to expect too much of him but whenever we had him cheaply it seemed to take his team-mates by surprise and the crowd were at least temporarily subdued, and it seemed to have a bad effect on the team's morale. It was as though if Gavaskar could not score runs against the West Indies then no one could.

Madras was a dead match as far as we were concerned, though our players were anxious to make it 4-0 as a way of making India pay for their temerity in beating us at Lord's. It still hurt. Gavaskar was obviously not happy with his form so that when we got to Madras we were not unduly shocked to discover that after consultations with Kapil Dev and the selectors, he had been dropped down from his customary position as an opening batsman to number four in the order. As a tactical change it was somewhat belated; the series was won and lost and there did not seem much point in it except that we felt he no longer had the nerve to take on the new ball bowlers. On a personal level I believed I had won my battle with him and from a psychological point of view, they could have boosted mine further only by leaving him out of the team altogether. Here was the 'little master', hero of all India, opting out of a clash with what I will concede was still very much a young bowler coming to terms with his new role. If ever I needed confirmation of my blossoming skill, I received it here in Madras with that one small change in the batting order.

Gavaskar, though, was to have the last laugh. I may have played my part in removing him from having to face the new ball but he was by no means beaten. I should have realised that a batsman of his quality would flourish anywhere, even at number 11. We batted first, all made starts and got out, and between us collected 313 of which I scored 38. Then it looked as if Gavaskar's decision had rebounded on him when Roger Harper at slip took catches off successive deliveries from me to send back Gaekwad and Vengsarkar without a run on the board, so here he was taking on me - and the new ball anyway - in virtually his old position.

Roberts and Harper took one wicket each at the start of the fourth day and India were a perilous 69 for four. I began my first over and from the second ball saw Gavaskar edge a lifting ball to third slip. We danced in celebration, I raced down the wicket and then turned to see the umpire absolutely unmoved. I could not believe my eyes. Not out was the verdict. To say we were shocked and disgusted would not do justice to our deep dissatisfaction. Gavaskar was out and he knew it, but, as I was saying, you have to knock his stumps out in India and then hope it's not a no-ball. Gavaskar duly ground on after this unexpected 'life' and when he reached his inevitable century none of us could find it in us to applaud except, I'm told, Richardson, the 12th man. When Kapil Dev later called a halt, India, their recovery complete, were 451 for eight and Gavaskar the little matter of 236 not out. I suppose I should have been happy with my five for 72 from 26 overs but I can never forgive that decision which set him on his way. India's lead was 138 and at 64 for one in our second innings we played out time for a draw. Man of the Match, just to irritate us still further, had to be Gavaskar and, if nothing else, it showed how a player of his class can never be written off.

Even if he did have the umpire on his side, I learned at Madras the importance of never under-estimating anyone, to treat all batsmen with respect - particularly someone of Gavaskar's innate and timeless talent. He is, now that Boycott has faded from the scene, the last of a generation of batsmen who at Test level had the skill, the temperament and the self-discipline to bat all five days of a match if necessary. One-day cricket is blamed for the way batsmen behave now, getting out to all manner of deliveries because they have been taught quick runs should gain priority over a long innings. I mean it as no disrespect to the many fine batsmen around the world when I say Gavaskar is the end of a breed. His type of batsmanship requires deep dedication, composure, massive self-control and a technique born of the textbooks. We may never see his like again.

I don't hold completely with the theory about one-day cricket being the ruination of the long-innings batsman, although it may have played a part. Variations in wickets, different demands, better bowling-in-depth are all, I believe, contributory factors. Anyway, whatever the machinations of the umpires, with 33 wickets at 18.81 each I had equalled a West Indian record for the number of scalps in a series, held jointly by Alf Valentine and Colin Croft, and I was now looking forward to taking on the Aussies again in the Caribbean after the one-day internationals in their country.

The Australians were a big disappointment when they came to the West Indies in March and April 1984. If ever there was substance to the argument that one-day cricket can destroy players then the present crop of young Australian batsmen are living proof. I know we beat India with some ease the previous year, and in subsequent tours New Zealand and England were also overcome without too much difficulty, but of the lot, the Aussies were the poorest and only the weather saved them from a five-nil thrashing.

The Australians have always been renowned for their competitiveness and their willingness to scrap for every run and every wicket but over the years that famous national characteristic has become less apparent in our clashes with them. I am sure it is only temporary but I feel cricket in Australia has reached something of a low point. Allan Border would be a contender for a place in any Australian team in any era. He personifies all that is best about the Aussie cricketer of old. Add to his impeccable technique a refusal to be ground into the dust by any bowler or combination of bowlers and you have an outstanding batsman and a player we all respect and admire. As if by contrast, the vast majority of his team-mates showed no inclination for the fight which they knew they would require against us. Greg Ritchie of Queensland and Wayne Phillips of South Australia are both capable of getting substantial numbers of runs at Test level, but in my opinion they are far too flashy ever to pose consistent threats and certainly not against the depth of quality bowling we possess.

Not long ago I was saying one-day cricket cannot take the blame alone for the diminishing number of big-innings batsmen and yet when it comes to the Australians I can hold no other reason than the preponderance of limited overs matches responsible for the dearth of international calibre cricketers. The South African rebels took many of their present crop of Test-class players out of selection. The likes of Terry Alderman, Graham Yallop and Kim Hughes would still have been contenders, as might several more such as Carl Rackemann and Steve Smith - they desperately missed Alderman in England in 1985. Yet they had a full complement of players from whom to choose their squad for the Caribbean since the concept of a rebel tour of Australians to South Africa had not by then become reality. In Australia they play only a handful of Sheffield Shield matches plus a game against the touring team, a maximum of 11 first class matches and the rest is one-day cricket. There is the domestic limited-overs competition and then the World Series Cup, some 18 one-day matches for any youngster graduating to the international side. It means the first-class game no longer maintains priority and it means the Australians have bred a whole generation of cricketers in a rush, sacrificed on the altar of television. I believe it will be a long, long time before they re-emerge as a power, because only Border of their present players would force his way into contention for a World XI.

Young Craig McDermott has the potential to be the latest in a long line of distinguished fast bowlers but there were signs in England he had seen too much action already in his short career and he needs careful handling if he is still to be taking Test wickets in 10 years time. As for Alderman, he achieved nothing against us but he was the man the Aussies missed most in England in 1985. His ability to swing the ball both ways, learned on his native Perth wickets, would have gained him mastery over Gooch and Robinson, of that I'm sure, and I feel he might have got somewhere around the 42 wickets he took four years earlier. Our own series against the Australians proved to be something of an anti-climax. A bad knee kept me out of the first Test in Guyana where, having been set 323 to win, both Greenidge and Haynes scored unbeaten centuries when we closed at 250 without loss. Rain intervened there as it did in Trinidad for the second Test when I returned in place of Winston Davis. Border was marooned on 98 not out when Australia lost their last wicket at 255, then Dujon was top scorer with 130 as we built a 213-run lead. Once more their resistance was negligible apart from their captain, who averted defeat with a defiant unbeaten 100 as the match ended with them 299 for nine, only 86 ahead. I managed only two wickets in that match for all my effort.

With draws in the opening matches, it was important we put pressure on the Australians by winning the third Test in Barbados. If we won there on a hard, fast surface we felt they would struggle to equalise. I figured that to get among the wickets I would have to bowl a little slower to allow the ball to swing more. The result was that I took 19 wickets in the next three Tests, all of which we won. The Australians must have spent the rest of the tour wondering how they contrived to lose at Bridgetown after scoring a creditable 429 in the first innings in which Phillips, batting at eight, hit 120. Even so, we replied with a massive 509, Haynes and Richie Richardson contributing hundreds. Australia only had to bat sensibly in the second innings to get away with a third draw but Holding and I exposed the lack of grafters in the team by running through them in fewer than 44 overs. I finished with five for 42 and Holding took four for 24 as they collapsed to 97 all out. In my view, that finished them. In the fourth Test at Antigua they were a demoralised outfit, running into Viv Richards on his home territory where he responded with a truly magnificent 178, upstaging what would normally have been a match-winning innings of 154 from another Antiguan, Richardson. They were the foundations of our 498 in reply to their 262 in which only Border - again - with 98 stayed around long enough to trouble us. Knowing they had no real chance, unless the weather intervened once more, they were all out for 200 second time around to provide us with victory by an innings and 36 runs.

We were forced to admire the strength of Border's character, his sheer refusal to surrender, during the last Test at Kingston where we won by 10 wickets. He was 60 not out at the end of the second innings, standing firm while all around him gave the impression that the quicker they got out, the sooner they got home. In that second innings I took five for 51 to add to the three - including Border - I picked up in the first innings but, looking back on it now, it was almost devalued by the lack of heart and courage shown by the Australians. By the end of that very one-sided series, the Australians and ourselves were glad to see the back of each other since the Tests in the Caribbean had followed on so swiftly from the one-day internationals in their own country, much of which had been under floodlights.

I'm often asked about floodlit cricket. Let me say immediately, I don't much like it. It is only a personal opinion and I readily acknowledge how well it has been received in Australia. The crowds love it - and they pay our wages. In Australia it is all a great occasion, the matches starting in the afternoon and finishing at about 10.30pm. They can get hysterical, lifted by the undeniable excitement of white balls, coloured clothing and an American-style razzmatazz which may not go down too well at Lord's but is lapped up at Sydney and Melbourne. As far as I'm concerned a little of it goes a long way.

Let me explain from a player's point of view why most of us in the West Indies camp are against it, or at least so much of it. As a bowler I find the ball is harder than a normal one and is too heavy for my particular liking; it also swings to an extent that I find makes it difficult to control, although I will concede the white ball is much easier to follow than a red one. Easier that is, for the spectator seated high in those wonderful new stands at the SCG or the 100,000-seater stadium at the MCG. As a player, closer to the action, the ball is often impossible to see in the lights, which accounts for so many dropped catches or misfields. Twilight is the worst time to be playing, either as a batsman or as a fielder. The ball is desperately difficult to pick up in the semi-darkness before the lights begin to dominate the arena. Everyone struggles at that time of day and it is a time at the end of the first innings when things can be fairly crucial.

The following year, 1984-85, we played in 13 one-day internationals in the World Series Cup and another four in the World Championship of Cricket which followed. I found it all a real bore. While admitting there will always be a market for floodlit cricket, I think there is too much of it and if Packer's men are not careful they will kill the golden goose. It was the first time in cricket where they first started using 'make-up' to cut out the glare from the lights when the Australians drew black lines under their eyes. We in the West Indies dressing room took it as a great compliment. As the saying goes, imitation is the greatest form of flattery.

* Marshall was not to know then that the Australians were preparing to dominate world cricket in the nineties every bit as much as the West Indies had done in the eighties. When he wrote this chapter there was no sign of a revival in Australia where the Packer years, and to a lesser extent the rebel tours to South Africa, had taken a toll. While Australia was laying the foundations for their resurgence through the academy system, the seemingly invincible West Indians began to decline alarmingly. Dr Rudi Webster, his close friend, said Marshall wanted a cricket academy in the Caribbean: "He felt that in the absence of an academy, more attention should be paid to the Northern Telecom youth tournament for replacements for unco-operative and unproductive players. He felt that these youth players were not given enough exposure, which he insisted was a catalyst for development."

Meanwhile, with Marshall now at his speed peak, he was cutting a swathe through moribund county ranks. Derbyshire's Devon Malcolm, Jamaican-born and Yorkshire-raised, took 128 wickets in 40 Tests for England and was a regular opponent: "I remember once at Southampton and Derbyshire were cruising. We thought the game was won but Mark Nicholas just kept Marshall back until he was ready to unleash him. We probably needed about 100 to win with eight wickets in hand and Nicholas had no problem. He said, ' look, as soon as I get Malcolm on I know he will do the job.' Within 30 to 40 minutes, to our horror, the game was Hampshire's. Malcolm just came on with his skill - away swingers, inswingers - we could not believe anyone could have such control. We knew he was a magnificent bowler but we had hoped it would be too much even for him to fashion a win when everything pointed to a defeat for his team. We thought we had Hampshire but Malcolm just turned it up and we were blown away in no time." Devon Malcolm was among the mourners at the funeral.

13.

One-Armed Bandit

IAN BOTHAM MIGHT WELL HAVE saved me from disciplinary action and even, it's not too far-fetched to suggest, being sent off in a Test match. I shall never know if that particular course of action was going through the mind of the umpire Dickie Bird as he issued me a warning about bowling too many bouncers at the English batsmen at Edgbaston in June, 1984 but things were getting a bit bleak until the big man intervened.

I must admit to being pretty psyched up for this match; the papers had been on about it for days and the pressure of the dawn of a new day and a new series had got me a little excited. It was the match when poor Andy Lloyd ducked into a short ball of mine and had to be taken to hospital with concussion: passions were certainly running high. The sight of a batsman being taken off like that could have affected the way I was bowling but I was determined I must carry on using my usual methods. In spite of Lloyd's injury I resolved to continue my policy of bowling the occasional bouncer and it was up to subsequent batsmen to get out of the way - or hook if they were quick enough. They were, after all, supposedly international cricketers. Botham, for one, was going to get his share.

In retrospect Lloyd was as much a victim of the English policy on pitches as he was of a bouncer that simply never got up. They tried to take the sting out of our bowling by deadening the tracks but instead all that was achieved was a succession of variable and unpredictable wickets on which a batsman could never be sure of the bounce. Lloyd was the first casualty and no one was more upset about it than me and as they carried him away for treatment I was close to breaking down. I like to get a batsman out fairly and squarely, not to maim or injure anyone, and it was a measure of my resolve that I put it behind me and attempted to carry on as if nothing had happened. I knew Lloyd's injury was not my fault and, to his credit, he acknowledged as much when I saw him later. All the West Indian players felt desperately sorry for the man in his first big match, coincidentally on his home ground and in front of his own Warwickshire supporters. I hope he gets another chance one day, but he knows that if it is against me he will get exactly the same sort of treatment.

Boos and cat-calling emanated from the England fans whenever I bowled anything remotely resembling a bouncer at Lloyd's successors after his premature and sickening exit but I was not going to tone down my methods to suit them. Botham came in at number six and we all know how much he loves to hook and how he relishes the short ball. I stationed a man at long leg and the battle was on; he knew I was going to feed him a diet of short-pitched deliveries and I knew he would go for them. That's his style. I was prepared to concede a six or two if it meant he would ultimately fall into my trap and he was ready to ride his luck. The contest began and the bouncers rained down on England's greatest hero.

Dickie Bird is a great character and a first-rate umpire. I have no doubts he has never made a decision when he hasn't had the game's interests at heart. He was obviously watching my battle with Botham with increasing agitation. One particular bouncer Botham failed to see and it just missed him. The next struck him on the helmet and that was too much for Dickie. He called over Clive Lloyd and, in the light of what had happened earlier, he felt he ought to defuse what he must have felt was an emotion-charged situation. 'I'm going to have to warn Marshall about persistent bouncers,' he told Lloyd. I almost got myself into trouble at this point with a needless, but heartfelt, riposte when I replied to Bird, 'You wouldn't be saying that to me if he had hit that ball for six instead'.

Dickie was a bit surprised that I was offering an opinion at such a delicate stage in the proceedings. It was then that Botham came to the rescue. He could see I had talked my way into trouble. 'That's all right,' he said. Bird seemed appeased by Botham's intervention. He was acting, after all, with the batsman's safety in mind and with that reassurance a warning was all I got, though I must admit I felt bad about it. I was merely using every delivery available to me and while I concede it may have looked like I was trying to intimidate him with so many bouncers, it was a genuine tactic against a recognised batsman. I was pitching short to get him out, not to kill him. Botham is a good friend of mine and there is a deep mutual respect. I can pay him no greater compliment than to say I wish he could play for the West Indies since any team in the world, ours included, would gladly welcome him. In this case if the batsman concerned had not been a compulsive hooker I would not have bowled him so many bouncers. As it was Botham needed no protection and went on to make a top-score of 64 in the England first innings total of 191. Andy Lloyd, of course, did not return and took no further part in what has been his only Test. My only wicket in this innings was that of Nick Cook, batting at 10, and I suppose the injury and the warning served to cramp my style a little. It was then that England's bowlers let them down and this is an issue I should like to touch on.

When the game's historians look back on that first 'blackwash', a comprehensive five-nil thrashing, they will point to the mastery of the West Indian fast bowlers. Of course we played our part but in my view it was the failure of the England bowlers and the indifference of the fielding which was the main reason for their failure to at least reduce the margin of defeat. In saying this I realise they never had bowlers to match our pace, however most of the wickets at the Test matches were not particularly helpful to us. They were made for the medium-pacer who could get a bit of movement and take advantage of the variation in bounce. The England bowlers failed to do this and allowed themselves to be steamrollered even when the conditions suited them better than us. Sure, we bowled well at times but it was the England bowlers who lost that series for them, not the batsmen.

At Edgbaston, after Bob Willis had taken two early wickets, they allowed us to build a colossal total of 606 in which Larry Gomes and Viv Richards each scored centuries and Lloyd, Baptiste and Holding half-centuries. The bowling was dreadfully wayward and it seemed to us England, defending a small score of their own, were simply going through the motions, hoping for rather than planning for wickets. They were quite obviously a thoroughly demoralised team when they came off the field and only Geoff Miller, by virtue of bowling a mere 15 overs, had not got three figures against his name. England gave the impression they had not expected anything other than a beating - and they duly got it. Joel Garner, four for 53 in the first innings, took five for 55 this time and we were the winners, by the incredible margin of an innings and 180 runs.

It was during that second innings that I ran into more bouncer trouble with umpire Bird. Willis was holding us up with a plucky performance as last man. Indeed the last wicket pair, he and Downton, put on 42 valuable runs and since we were on the brink of victory, they began to exasperate us with their defiance. After pitching the ball well up to him, I thought it time Willis had a surprise - partly to show him that even as a number 11 he was not immune to a bouncer and partly because I wanted him to think twice about plunging forward on the front foot with that great reach of his. I let go a short one and it flew over the top of his startled frame and went first bounce to the fine-leg boundary. That was too much for Bird. With an admonishing finger, he told me to cut it out. 'It's too early to bowl like that at a tail-ender,' he said. This time I didn't argue: Willis didn't last much longer anyway. I suppose one day someone will be sent off in a Test and in all seriousness I'm not sure I was that close to going during my battle with Botham, not that I shall ever know. England really ought to have done better at Edgbaston. It was a good wicket to bat on and they should have been able to stick around for a draw, even allowing for Andy Lloyd's absence.

Lloyd was not the only rookie ruined on the poor wickets we encountered at Test matches that summer. Paul Terry, a close friend of mine and a team-mate at Hampshire, was another. Terry had his left forearm broken by a delivery from Winston Davis which just never got up as much as he expected in the fourth Test at Old Trafford and, like Lloyd, took the best part of a year to get over the trauma. There was no doubting in my mind that he had deserved his chance with consistently high scores over the previous season or two and, though I know I'm biased, I was pleased he was selected for his country because I recognised in him a player who was able to get in line to the fast bowlers and to play straight. Sounds simple enough, but such a tactic requires skill and bravery and there are surprisingly few around in England who have either that ability or the inclination to face up this way to bowling coming at them at around 90mph.

Most batsmen play top-class bowling away from their bodies and I need only an over or two to realise who likes the quick stuff and who does not. You might say it's easy for me to deduce this as the 'executioner' at the other end, firing down the missiles, but in my view if batsmen want to be taken seriously then they must show the application and the right technique. Terry was one who did have the ability. I had faced him in the Hampshire nets and had always been impressed by his unflappable nature, his skill and his ability to get in line. Gordon Greenidge, his opening colleague at Hampshire, felt much the same way: We were genuinely delighted when Paul was selected for the third Test as England's selectors searched desperately for a combination they thought might at least stem the tide. They had made one positive move by bringing in the Nottinghamshire left-hander Chris Broad for the very same qualities of solidity and courage which later persuaded them to bring in Terry at Headingley. Broad did well, persevered better than most, and ended by averaging 24.37 from his four matches. Quite why England then banished him to the wilderness of county cricket again I shall never know. The West Indian bowlers came to respect his single-minded determination and it will remain a mystery why, having done a competent and thorough job, he was dismissed as suddenly as he was selected. Obviously someone in the England hierarchy had decided he was not really good enough. After bowling at him in four Tests I can only say that in my opinion he deserved a better fate.

Chris began with 55 at Lord's in England's first innings score of 286 and with Botham taking a typically phenomenal eight for 103, England even had a healthy lead of 41. From that position they should never have lost. I had taken six wickets for 85 in that first knock but England were now in a powerful position to force a positive result. Their batsmen battled away and Allan Lamb, who enjoyed a great series against us, hit 110 to enable them to declare at 300 for nine, leaving us 342 to win. English hearts were rightly raised - and quickly dashed. The England batsmen had done all that could have been asked of them, but now it was the frailty of the bowling which was to let them down again. We were worried but Greenidge, raised in England and often thought to be a player better suited to English conditions, made a mockery of a challenging declaration. Gordon made an unbeaten 214 and Gomes scored 92 not out as England were given a severe thrashing by nine wickets. In spite of having faced him in county cricket for many years, Willis, Botham, Pringle, Foster and Miller fed Greenidge's strengths outside the off-stump - and the rest was humiliation for England and their disbelieving supporters. There is no way a team asked to score more than 300 runs in the second innings of a Test match should be allowed to do so for the loss of only one wicket. There was no way also that Botham (nought for 117 in the second innings) should have shared Greenidge's Man of the Match award.

After a defeat of that proportion England, in my opinion, threw in the towel. The selectors could have made as many changes as they liked for the third Test but it would have made no difference because the players had given up. We could recognise the tell-tale signs of acceptance of their status. For a whole variety of reasons I shall never forget Headingley 1984, not least because I thought it was going to be my last match of the tour when, after bowling only six overs in the first innings, I was struck on the thumb while fielding at gully and a visit to hospital confirmed my worst fears of a double fracture. The doctor ordered me to take no further part in the match and to stay out of cricket for 10 days. The forearm was duly put in plaster and I returned to the dressing room to watch morosely as Allan Lamb made 100 out of England's 270 and then see Gomes push us towards a small first innings lead.

Gomes started to edge his way towards a well deserved century when Joel Garner went out to join him with everyone, including myself, assuming he was our last man. I must say the injury was not hurting too much now that it was encased in plaster and it was put to me, jokingly at first, that I could go out at number 11 if required. I thought about it. Why not? I was prepared to have a go, I responded, and Lloyd said that if I felt I could hold a bat and that it would not in any way further damage my finger, then I should get changed and be ready to go in. Garner was run out attempting to give Gomes, on 96, the strike. With several players helping me put on my pads and other vital necessities of a batman's equipment, I ran down the steps to join a very surprised-looking Gomes. He thought he had been marooned four short of his ton and I think he feared the end, in spite of my foolhardiness, was not far away.

It was only after I got out in the middle that I realised there was no way I could use both hands to bat so Larry told me simply to just block the ball if at all possible. I faced eight deliveries and from one of these hit a four with one hand! It must have looked cheeky but by then Larry had got his century and I knew I couldn't last much longer. The Headingley crowd did not know whether to laugh or cry at my one-handed, almost mocking antics. I didn't indeed last long after my boundary but I suspect my little intervention damaged England's morale rather more than it did my thumb. We were all out for 302 and I suppose many people, shocked by my arrival in haste as a batsman, thought that it would be my last contribution to the match. I had thought much the same way but as I left the field it occurred to me that since I was a right-arm bowler and my left hand was causing me no pain in its cast, I might give it a go in the England second innings. In the dressing room I tried it out and once again Lloyd left the decision to me. I said I was prepared to attempt bowling in the knowledge that even if I was defying doctor's orders I could always come off again if things got painful.

When they saw me coming out to bowl there was a look of absolute disbelief among the English batsmen and I walked straight into another contentious issue. The England openers wanted me to cover some of the white plaster with pink adhesive tape because they feared it would disturb their concentration. I was happy to do that as long as it meant they had no other excuses and when Lloyd asked me if I wanted to share the new ball with Joel, I accepted the invitation greedily. I had a few doubts about fielding, and catching in particular, but none at all about bowling and I was soon on my way to my best bowling performance in a Test match - seven for 53 from 26 overs - and I was by no means bowling at my fastest. England were all out for 159 and we went on to complete the win by eight wickets. Gomes was Man of the Match for his gritty 104 in our first innings at a crucial stage in the match but the newspapers had no doubts who had been responsible for England's demise. I can still see the headlines now: 'Thumbs Up, Marshall,' said one. 'One-arm bandit,' was the consensus of most of the others with frequent references to my 'single-handed' destruction of England.

It was only after this win that I heeded the doctor's advice, somewhat belatedly, and stepped down for the fourth Test at Old Trafford. Winston Davis came in as my replacement and it was from one of his deliveries that Paul Terry broke his forearm, the ball - an intended bouncer - never getting up. He, more bravely than I, came back as last man in England's first innings with his arm in plaster underneath a sweater, but in retrospect it was a futile gesture. Only two more runs were added as England attempted to stave off the follow-on after we had made 500. We all felt very sorry for Terry, a new young batsman trying to make his way in the game, but there is never much room for sentiment in Test cricket. For all our commiserations, Greenidge's 223 had given us a 220-run lead and with Terry unable to bat again, England folded to 156 all out.

All that was left to us now was to complete the 'blackwash' at The Oval and this we achieved by 172 runs. I was fully fit again and my five for 35 helped set up a first-innings lead of 28. Desmond Haynes made 125 in our second knock and England were left 375 to win. Garner and Holding took nine wickets between them and not even a typically flamboyant 54 from Botham could ward off the inevitable. Greenidge, with 572 runs at an average of 81.71, was rightly named Man of the Series and, for all the many incidents, I had to be happy with my 24 wickets at 18.20 each.

I was now established at my peak as the most effective bowler in the world and possibly the fastest also; other people were saying this about me. I have never been less than honest with myself and I think, unduly immodest though it may sound, it was probably true. Actually I had learnt I did not have to keep proving I was the fastest in a macho sort of way. Experience has taught me to use speed as a weapon, though by no means my only one. Those seven wickets at Headingley, for instance, for all their notoriety, were put together as much by swing and guile as sheer speed. My own belief in my new-found eminence was confirmed by the record books. My five for 35 at The Oval was the seventh time in my last 10 Test appearances I had taken five or more wickets in an innings.

By the time the West Indian squad set off for Australia and five more Tests from November, there was a strong feeling of near invincibility. We had won our last eight Tests but, unlike the period when we lost to India in the World Cup in 1983, we were by no means complacent. We knew we were going to have to work hard to maintain our position as the best team in the world. Gone was the era of the calypso cricketer; we were now a tough, uncompromising group of players, hardened by battle and galvanised by the occasional failure. We did have one memorable disaster in Australia, in the fifth Test on a sharply turning wicket at Sydney, but by then we were already three-nil up in the series. If you have to lose a Test match then it might just as well be in such circumstances.

The first Test was an extraordinary affair on a traditionally fast WACA wicket at Perth. Centuries for Gomes and Dujon and then Australia all out for 76 (Holding six for 21) and 228; victory to the West Indies by the gigantic margin of an innings and 112 runs. The Aussie press, never slow to criticise at the best of times, singled out the captain Kim Hughes as the culprit in this national 'disaster' and the writing was on the wall by the time he broke down in tears reading out a prepared resignation speech after the next Test at Brisbane shortly after we had won again, by eight wickets on the fourth day. Hughes's batsmen let him down at Brisbane amid strong dressing room rumours the players no longer wanted him as their captain. As a victim of player-power and hunted down by the media, Hughes made a pathetic figure as he bade farewell to top-flight cricket and prepared for his defection to the South African rebels. After I had taken five for 82 in the second innings we only needed 23 to confirm Hughes's misery.

At Brisbane I hit 57 in our first innings total of 424, which gave me almost as much satisfaction as the wickets I took to precipitate our victory. It was at Adelaide in the third Test that I took 10 wickets in a match for the first time at this level. My haul cost me 107 runs but my figures were still bettered by Geoff Lawson, who took 11 in the game, though it failed to save his side, with Border at the helm, from defeat by 191 runs. It was Adelaide's centenary Test and our win, as easy as it sounds, went a long way to spoiling a distinguished party and occasion.

We really ought to have made it 4-0 at Melbourne but Lloyd's delayed declaration because of injuries to key bowlers gave Australia, at 198 for eight, the time and opportunity to hold out for a draw. My own contribution to this match was another five wicket bag (five for 86 in the first innings) and 55 made in nearly three hours. It was the fourth successive innings in which I had taken five or more Aussie wickets and by just presenting the facts I may give the impression of being slightly blasé about it all. I can only say I have never taken anything for granted. I always have to work for my wickets, always have to look for new ways of getting batsmen out. Just as batsmen get predictable with their strengths and weaknesses, so too do bowlers. In a long series batsmen can take steps to counter a bowler so it was up to me to vary everything just to keep them guessing and off balance.

Off balance is exactly what we were at Sydney when we lost our first Test match for nearly three years and our first by an innings for nearly 16. I suppose we should have been forewarned because New South Wales, at the same SCG arena, had beaten us earlier in the tour by 71 runs with the spin bowlers Murray Bennett and Bob Holland taking 15 wickets between them. Not surprisingly Bennett and Holland were called in for this particular Test and then we hardly did ourselves any favours by leaving out our only specialist spinner, Harper, in favour of Walsh, a fourth seamer. Our reliance on pace over the years might have clouded our judgement that day but we certainly paid for that decision. Wessels scored 173 as Australia recorded 471 for nine declared, their biggest score against us for nine long seasons. My figures of nought for 111 just about summed up the wicket and the ease with which Australia made their runs.

We should have guessed it would take spin, even though we had no one to exploit the conditions. It was only when it was our turn to bat that we found out the awful truth. I have to say in mitigation that the wicket was a poor one for a Test match but we did not help matters by batting as if we did not care too deeply about the outcome. At 160 for six I went out to bat still not fully appreciative of how much it was turning. Dujon greeted me at the crease. 'We have a real turner here,' he advised me. I didn't believe him. 'No, it's not,' I said, dismissing his warning. Holland was bowling his leg spinners and the first ball I received pitched outside the leg stump and went narrowly over the top of the off stump. I was absolutely dumbfounded. Dujon smiled from the other end. 'See what I mean,' he said. It made no difference as I was stumped soon afterwards, going down the wicket in an attempt to smother Holland's prodigious spin. Holland, at 38 only new to Test cricket, and Bennett snapped up our last five wickets for three runs and, horror of horrors, we were made to follow on.

The spinners ran through us again and, although I batted nearly an hour and a half for an unbeaten 32, we lost by an ignominious innings and 55 runs. Holland finished with match figures of 10 for 144 and Bennett, the left-arm spinner, took five for 124 to emphasise how much the wicket was turning. Derek Underwood would have been in seventh heaven in Sydney that match and for once we discovered what it was like to lose a match with more than a day to spare: it is not a nice feeling. My only consolation was a prize for being named Man of the Series, some reward at least for my 28 cheap wickets.

Two brief and cricket-filled months later, I was to be Man of the Series against New Zealand in the Caribbean as the West Indies roadshow moved on again, the players somehow shrugging off a year of almost continual involvement to take on the Kiwis for what many saw as the return contest in a grudge started in 1980 when we lost a deeply strife-torn series in New Zealand. It was a contest many of our team were anxious to continue and a record I, for one, was keen to put to rights.

Ian Smith, the New Zealand wicket-keeper, has earned a reputation as a determined lower-order batsman who can hit the ball a long way when he desires but I have never seen a man more scared of me than him. Let me explain the background. The first Test at Trinidad was drawn, largely because of rain, and the second, dominated by Martin Crowe's 188, went the same way in Guyana. It was while he was making a watchful 53 in more than three hours that I began to psyche-out little Smith. At the end of the match I said to him: 'Wait till you get to Barbados. Then I'll sort you out.' Instead of laughing it off he took it very much to heart and obviously began to dread the next Test. What's more there's no doubt he spread the word around his dressing room so that by the time we got to Kensington Oval they were already a beaten team. They were expecting all kinds of unmentionable deeds to take place on this super-fast wicket and they never happened. By then, though, it was too late. We had rolled them over by 10 wickets and I had removed the trembling Smith cheaply twice. They were all out for 94 and although they fared better in the second innings when they made 248, I finished with match figures of 11 for 120 - and for that I have to thank their frame of mind. They were petrified and Smith himself was genuinely frightened while he batted. I can't say I have any regrets about resorting to psychological methods to sort out the New Zealanders. We were out for revenge and, even though I hadn't played in any of the Tests on the previous tour, I bowled aggressively throughout the series just to show them we were the bosses. The hurt had stayed with us. We remembered the poor umpiring (they gave up showing action replays of decisions on television) and the excuses which had followed and there was no question of us showing them any mercy now.

There was more ill-feeling at Sabina Park for the last Test and it emanated from a spell of sustained short-pitched bowling by Richard Hadlee, their one bowler of real quality. Hadlee thinks about every delivery but I cannot understand why he decided to unleash a series of six successive bouncers at our number 10 batsman, Garner. Two were delivered at the tail end of one over and four in a row in the next. I realise some would say we were getting a taste of our own medicine, but we were outraged. When it was time for us to defend our first innings score of 363, Garner and I ripped into them with a real sense of grievance in our bellies. The outcome was another batting performance of real fear from the New Zealanders and a broken arm for Jeremy Coney, their vice-skipper. I will admit now that we knew what we were doing and although Coney, Geoff Howarth and their manager Dr John Heslop complained about our tactics, there was no official objection and we went on to win by 10 wickets. In my view - despite their whinging - we certainly did not overuse the short ball. I could see they were playing the short stuff badly and in my case I was successful in exposing this weakness.

* Marshall made his success in this period in the mid-80s sound disarmingly easy. By his own account, and his figures support this, he was getting wickets anywhere in the world and against all types of opposition. Tim Tremlett, a playing colleague at Hampshire and coach there later, told Meridian Television that Marshall was meticulous in his preparation: "He would always be on the phone discussing future opponents with people who had recently played against them, hoping they might give him some useful information. Better still, he would obtain videos from all over the world of players he had not yet encountered so that he could analyse their weaknesses and strengths." Tremlett was among those to cross the Atlantic to pay his respects, and those of his indebted county, at the funeral.

David Gower remembered the one-armed bandit affair only too vividly, being on the receiving end: "The classic Marshall destruction of England was in my first series as captain when he broke his thumb, got Gomes his century and took seven for almost nothing. Just when we were thinking we had one less fast bowler to worry about he came back and bowled us out. He was a lovely guy to be with, apart from his cricketing ability. He was typical of Barbadians who have a good reputation for keeping a smile on their faces."

14.

'Blackwash'

ENGLAND ARRIVED in the Caribbean fresh from an Ashes victory and in the firm belief they were now the second best international team in the world. Three months later they limped home, the victims of another 'blackwash'; another five-nil annihilation. The good work built up over two series, one in India, the other against a very ordinary Australian squad, had given England a false idea of their own status. They blamed injuries to key players, our array of fast bowlers and the uneven bounce of our pitches.

I will concede there were valid arguments to support those theories yet I believe England did themselves no favours. Speaking as the player named Man of the Series for my 27 wickets in five Tests I like to think I know what I'm talking about when I say that many of the English players went with a defeatist attitude, expecting the hiding they ultimately got. Yet I reckon the series was lost before the players even set foot in the Caribbean. It slipped away in the committee rooms of Lord's - or wherever it is England's selectors choose their teams. When I saw the names of the players down to tour the West Indies I could not understand how they picked some of the names or for what purpose.

On the plus side I was pleased England had taken the bold step of taking the somewhat injury-prone Greg Thomas. The Glamorgan bowler is genuinely quick, strong and very hostile and although his selection raised a few eyebrows among the public, whose knowledge of Welsh cricket may not be all that strong, I for one had been impressed by his performances in county matches. I first encountered him at Southampton and I even went as far as giving him a few tips because I could see that here was an outstanding young talent. As England scratched around for players against the Aussies that summer I gave him a plug in my column in the Daily Mirror and, although I expected nothing to emerge from that, I did hope someone in authority would take the trouble to venture west of London to have a look at him. As it turned out, Thomas more than justified his selection and earned the respect of all our batsmen in the course of the Tests in the West Indies. Why he was later ignored I cannot comprehend.

In the absence of another bowler of real pace, Graham Dilley of Kent, I could not see how England could fail to call up David Lawrence of Gloucestershire. Perhaps they thought they could not afford to take two rookies on such an important tour - instead they sent him out to Sri Lanka to bowl his heart out on dead spinners' tracks. In the West Indies, where the wickets can be concrete-fast, it is usually speed which wins Tests, not medium-pace English seamers. With Thomas coming in from one end and Lawrence the other, I'm convinced England would have got far more of our batsmen out than they did. Lawrence had been outstanding for Gloucestershire in taking 85 wickets in 1985 and, while admitting his action is a bit ungainly and he was still raw, I am positive he was a chance worth taking.

Instead England kept on the safe side and selected four medium-pace seamers of the sort who never achieve anything in places like the West Indies. Botham was one of them, of course, and there was no doubting he deserved to be on the plane to Barbados, but it was a source of mystery to me why Richard Ellison, Neil Foster and Les Taylor were all named in the tour party. Even allowing for the lack of depth of quick bowling in England it beat me why all three were chosen. I certainly respect them as bowlers in the helpful conditions provided in England or New Zealand, but I knew they would be ineffective in the Caribbean - and so it turned out to be. Poor old Taylor, a late entrant to Test cricket the previous summer, was injured at an important time and was little more than a passenger for a majority of the tour. He made a lonely figure playing golf by himself at England's base in Barbados. Foster and Ellison both only took seven Test wickets at more than 40 each in both cases. Enough said. They were the wrong horses for this particular course whereas Lawrence, for all his youth and inexperience, would have troubled even the likes of Greenidge and Richards. Gordon had spoken highly of him after facing him in county matches and since bowlers are credited with winning matches, I think England made a big mistake in their choice of the quick bowlers.

John Emburey and Phil Edmonds are the best pair of spinners, and

I emphasise pair, in the world and with Guyana predictably declining to offer hospitality to anyone tainted by South Africa, England's hopes rested on Trinidad where two Tests were scheduled and where the Port of Spain wicket traditionally favours the tweakers. Some of the other tour selections did not bear close scrutiny. I have nothing against Paul Downton but I'm not alone in believing that, quite simply, he is not the best wicket-keeper in England. I know he is a brave and solid batsman but there are many better candidates in my view; his deputy Bruce French for one, Steve Rhodes, Jack Russell and Bob Parks among others. My own choice would have been Jack Richards of Surrey. Jack had struck me as a much-improved batsman and a thoroughly competent wicket-keeper who could have filled the dual role in both the Tests and the one-day internationals.

I relished the prospect also of firing away at some of the batsmen England were bringing out. On the quicker wickets I fancied my chances against Graham Gooch and Tim Robinson for a start. Robinson, who had made such a bright start to his Test career, would, I suspected, find the pace too much for such a basically front-footed batsman. I would have selected his Nottinghamshire colleague Chris Broad in his place. A sturdy, no-nonsense batsman like him would have stood up better to our quick bowlers without question. I would also have had Wilf Slack in the England team if I had been one of their selectors. He had been in outstanding, form for Middlesex in 1985 and had a working knowledge of Caribbean wickets as a member of the Windward Islands team in the Shell Shield competition. Slack is a good performer against fast bowling and I was rather surprised to see his name in the B squad instead. An ability to stand up to people like me was the reason David Smith of Worcestershire became, with Thomas, the rank outsider in the tour party. It was said that Smith had earned his chance by the way he had fearlessly taken me on at Portsmouth and scored 112 and 87 in a county match. That may have been so and I am the first to agree how well he played in that particular game, but if I had been choosing the team I would have wanted a greater depth of evidence to suggest that, at nearly 30 years of age, he could do the same at Test level. Even so, I thought it was worth a gamble taking Smith because he does hit the ball hard and no one could ever accuse him of being scared.

For all the planning and thinking that went into composing the England squad, I believe the series was won and lost in one crucial incident in Jamaica in the first of the one-day internationals. England had hardly got off to the best of starts in any case, losing to the Windward Islands in St Vincent, and there was obviously a suspicion growing among their players that the wickets were going to be so bad that the West Indian fast bowlers were going to be unplayable. I imagine these fears were confirmed when Mike Gatting, in prime form, took a bouncer from me on the nose. Let me say straight away the sight of blood spurting in all directions absolutely sickened me. As the other West Indian players rushed to his aid I couldn't bear to look. I could feel myself close to passing out, my head went dizzy and I thought I was going to be sick. I realised he had been seriously hurt but I didn't dare go to him and discover what had happened. As medical help was rushed from the dressing-rooms to him I stood at the other end trying not to faint. I hate the sight of blood in any circumstances and I really thought they might have to carry the two of us off at the same time! I went to pick up the ball and to my horror I found a piece of Gatting's nose bone lodged in the seam. I dropped it like a hand-grenade, the feeling of nausea surging back.

It took me many minutes to regain my composure and my appetite for battle after Gatt had been lead away in deep distress. I recovered; England did not. I sensed their morale was carted off to hospital with their vice-captain and they came to the joint conclusion, there and then, that there was no escape from the second successive 'blackwash'. Cynics will say that I could not have been so upset if I somehow still managed to take four wickets in a six-wicket win but, as the other players told me, I had to put the incident behind me as soon as possible and get on with my job. Afterwards I went to see Gatting, who had played his hook shot too late, and when he told me it had been his fault, not mine, I was greatly relieved.

It was against this background, Gatting's terrible injury and his need to fly home for treatment, that England went into the first Test at Sabina Park with rapidly diminishing enthusiasm. Many of their top players, Gooch, Gower and Botham to name but three, were struggling for form and one of their leading batsmen was possibly out of the series. They knew also that Sabina Park had already produced a wicket where anything might happen. Added to that was our fearsome new fast bowling discovery, Patrick Patterson. Patterson had looked fast on occasions for Lancashire but had paid the penalty for bowling too short in English conditions, so that it must have been something of an unhappy surprise for the tourists to find out what a different proposition he was on his native tracks in the Caribbean. In terms of sheer speed some critics were even saying the strapping Jamaican was as quick as me, and in little spells there was no doubt he was. I think England had been hoping that on the evidence of indifferent seasons for their counties, Joel Garner and Michael Holding might not be the forces they once were. On the contrary, both produced some vintage displays to complement Patterson and myself and to help form a quartet of pace bowlers every bit as lethal as anything we had unleashed in recent years. Faced by four of us coming in at them in rotation, England hardly batted for more than 50 overs in any innings throughout the five Tests. Holding could still bowl as fast as any of us when he wanted while Garner's awkward lift and bounce was as dangerous as it had been in his prime.

It was the bounce, or occasionally the lack of it, which undid England in the first Test when Patterson took four wickets in the first innings and England were shot out cheaply for 159 and 152. Richard Ellison, somewhat confounding my belief he would not be effective in the West Indies, managed five for 78 in our total of 307 but we needed only five runs to win. My own job, as I saw it, was to establish some kind of hold over Gooch and Robinson, much as I had attempted to do with Gavaskar. Gooch batted soundly in the first innings for 51 but I bowled him before he had scored in the second which gave me a tremendous psychological lift so early in the series. He, though, must have thought he had got the better of me again by the masterful way he made 129 not out in the next one-day international in Trinidad. My figures of nought for 59 spoke for themselves as England deservedly levelled the score in internationals and it ought to have given them a boost for the Test match which was to follow on the same ground.

It was my 42nd Test and it was to provide me with my 200th wicket. England never looked at ease as Garner, Patterson and myself took nine of the wickets as England made 176 in their first innings and I even made some runs (62 not out) in our response of 399. I could see that the wicket would be more use to me second time around and that if I were to cut my pace slightly I could get the ball to swing. It duly paid off with four more wickets, one of which, Paul Downton leg before, gave me my 200th. My match figures were eight for 132 and they were enough to guarantee me the

Man of the Match award. Had England batted more resolutely in the first innings one of the spinners, Edmonds or Emburey, might have deprived me of the accolade. As it was, we only needed 93 to win and we did so, not without an alarm or two on a turning pitch, by seven wickets. If we had been chasing another hundred or so it might have been very different but Emburey and Edmonds, for all their guile and skill, did not have enough runs at their disposal and we escaped, a little thankfully. All touring teams are frightened of playing in Barbados. I have said how India, Australia and New Zealand had expected to be rolled over on the quick wickets of the Kensington Oval and were not surprised when they were. England were much the same. They guessed it would be a fast track and possibly a bit uneven as well.

By now there were rumbles of discontent about the number of bouncers the English batsmen were having to contend with, but after we had beaten them by an innings and 30 runs in front of about 4,000 of their own supporters it was revealed that England's bowlers had sent down more bouncers than we had. Greg Thomas performed well for England in our first innings score of 418 to take four for 70 and looked competitive and very fast at times, yet dropped catches let us build a bigger score than we ought to have done, with Richie Richardson badly missed in the covers by Gooch when he was still well short of his eventual 160. Once more we shared our wickets as England, to the disappointment of those holiday-making supporters, failed to go the five-day distance, all out for 189 and 199.

By now also, after three successive Test defeats, David Gower's captaincy was coming under some scrutiny from those ever-willing to find a scapegoat for the inevitable. David's languid approach may give the impression of being uninvolved but I found it difficult to understand how he could have possibly altered the results which went so comprehensively against him. I was a little sorry for him when Mike Gatting, fully recovered, replaced him during the series against India in the following summer, though no captain can expect to survive such a crippling run of defeats. Barbados, for all its seductive beaches and wonderful tourist attractions, must have been a miserable place for the England entourage after that defeat and I was not alone in forming the impression that many would rather have been sampling the cold reality of an English spring than be moving on to Trinidad for more of the same punishment - unfortunately for them that was exactly what they got. Defeat in both the one-day international, by eight wickets; and in the Test, by 10 wickets.

Trinidad, as at other Tests, had its share of England followers. They must have been rather surprised how they almost outnumbered West Indian supporters, at Barbados in particular. This is not necessarily due to lack of enthusiasm, nor to any sense of seen-it-all-before complacency. They should have been at the Kensington Oval earlier when Jamaica were playing Barbados for what amounted to a Shell Shield decider. On the one side were Holding, Patterson and Walsh. On the other myself and Joel Garner spearheading the Barbados bowling. This was nation against nation and a time when the Caribbean passion for the game runs really high. We were getting crowds of 15,000 for this battle, which I'm happy to say was won by Barbados by 67 runs. It gets back to what I was mentioning earlier about the West Indies being the federation, not the national team.

In Antigua for the fifth Test it was different. Even the holidaymakers were outnumbered by locals desperate to catch a glimpse of their hero, Viv Richards, and the heir-apparent to his crown, Richie Richardson. Perhaps it is because they do not see as much first class cricket in Antigua as they do in Barbados or Trinidad but their delight in having the relatively new experience of a Test match is always a joy to behold for the players. Except, of course, in this case the English, demoralised and defeated. All they could possibly hope to achieve was to avoid the embarrassment of 10 successive beatings by the West Indies. At one stage it looked as if they might actually do that. Haynes made 131 and I hit 76 in our first-innings total of 474, but the England reply was positive. Gower looked to be on his way to a century, which might have at least got the critics off his back for a day or two, until I got him for 90 and they were all out for 310.

Then came one of the most explosive innings it has ever been my good fortune to witness. I almost felt sorry for England as the great Richards, fired up by the home crowd baying for something exceptional, duly provided it in the most spectacular display of big-hitting. Seven sixes and seven fours flew to all parts of the ground as he raced to 110 in 58 balls, reducing the best of a nation's bowling to pathetic impotence. Botham, still two tantalising wickets short of Lillee's world record, was made to wait as Richards took him and his team-mates apart with a display of sheer ferocity.

England were left a day and a half to get 411, and since they had never batted that long before in the series we had every hope of completing the 'blackwash'. England were 33 for two at the close of the fourth day and with Harper's spin doing the damage on the last, we won with nearly 15 overs to spare. Richards was named Man of the Match and I, for my 27 wickets at 17.85 each, emerged above Garner, Richards and Haynes, the other candidates, as Man of the Series. I could hardly have been happier than to have returned to Hampshire for the 1986 season at 28 years old, in my prime, the fastest bowler in the world, a vital member of the best international team in pursuit of the 83 wickets I needed for my 1,000 in first-class cricket. I required now only some measure of success with my county to complete my contentment.

When I finally reached that magic 1,000 mark it was more than just a milestone to me - though the sight of Martyn Moxon's somersaulting off stump was pleasant enough in itself? Plenty of bowlers who had never played anything other than county cricket had achieved that and more, but in my case it was something to celebrate. I had joined a highly elite band of just four West Indians who had taken 1,000 first class wickets. What's more I had done it in just over eight years, one of the quickest since the Second World War. It was as much a dream fulfilled as seeing the house I had conceived in my sleep become a reality of bricks and mortar on a hillside in the St Michael district of Barbados in 1985.

Like most of the West Indian players, many from humble backgrounds, I have been careful with the money I have earned over the good years in readiness for the decades when the living might not be so easy. It was during the 1981 Antigua Test match with England that I awoke at 2am, my mind a frenzy of ideas. Grabbing a pen and paper I drew up the plans for what I have always thought of since as being my dream house. I surprised even myself at the detail I was committing to paper and when my ideas had exhausted themselves I took them to a friend in Barbados and, with the money I had saved from seven years non-stop cricket, I was able to get him to make them look something like a potential home. Now, high above the tourist hotels and beaches of St James', with a clear view of the Caribbean, is the house of that dream on a split-level with three bedrooms, a circular video and record room and a separate flat downstairs where in time my mother will live. I can think of nothing more gratifying than coming home from a long, hard spell abroad to the warmth of Barbados and seeing again my house, a sort of monument to all I have worked so determinedly for.

Of course I have been lucky to avoid a career-breaking injury or the sort of controversy which has dogged some of the game's other top names. I have kept fit and I have never smoked. I'm neither a big eater nor a big drinker although I have been known to knock back a brandy or two at the end of a day's play or at a party. I have been fortunate also to have had many good friends among the West Indian players and those at Hampshire. They are not just team-mates, they are pals. I have a house also in a suburban area outside Southampton on the same estate as Gordon Greenidge and Desmond Haynes, who happen to like Southampton, and several of the local football club's international players. One day, and it will be a sad one, I shall say goodbye to Hampshire and I shall sell the house and retreat to my dream home on the hill to start a new life, possibly away from the game which has been my whole existence since I was a teenager. Then it will be time to settle down, to think of marriage and to fill my home with the happy laughter of three or four children. I already have a daughter, Shelly Andrea, born on 24th November 1984 and she's the pride of my life. Her mother, Andrea, is a cashier at a restaurant in Bridgetown and I love our baby more than anything else in the world. At the moment I have no marriage plans because constant travelling around the globe is not conducive to it.

I have noticed how some players lose their appetite for sport when they marry, as other priorities take the place of wickets and runs. I still have wickets to take and runs to score but in a few years when the bounce starts to drain from my run-up and when mediocre batsmen start to hook me for six, I shall know it is time to make way for a new generation of hungry young West Indians with a point to make and a living to earn. I'm not looking forward to it because everyone would like to defy the years; to believe *anno domini* might somehow be avoided. Right at the beginning of my career, a wise old head told me: 'What goes up must come down'. I have often thought about that in the growing awareness of its accuracy. I am at the top of the ladder and I'm enjoying every minute of the fame, the notoriety even, and the adulation. It is great to be recognised. It is great also to travel the world at somebody else's expense and to be greeted as a hero wherever I go. I have yet to find it hard to bowl fast. One day, though, the legs will get stiff and tired and I shall start slipping down that ladder and then I hope I will have the foresight and maturity to know that it's time to pack my bags and retreat to Barbados. At the moment I still have goals I want to achieve on the cricket field and I shall pursue them with the same dedication and single-mindedness which I like to think have been the hallmarks of my performances over the years since I first realised cricket would be a way off the poverty line.

I'm a lucky man. I have two nice houses, a sponsored car with Hampshire, a bright red BMW at home and money to spend whenever I feel like it. Not many of my contemporaries in the Caribbean can claim any of that and it is an indefinable ability to hurl a cricket ball from one set of stumps to another, 22 yards away, faster than anyone else which has put it all on a plate for me. I know I have been fortunate. Every time I go back to Barbados I can see with my own eyes how many families, despite the paradise in which they live, are struggling to get by. Yet no one resents my comparative riches. I have only to drive the BMW out on the main highways to have people I have never met wave to me or flash their lights as they go past. I am someone they look up to, not envy, because I provide that ray of hope for so many other Barbadian kids, playing cricket like I did under the palm trees. One day they could be the new Malcolm Marshall. One day it could be some skinny little lad from nowhere who knocks me off the top of that ladder. When I finish in my mid 30s I shall go home and look for the next set of Marshalls, Garners and Daniels. I have had so much fun, so much wealth from a game I love that I feel it is only right I should put something back into it. Perhaps I shall become a coach, scouring the island among the dusty villages, the cramped back-streets and under those palms for a youngster I can help develop, nurture and see rise, in my place, as a West Indian cricketer. Such a discovery would give me tremendous pleasure and then at least I would have wiped the slate clean.

It all comes back to me, how I used to listen over the crackling airwaves to that great commentator, John Arlott, ironically a native of Hampshire, painting a picture - not just commentating - with that distinctive accent of his. He told us, thousands of miles away, about the bunting hanging from the beams at Lord's and about the seagulls standing imperiously around in the outfield, defying anyone to disturb them. It was he who made the game come alive in my imagination and fuelled my desire to become the new Sobers. For that, I shall always thank him and perhaps I have repaid him with what I have done for his county. Incidentally, I like to think I do a very passable imitation of the great man!

Tony Cozier has chronicled our rise to the top as the West Indies' number one cricket reporter. We call him the West Indies' leading wicket-taker because every time he comes on the radio, a West Indian wicket falls. He is another who, in more familiar tones, relayed every minute detail of what my heroes were doing on the cricket pitch, making me realise, with a bit of luck, I too could rise to the top. Luck does play a part, of course, but the important thing is to seize the opportunity when it presents itself. I was lucky to have got into a Test squad after only one first-class match; I was lucky to have been taken on by Hampshire at the same time without having been seen by any of their officials; I have been lucky also to have been part of possibly the greatest international side of all time. I like to think I have taken those pieces of good fortune and worked on them to my advantage. You cannot take 1,000 wickets in eight years without knowing a thing or two about bowling fast.

Thanks to cricket I have travelled from one end of the world to another, and many stops in between, and found friendship everywhere. When I go back to Barbados, invest some money in bonds or something similar and open a sports goods store, I shall think back to all those friends I have met and the matches I have played in. I suppose I run the risk of finding that life after cricket could be an anticlimax but I don't think it will. It's a question of discovering new priorities. In the meantime I shall continue to revel in every minute of my life as a professional cricketer. Mine has been the fast way to the top. I am proud to be among the great cricketers produced by the West Indies. I am proud also to be considered the world's top fast bowler and I will not give up my crown easily. Here's to the next 1,000!

---

* When he wrote this final chapter early in 1987 there were nine more years ahead of him in first class cricket as a player, and perhaps for three or four of those he was the world's fastest bowler. To the surprise of many at the time he admitted when he was 30 in an interview in Barbados that he was not quite the bowler he had been in terms of sustained pace. He was now

starting to rely on guile and experience, as he always knew he would have to one day. There was never a sports goods store for him to retire to; cricket had bitten too deeply to allow him to walk out as suddenly as he had appeared. Instead he was quickly lured into a coaching role so that he was soon putting something back into the game he loved.

As for the England teams he faced over the years, he was always surprised at selectorial choices and in that he was not alone. In his view, expressed vigorously but fairly in his Daily Mirror column over eight years, there were too many players in England of a similar standard and very few of them in any way outstanding. They were chosen for England on what seemed like a whim and jettisoned almost immediately, hence the long list of one and two-cap wonders. This he perceived was the fault of the county system where reputations were made and then exposed as false in the white heat of international competition. What also saddened him was that when he first came to England in 1979 every county had Test-calibre players. By the time his own playing career ended this was no longer the case. He liked a contest and genuinely hoped that all nations, England included, picked their best players all the time.

The key to success was being prepared to give 100 per cent on every occasion and it was this quality to which the former Somerset and England spin bowler Vic Marks, now cricket correspondent of The Observer, referred in a fascinating insight. In his obituary, Marks wrote: "Most cricketers try pretty hard in the Test arena - though Marshall always went the extra mile - and generally the great ones coast a little when returning to the counties. Marshall would never do that even on a drab day at Bournemouth. There was a peculiar tension when batting against Hampshire in the eighties. Even when he was grazing at mid-off you were conscious of him; you could not avoid glancing in his direction, checking his movements: 'When is he coming back? How much more of Nigel Cowley (an off-spinner) will I be permitted? He's had a word with the captain. He's loosening up'. Invariably he did come back and the sternest of challenges ensued. Like all the great West Indians, he never said a word to you. There might be the odd glance, an icy stare or a knowing smile, but sledging was demeaning - to him - and with such pace in his armoury, it was a redundant weapon anyway. 'Cappy,' he would chime in his slow, high-pitched Bajan accent (when he and Garner were together, he speeded up and they were indecipherable to those of us born on this side of the Atlantic), 'mid-off's a waste of time: put him in slips. Square leg to short leg.' Then he would glide in at pace or maybe dally with his victim with an assortment of swingers (on balance, I preferred the latter). The contest was fierce and usually one-sided, but after stumps he would be chuckling away with anyone."

PART THREE

1.

International Years 1986-1992

MALCOLM MARSHALL CONTINUED to remain an integral part of the West Indies attack until March,1992, a month before his 34th birthday. He might have expected a year or two more but he was shrewd enough to realise that the end had been reached after the World Cup in Australia and New Zealand when the much-fancied West Indies gave a hint of the decline to come by failing to reach the semi finals.

There is never an easy way to tell a great player that his days at the top are over. The West Indies Board of Control originally claimed he was injured, but there was no doubt he was one of the scapegoats for finishing sixth. Marshall took his exclusion with dignity, made no public comment about it and prepared instead for the final phases of his playing career with Hampshire, in South Africa and for one season in the leagues in Lancashire. By the time he had finished he had collected 376 wickets in 81 Tests, at that stage making him by a long way the most successful of all West Indian bowlers. Courtney Walsh, by virtue of having played many more matches, was later to overtake him in terms of wickets taken and Marshall was typically among the first to congratulate him. Walsh had been a contemporary of many West Indian triumphs they shared as players and when Marshall became coach he came to rely on Walsh and Curtly Ambrose to spearhead the attack.

So it was in 1986 when the West Indies toured Pakistan with Garner and Holding choosing to rest and Walsh and Marshall being joined by the Trinidadian Tony Gray, later of Surrey. Slow wickets, uneven bounce and one astonishing West Indian collapse meant the series finished level 1-1 with a third match in Karachi being drawn. It was in Faisalabad that the West Indies fell apart in such uncharacteristic fashion, all out for 53 to record only their fourth defeat in 57 Tests (30 wins). Revenge came at

Lahore and it was a measure of the West Indian predominance at the time that their win in three days by an innings and ten runs was the third time that year that opponents had been routed inside three days. The West Indies might well have won the decider in Karachi but the umpires took the players off for bad light with nine overs remaining and with Pakistan a wobbling 125 for 7 in their second innings. Marshall's 16 wickets in the series cost him 16.62, but there was still plenty more, perhaps too much, cricket still to be played that winter.

There was a one-day tournament in Sharjah and the World Series Cup in Australia to be contested before a tired and weary West Indian party made its way to New Zealand for what proved to be a hotly-contested three match series, each side winning once and the other match in Wellington being notable for Holding's retirement (60 Tests, 249 wickets) and Marshall reaching the coveted double of 1,000 runs and 100 wickets in his 49th appearance. In Auckland, where the West Indies won by ten wickets, the redoubtable Greenidge wore sun glasses in making a match-winning double century in an innings which included seven sixes. At Christchurch, however, the Kiwis levelled the series emphatically on a wicket left damp by incessant rain and inflicted on the West Indies their first defeat inside three days since 1964-65 at Port of Spain. Marshall played no significant part in the proceedings, his nine tour wickets costing 32 each.

Back in England in 1987 Marshall was preoccupied with his benefit season with Hampshire, but the playing highlight was undoubtedly the match between the MCC and the Rest of the World at Lord's to mark the MCC's bicentenary, a chance not just to settle an old score or two but to prove conclusively that of all the bowlers playing in cricket at that time he was the best. The MCC had assembled two powerful, almost fantasy sides with Gatting leading one team and Allan Border the other. Gatting's team was made up of himself, Greenidge, Broad, Gooch, Gower, Rice, Hadlee, Shastri, Emburey, Marshall and French. Border was among a line up which included Gavaskar, Haynes, Vengsarkar, Miandad, Dujon, Imran, Kapil Dev, Harper, Walsh and Abdul Qadir. Which mischief-maker had pitted Marshall against Vengsarker has never been identified but The Guardian's Mike Selvey revealed earlier how in this match Marshall had stepped up a gear in his battles with Gavaskar and his Indian compatriot. What annoyed Marshall as much as having an lbw appeal against Gavaskar turned down from the legitimate first ball was having Desmond Haynes dropped from his second in the slips. Vengsarkar was out to that brute of a delivery from Marshall described by Selvey and at the conclusion of a drawn game he was named bowler of the match. The £2,000 cheque was pleasant enough reward but the knowledge that he had out-bowled all the others from either side unquestionably gave him the greater satisfaction, pride of performance being a strongly motivational factor.

Not surprisingly, after so much cricket in so many places, Marshall chose to rest during the winter of 1987-88, opting out of the World Cup in India and Pakistan, the warm-up tournament in Australia and a short tour of India. If the West Indies Cricket Board were upset by his decision they did not let on for fear of alienating their main bowler and allowed the golden goose to return to Barbados for a few months recuperation in the sunshine. The tour of England was on the agenda for the summer of 1988 and if it was a case of working out priorities then England took precedence.

It was around this time that Marshall met Connie, later to become his wife and mother of their son Mali. It was around this time also that Marshall rediscovered his passion for road tennis, a game played in Barbados more seriously than many outsiders are aware. Rawle Maycock recalled how Marshall was an enthusiast and brought Viv Richards and Desmond Haynes along to the Station Hill area for a game or two. He even sponsored a tournament in Deanes Village, St Michael. Maycock said, "Malcolm donated some of the biggest trophies that were ever given out at road tennis. The people of Deanes Village and Station Hill will mourn the loss not just of a great cricketer but also a road tennis champion. He was well-liked and would hang around with the fellows long after the games were over."

Marshall prepared for England by taking 27 wickets for Barbados in the regional competition after being appointed captain. Barbados finished fourth, but he made local headlines for being fined 250 US dollars after accusing the umpires of cheating in a match against eventual champions Jamaica. This did not stop him from taking part in Pakistan's spring tour of the Caribbean though he missed the first Test in Guyana through injury. The second in Trinidad was drawn and the third in Barbados remarkable for a statistical quirk; Abdul Qadir became Marshall's 250th Test victim, the match after Marshall had been Qadir's 200th. In the event the West Indies won by two wickets and Marshall's nine wickets over the two innings won him the man of the match award, all of which was the perfect build up for England when the great bowler was to experience his finest hour.

If Marshall had been the one-armed bandit in 1984 he was the supreme destroyer that summer four years later; indisputably man of the series, twice man of the match and completely dominating a shell-shocked home side. Only Graham Gooch stood in his path, his 146 in the first Test at Trent Bridge enabling England to precede four emphatic defeats with a draw, but the affect was the same. Marshall took 35 wickets in the series at 12.65, both the number of wickets and the average at which they were obtained are records for any series involving the West Indies.

Gooch may have saved England at Trent Bridge but Marshall claimed the first of his man of the match awards for his six wickets in the England first innings. He should have got another at Lord's in the next Test where the West Indies won by 134 runs but his final analysis of ten for 92 was not deemed to be enough, though his six for 32 in the first innings was the best ever by a West Indian at cricket's headquarters. There was no denying him in the third at Old Trafford, his seven for 22 proved to be his best in Tests and set up a West Indian win by an innings and 156 runs. By his own incredible standards the fourth at Headingley was almost a setback. He 'only' took five wickets in another one-sided encounter, but along the way came his 100th against England, the match being marred by racial abuse from some sections of the crowd.

By the time the players reached the Oval for the last match England were a battered and humiliated outfit, longing for some respite after using four different captains in a shambolically familiar attempt to alter the inevitable. There was little opposition of substance as the West Indies duly completed the task of demolishing England and it was all over 20 minutes after tea on the last day when Gus Logie drove Philip DeFreitas for the winning boundary. Marshall's case for being man of the series was irrefutable and if there was a high point to his career then this was surely it. Here he was at 30 years of age in his bowling prime and with a trail of destruction in his wake to prove it. His one-armed bandit antics of 1984 may have brought him public recognition and a place in the history of cricketing oddities but his performances of four years later elevated him to a higher plane altogether, a plane not achieved by many, if any, others. Later he was to look back on that series as his greatest, for the ease with which he sliced through a supposedly international opposition and as the time when it all came together; pace, guile, cunning, variation, knowledge of opponent and mental strength. His finest hour, no doubt.

If anything his exertions in England produced a reaction when the West Indies rattled on to Australia for an equally demanding four months from October 1988. The Australians were still putting together a combination which would dominate the 1990s as readily as the West Indies had done in the 1980s. The academy system was about to bear fruit and the finishing touches were being applied to a squad which would crush England in the Ashes series of the following summer. But in 1988-89 the West Indies ruthlessly reminded them that there was work still to be done, the holders of the crown of world cricket champions putting Allan Border's young pretenders firmly in their place. The West Indies won the first three Tests in Brisbane, Perth and Melbourne with Marshall, who had an otherwise undistinguished series, reaching a personal milestone when he had David Boon lbw in Melbourne for his 300th wicket in his 61st Test.

Since he was still several months short of his 31st birthday he had every reason to suppose there was time and opportunity to reach 400 and beyond, but this was not to be. In this instance in Australia he managed only 17 wickets and where he had been the chief instigator of England's downfall a few months before, here it was Ambrose with 26 wickets at 21.46 who undermined the Australians. At Sydney, with the Sir Frank Worrell Trophy already won and lost, Marshall gave a superb demonstration of his potency even on the most unhelpful of wickets when he took five for 29 from 31 overs in a match otherwise remembered for the little used spin of Border whose figures of eleven for 96 proved decisive and to this day remain the best by an Aussie captain. The drawn fifth Test in Adelaide, apart from providing Greenidge with his first Test century in almost 14 years in Australia, was notable for some dubious umpiring decisions and both Marshall and Haynes openly showed dissent at verdicts which went against them. They were not punished.

When India visited the Caribbean the major talking point, particularly in his home island, was whether or not Marshall could overtake Lance Gibbs' West Indian record of 309 Test wickets. It was ironic considering how pace had dominated West Indian attacks almost exclusively for a decade or more that Gibbs should be a spinner, and he was a good one, himself waiting until almost the end of his career to overhaul Fred Trueman's then world record of 307. "Whoever beats that will be bloody tired," was Trueman's famous remark on being asked about his record but there was no sense of tiredness, only eagerness, when Marshall neared his target.

With the first Test in Guyana almost predictably ruined by rain the scene was set with impeccable timing for the next in Barbados. The whole island was willing him to succeed and to succeed in front of them, so much so that a calypso was created to mark the occasion as if to remind him of what was expected. He remembers going to bed one night during the match a solitary wicket away from overtaking the Guyanese-born Gibbs. "I was one short overnight and the radio station played a song written in my honour called 'Hit It O Maco O Maco Hit It' over and over again as if they knew I was listening. Finally, after lunch the next day, Dujon caught Azharuddin from an outswinger. I was overwhelmed with pride." The West Indies duly won there, Port of Spain and Kingston, his eleven wickets for 89 earning him yet another man of the match award in Trinidad.

Apart from two limited overs tournaments in Sharjah and India late in 1989, there was no more international involvement for Marshall until early in 1990 when England were invited to the Caribbean, and they must have been dreading meeting him again so soon after his one-man destruction of them only two years before. But they were spared his sword largely as the West Indies gave hints of the struggles to come in labouring to a series victory and not without considerable discomfort and occasional embarrassment. Marshall missed two of the Tests and took only three rather costly wickets, so that after a summer with Hampshire he was looking forward to discovering his true form on the short tour of Pakistan towards the end of 1990, but even there it did not quite work out for him. In only one match, the second at Faisalabad, was Marshall able to make a telling contribution, his four wickets in 13 balls setting up victory inside three days, but in the third and last in Lahore he failed to take a wicket. (It was here incidentally that one BC Lara made his Test debut). Therefore, it was not unreasonable to suppose that the West Indies hierarchy might have been a little worried about Marshall's apparently declining powers and, with it, declining success.

By the time Australia came to the Caribbean in early 1991, Marshall was approaching his 33rd birthday, but still regarded as a vital member of the pace-reliant attack which had stood the West Indies in such good stead for so long. The sides were contesting the Sir Frank Worrell Trophy even though it had gone missing in 1984-85, but spectators would have been unaware of such a comparative irrelevance as the series was marred by bad feeling and altercations, major and minor, at most of the matches. The West Indies were leading 1-0 when the fourth Test began in Bridgetown and it was another of Barbados's favourite sons who stole the show, Greenidge batting for more than eleven hours on the eve of his 40th birthday for a match-winning 226, but it was here also, almost unheralded, that Marshall claimed his 350th Test wicket. Greenidge's century opening partnership with Haynes was their last together and his double century was the highest score by a West Indian against Australia. Sadly the next Test in Antigua, which Australia won by 157 runs, was Greenidge's last and it coincided with his landmark birthday. Richards announced that this was his final home series and it was plain to see that the great order was beginning to break up after 15 years on top of the world. Marshall's 21 wickets at 20.81 hardly indicated that his own end was nigh and there was time still for one final tilt at the English in his own private killing grounds around the counties.

England had always provided him with rich pickings and at 33 it was apparent to all but the most optimistic or sentimental that this was to be his last major tour of England. What no one had anticipated was that this was also to be his last major tour anywhere. While Viv Richards was now approaching 40 there seemed to be enough playing life in Marshall after the Australian visit to the Caribbean to suggest more battles to be fought and won in other corners of the cricketing globe. Not that Marshall performed badly in England in 1991 either, his 20 wickets being gleaned at a highly satisfactory 22.10 each but overall it was a poor summer for the West Indies, drawing the Test series 2-2 with Greenidge being forced home by injury before the tour had begun in earnest, Richards winding down to retirement and Lara hardly figuring. The West Indies were on the back foot from the moment Gooch's 154 set up a win in the first Test in Leeds so that it was not until the third Test that the West Indies finally levelled. The West Indies won the fourth Test and England the fifth thanks to Phil Tufnell. The fifth Test was always going to be the last for that great warrior Richards and it was duly and properly acknowledged, but it was also the last for Malcolm Marshall. It was not an auspicious way to go out of Test cricket; nought and 17 with the bat, one for 62 in the first England innings and one for nine in the second. It was perhaps fitting that Graham Gooch, an adversary throughout his career, should be his last victim, lbw for 29.

There was nothing during the tour to lead any observer to believe that Marshall was on his way out; on the contrary, many believed he would remain the cornerstone of the West Indies, possibly even as captain, for a critical year or more, a view which was reinforced when he took four for 18 against the Australians in Melbourne – his best performance in one-day internationals – in the run-up to the World Cup of 1992. But here the international story ends. With Richie Richardson as captain the West Indies had a poor World Cup and although he played in five matches he missed the last two against Sri Lanka and Australia. Failing to qualify for the semi finals was seen as something akin to a disaster in the Caribbean and heads had to fall; Marshall's was one of them. The Caribbean authorities said that Marshall was injured, Marshall said he was not and with that an illustrious career ground to a halt.

Not wishing to make a fuss, as some of his contemporaries had, he slipped quietly away, his stirring deeds still fresh in many memories. Having made such a sensational entry to international cricket after only one first class match, Marshall almost certainly felt to be in its debt so that at least he bowed out with dignity. It would have been nice for him and his many supporters around the Caribbean and elsewhere if he could have gone like Richards with a fanfare and tributes from friend and foe. This he deserved at least and it was a shame that he should slip away, paying the penalty for collective failure in a one-day tournament. He never cared much for one-day cricket anyway. The board of control, perhaps mindful that their wonderful team was breaking up through old age, might have been looking to make sweeping changes so that Richardson could lead a team of newcomers, eager to learn and desperate to emulate.

As Marshall discovered to his cost when he returned to the fold as coach later, this was not the case. The cupboard was all but bare; no new Richards, no new Greenidges and definitely no new Marshalls. In the Caribbean and in Hampshire there are all kinds of worthy plans to commemorate his life's work, and rightly so, but if it was possible to ask the man himself for the most fitting memorial he would surely ask for the emergence of a new, vibrant and powerful West Indian international side with its own set of heroes and icons. They would play the game to win but they also would play with a smile on their faces. If the English opposition contained a Hampshire player or two nurtured and raised in his ways he would have felt everything he had done and believed in to have been very worthwhile.

2.

South Africa at last

THE ONE UNEXPECTED BONUS of no longer being required by the West Indies was that Marshall could embark on a career in South African provincial cricket. In tandem with his last few northern summer years with Hampshire, Marshall spent four years with Natal as their overseas professional at a time when the South Africans were emerging from their self-inflicted isolation during the Apartheid era.

Many West Indians had gone there before him, risking bans at home and personal isolation to take up lucrative contracts with provincial sides. Some, like Sylvester Clarke, Franklyn Stephenson and Eldine Baptiste, had stayed on after the rebel tours had concluded even though at that stage South Africa was still a cricketing no-go area in the official sense. When Nelson Mandela was freed, Apartheid officially dismantled and South Africa readmitted to the ICC, there was no longer a reason not to go. The South Africans were desperate for international competition and to take on and be with players they had only ever been able to read about or see on television.

It's fair to say that those West Indians who had already been playing in South Africa were not top notch. Many, like Clarke and Baptiste, had played Test cricket but had not held down regular places but Clarke and Stephenson, for instance, had been able to combine county careers with playing in South Africa and had made a decent living in doing so. There were other reasons to go. Gordon Greenidge recalled: "Maco had heard all about the likes of Barry Richards, Eddie Barlow and Mike Procter and wondered what it was like to play against these sort of people, to find out what had made them so excellent. It was as if a dimension to world cricket had been missing. The Smith brothers, Chris and Robin, were also part of the same background and I think he was curious." Desmond Haynes agreed that South Africa had always intrigued his old friend. "After that time when they tried to get him to join the rebel tours it was always in the back of his mind that he would like to play there one day, but all the while Apartheid existed there was no way he was going there. When the chance did come he went there determined to show a few people what they had been missing all those years. There was definitely an element of 'I'll show you'. It was a good way of completing his career, a new challenge to be faced and overcome."

Haynes would later follow Marshall to South Africa to join the Cape Town-based Western Province and of all the players lured to South Africa post-Apartheid, they were the biggest and best known. The greasy spoon café incident in Southampton when Dr Ali Bacher failed to persuade him to join his rebel tour with a million dollar offer may have been ten years earlier but it had not been forgotten, either by the South Africans or by Marshall. But if Marshall had gambled on becoming a fixture in the West Indian side by turning it down, it was a gamble that had paid off handsomely. Had he gone to South Africa when Dr Bacher suggested he may have been a million dollars better off but he would never have become one of the great international bowlers.

The South Africans, freed from their constraints, came calling again during the county season of 1992 when Natal, the most English in many ways of the South African provinces, offered him a three-year contract. The terms were good and this time he was on his way. On his way, in fact, to the Indian Ocean port of Durban with its palm-fringed sea front and its warm, healthy climate. There was a luxury flat awaiting him near the ocean, a sponsored car and a belated chance to show a whole new public that he had not been the world's top bowler for nothing.

By now Marshall was 34 and therefore no longer capable of bowling over after over of blistering speed but he had learned cut and swing, in and out, angles of variation and other tricks which would ensure he overcame anything the South Africans had to offer. The long period of absence had taken a toll of South African cricket. Richards, Procter and Barlow were long gone and South African-born players like the Smith brothers and Allan Lamb, who were in their prime, had defected to England for the chance to play Test cricket. Kepler Wessels had also qualified for Australia by residence. Between them they had left something of a void and for others who had stayed behind, such as Clive Rice and Jimmy Cook, the return to the international fold was all but too late; their true calibre never properly examined. The lack of international competition meant that in 1992 the South Africans were not so much short of talent as short of top level know-how.

The arrival of Malcolm Marshall was therefore good for South African cricket as it stepped blinkingly into the international spotlight after the dark years and South African cricket, it transpired, was good for Malcolm Marshall. It restored his pride and gave him a whole new purpose so that the four years he spent playing for Natal were as happy as any he spent anywhere in cricket. "I love Durban," he told everyone on his return to more familiar territory. "It's a beautiful city." Coincidentally, the Smiths had been raised in Durban and their parents were still living there at the time. They had told him of the numerous and wonderful golf courses and the beaches and he was not disappointed with what he found. It became a home-from-home after Barbados and after quickly winning over an adoring public, there is no doubt Marshall revelled in the adulation. It would have been easy for him to have coasted through the duration of his contract. There was nothing to prove, as such, and if anyone doubted out there what he had achieved they could look it up in Wisden.

But that was not the Marshall way, never had been and never would be. Instead, he arrived in Durban in October 1992 determined to give value for money, and so he did. Making his debut under close scrutiny in Port Elizabeth, Marshall helped Natal beat Eastern Province by ten wickets and, his commitment and desire duly confirmed, he went on to enjoy a profitable first season. In five matches in the Castle Cup he took 28 wickets at 16.11, figures good enough to place him at the top of Castle Cup bowling national averages. His best performance was six for 45 against the powerful Transvaal in Johannesburg, but Natal could only finish third behind winners Orange Free State. The only disappointment for a man who still regarded himself as an all-rounder was a batting average of 10.87 from eight innings. This he was anxious to put right the following year, and he did so in spectacular fashion.

Jonty Rhodes was named Natal's captain for the 1993-94 season but he led the team in only four of the eight first class matches in the Castle Cup, Marshall taking over for the games against Border, Western Province, Northern Transvaal and Boland. The spectacular fielding of the irrepressible

Rhodes left an indelible impression on Marshall, who was ready to admit that in all his years in cricket he had never come across anyone like him for raising fielding to an art form. "The standard of fielding in South Africa is very high," he told his Hampshire friends on returning to England. "But this man Rhodes is something else."

By now Marshall's own willingness to become part of a team, to bowl all day if required, had won him many followers among inexperienced players. One of the young men coming into first class cricket at that time was Lance Klusener and they quickly became mutually admiring. Klusener remembered: "Malcolm was a fantastic bloke on and off the field. Everything we had been told about him was true. He came at a time when cricket in South Africa needed a few world class players to get some interest going and there were not many bigger names than Malcolm's. It certainly helped that he was black. Our own black people could see what could be achieved and looked up to him, but then everyone looked up to him. He was such an unassuming fellow and still a fantastic cricketer. He could have come to Natal, collected a nice pay day or two and taken it easy, and who would have blamed him at his age? But he gave everything he had and we all worshipped him. All the time he was telling you what to do and passing on tips about bowling. Shaun Pollock and I learned so much from him."

Robin Smith, naturally keen to discover what was happening back in Natal for whom he had played as a teenager, was told by Marshall that South African cricket was coming out of seclusion and would soon be a world power: "The two names he kept mentioning were those of Klusener and Pollock. He believed they had the potential to become famous all-rounders, not just good players but possibly great ones. A few years on and you can see that he was right." Marshall even wanted Hampshire to sign Pollock but he went later to Warwickshire instead.

Klusener was emerging in season 1993-94, but so too was Marshall the batsman. At the advanced age of 35 Marshall enjoyed his best single campaign as a batsman, averaging 60 in eleven matches and recording the highest score of his career, 120 not out against Western Province at Pietermaritzburg batting at number seven. The opposition, incidentally, contained his Barbadian contemporary Carlisle Best. "See what the world has been missing, Besty," he said with his huge grin. "Make sure you tell everyone." Natal had a strong batting side in those days. Pollock was playing, so too Test players Andy Hudson and Pat Symcox, while the man who missed out on a Test cap because of his country's isolation, Clive Rice, was still a force at this level.

Marshall also scored an unbeaten 73 against Boland to finish with a grand total of 420 runs and the only disappointment was that such a strong provincial side should only finish sixth. If there was a drawback to his new-found eminence as a batsman it was that his bowling suffered a little, as 19 wickets at 36.73 would indicate; in terms of wickets per average one of the least respectable of his long career. There were understandable mutterings that as a bowler he was finished, but if there was one lesson to be learned about Marshall it was never to underestimate him and the following year, now aged 36, he produced a set of bowling figures worthy of his prime.

In the summer of 1994, unheralded and largely unnoticed, Marshall played his last first class match in England for the President's XI against the touring South Africans in the Scarborough Festival. The gentle atmosphere of the world-famous Scarborough Festival is perhaps a strange place for such a warrior to depart and, befitting the occasion, he did so quietly with little contribution.

So, for what he thought would be his last in first class cricket, Marshall returned to Durban in November 1994 to fulfil the final year of his contract. For most of the season he was Natal's captain and it proved to be a superb year for the province and their leader. Winning their opening match against Franklyn Stephenson's Free State by nine wickets, Natal went through the season unbeaten, winning six of their eight matches and claiming the championship for the first time in 14 years. What's more, Marshall was named Castle Cup Player of the Season, a remarkable achievement for a man no longer at his playing peak but no more than he deserved for taking 35 wickets at the little matter of 16.17 each, much more in fact the sort of figures expected of the great Malcolm Marshall.

Natal had a strong blend of youth and experience and Marshall was by no means the elder statesman. Neville Wright, 37, Hudson and Symcox were all of a similar vintage, while at the other end of the age scale were Pollock and Klusener in their early 20s and a 21 year old wicket-keeper in Mark Buyns. Supporting Marshall as bowlers were Pollock, Klusener and Neil Johnson, all genuine all-rounders, and left arm swing bowler Ross

Veenstra, 22, combining to form an irresistible combination skilfully manipulated by their skipper during victories over Western Province, Transvaal, Boland, Northern Transvaal and Eastern Province. Only Border, in the last match, and Western Province escaped with draws, Desmond Haynes' unbeaten 70 for Western Province denying his old pal another victory. The blossoming Pollock remembered that season and the huge influence Marshall had in enabling Natal to clinch the title: "He was my mentor, of that there is no doubt. He thought I had some potential, which was a compliment in itself, and taught me so much about bowling; how to vary my deliveries, how to spot weaknesses, when to bowl fast and when not to. I was never able to thank him enough and I was terribly shocked when he died. I owed so much to him as a person and as a bowler and if I can go on and have a successful career it will be a tribute of sorts to him."

In the euphoria of the celebrations which followed the winning of the Castle Cup, Marshall was persuaded to come back for one last year. Natal were thinking that the three years of his initial contract would have been enough and that by then Marshall would have gone as far as he was going to go, but his contribution to the overall effort induced them to offer him new terms. He quickly agreed to one more season, definitely the last. Marshall had wanted to go out at the top, as many such players do, but the temptation was always to go on a little longer while there was still power in the limbs and command from the brain.. The old adage about being a long time retired ate away at him. He was Castle Cup Player of the Year, and it would be nice to do that again and maybe also retain the Castle Cup itself, but the fear was that by going on too long he might become a passenger or, worse still, an embarrassment, punished for his dimming reflexes by the sort of players who would have been his fodder in his heyday.

By then, of course, he was enjoying Durban as a city and there was talk of him becoming Natal's coach eventually, an ambition that was thwarted by his subsequent appointment as West Indies' coach but still a possibility at the time. The golf courses were an attraction he couldn't resist and among those who shared an occasional round was Nigel Cowley, his former colleague at Hampshire, who had moved out to South Africa to live at the end of his playing days.

Back he came for his swansong, season 1995-96, with his 38th birthday not far off and a coaching career beckoning. Natal again made him captain and they won their first four matches with some ease. The title-chase was on. Then came an extraordinary match at Bloemfontein against the Free State, extraordinary because of one final Marshall heroic. It was a match ironically Natal lost and in which Marshall did not take a wicket. Free State declared at 532-7 and Natal were quickly bowled out for 167. Following on and batting at ten, Marshall came in with Natal in danger of defeat at 378-8 only to produce a classic piece of batting which took him within a run of his eighth first class century. When last man Veenstra was out for 45, Marshall was 99 not out and Natal had comfortably avoided an innings defeat. Their reprieve was only temporary but for defiance and refusal to bow to the inevitable, it was a masterly performance and served only to enshrine him still further in the eyes of the Natal public.

Natal won their next match against Northern Transvaal so that the championship became talked about again, but the turning point came when Pollock was called into the national team and ordered to rest at a time when Natal were due to play Western Province. Without him Western Province were able to hold on to a draw at 273-7 in the second innings and only 81 ahead. With Pollock in the side they must surely have won. All of which brought Marshall to the 408th and final match of his career in February 1996 at Centurion Park against Northern Transvaal. The script did not go quite according to plan. There was rain about, very few spectators and Marshall lost the toss. Northern Transvaal were all out for 213 and Natal responded with 167-6 when the rain came and the match was washed out. His contribution was a modest 2-51 in the Northern Transvaal innings and there was no last chance to add to his total of 11,004 runs in first class cricket. The whole of his final day as a player was spent hoping the rain would cease long enough for him to go to the crease for one last knock. Instead, it all ended in a bit of an anti-climax. No parade, no banners, no standing ovation, nothing to mark the end of one of cricket's great innings. Just rain and memories.

Natal finished third and Marshall's 14 wickets had cost him 28.78 each. It was definitely time to call it a day. He will be remembered in South Africa as he was everywhere, with affection and admiration. Pat Symcox, a South African Test spinner and Natal colleague, told Meridian TV: "He was such an enthusiast that he got everyone going. All the players wanted to do well for him because they felt privileged to be playing with him. There was one guy, Brad White of Transvaal, who always looked scared of him. He used to nick a catch as soon as he came in against Malcolm and retreated to the pavilion. We named him 'Nick White' and Malcolm used to say: 'leave him to me'. When he got him out, as he invariably did, he would race down the wicket whooping with delight and smiling. That's how we will remember him: a great player but always smiling and enjoying himself."

3.

Hampshire 1986-93

MALCOLM MARSHALL WAS a Hampshire player off and on, West Indies' tour calls allowing, between 1979 and 1993 and in all the major competitions he took 1,065 wickets for them, 826 alone in the first class arena. Throughout the 1980s there was no more feared fast bowler in the world, but when he finally left the club as a player his Hampshire trophy cabinet, if not bare, certainly had plenty of room in it. Here was a man who had in his possession a World Cup winner's medal without even having played in the competition. But lesser domestic medals and accolades either eluded him completely or were much harder-earned.

Three times Hampshire, with Marshall as the bowling spearhead, were third in the County Championship in 1982, 1983 and 1990 and runners-up in 1985. Yet all he had to show for a decade of sweat and toil on behalf of his adopted county was a solitary winner's medal from the John Player Special League, the Sunday competition, in 1986, a poor reward for his efforts and a poor reflection on a powerful side which had Gordon Greenidge at its disposal until 1987 and Robin and Chris Smith at their best. There was also available plenty of high calibre county players like Paul Terry, Mark Nicholas, Trevor Jesty until 1984, Tim Tremlett and Nigel Cowley, Bobby Parks and Cardigan Connor. As a combined force they gained a reputation for bright, attractive cricket and collective under-achievement. Under Nicholas's ambitious leadership Hampshire were unquestionably a capable team but had not proved to be good enough to win anything worthwhile.

And so it proved until 1988 when the last of the (then) 17 counties to reach a Lord's limited overs final did so in the Benson and Hedges Cup but with one major absentee. Malcolm Marshall. The West Indies were touring England at the time and Hampshire had replaced him with the

South African all-rounder Steve Jefferies who, by Marshall's standards, was hardly a success, taking only 34 rather expensive wickets in first class matches but who used the grand occasion at Lord's to justify comprehensively Hampshire's decision to take him on. Jefferies in effect won the final against Derbyshire with an inspired piece of swing bowling in helpful early conditions to take 5-13 from ten overs so that Hampshire won easily in mid afternoon by seven wickets. Success at last for the team, but not for Marshall. He was elsewhere in England, sent a message of good luck and another of congratulations and left the rest of the team to bask in the national spotlight and envelop new hero, Jefferies, as he collected the Gold Award as man of the match.

At least Hampshire were proving to themselves and the outside world that they did not rely on Marshall and it all happened again in 1991 when the West Indies were touring England once more and the overseas vacancy was filled by the untried Pakistani pace bowler Aqib Javed. Marshall could only watch from the distance as his county won through to Lord's again, this time to the final of the NatWest Trophy. There is no doubt that a Lord's final, particularly the showcase NatWest Trophy in early September, is one of the great days of the English cricket calendar. The wonderful ground is full, the match is televised and there's a festive tinge to the air as the summer draws to a close. Like Jefferies three years earlier, Aqib Javed hardly filled the great man's boots in his only season with Hampshire. Allowing for his inexperience 53 first class wickets at 31 is not a bad return but well below what Marshall had been delivering in other years on a regular basis. Yet there was young Aqib Javed in his first season away from home at a Lord's final, something Marshall had never achieved. Not that Aqib made much of a contribution in the final itself (nought for 54 in 12 overs) but his teammates did. Robin Smith's match-winning 78 helped Hampshire overhaul Surrey's 240-5 with two balls to spare in near darkness. The trophy was held aloft jointly by the injured Nicholas and captain-for-the-day David Gower and a beaming Aqib clutched his winner's medal. Later Marshall was to admit to mixed feelings: "Sure I wanted the boys to win but I wanted to be out there with them. I was genuinely delighted when they won both those trophies yet there was a feeling that I might never get a chance."

So Marshall came back to Hampshire in 1992, now aged 34, and with a general feeling that time was running out. Several of his contemporaries were also getting on a bit in cricketing terms and he was not alone in thinking that it was now or never. The Benson and Hedges Cup began in the chill of April on a group basis and Hampshire's could not have been much tougher. There was Essex (Gooch, Hussain and Mark Waugh), Northamptonshire (Lamb and Ambrose), the traditionally strong Lancashire and makeweights Scotland.

It did not start well for Hampshire, being bowled out for 177 against Essex at Southampton, but Marshall was in no mood to be denied his day at Lord's. Nicholas recalled: "We had been bowled out cheaply. Marshall, who was desperate for a day at Lord's with his beloved county, won the match in minutes by trapping Gooch, John Stephenson and Waugh lbw to leave Essex on the ropes at five for three. He finished with four for 20 and the man-of-the-match award." Hampshire needed a century from David Gower to see off Northamptonshire in the next match by six runs while Marshall and Shaun Udal each took three wickets to account for Lancashire. It rained in Glasgow but Hampshire got the point they needed to get into the quarter finals.

Middlesex were the next opponents and 89 from Desmond Haynes, of all people, came close to getting in his friend's way, particularly as an injury prevented Marshall from bowling any more than five overs. David Gower, a man for the big occasion, saw Hampshire home and into the semis by six wickets. Southampton's cramped and antiquated County Ground was full for the semi final, near rivals Somerset saw to that, bringing plenty of support with them with Marshall now just one match away from the match of his dreams. Somerset chose to bat first and managed only 218–8. Marshall's one for 37 was overshadowed by Connor's four for 32 and a tight spell of bowling from Raj Maru who took one for 32 off eleven overs. Paul Terry's calm and patient 89 not out galvanised a six-wicket win and had Hampshire on their way to Lord's again – this time with a delighted Marshall. After 13 years, he was on his way to a Lord's final at last.

Even then there was something of an anti-climax about it because the match against Kent was completed over two days because of bad light and rain. On the Saturday the house was full, as was traditional, but when the match was actually finished on the Sunday there were large gaps on the terraced seating. So Marshall's finest hour for Hampshire was played out to a small gallery of devotees. Kent captain Mark Benson chose to bat first and, with the benefit of hindsight, it was the wrong decision because all the major Hampshire batsmen got among the runs, including Marshall, who made an unbeaten 29, accelerating as the end of the innings neared, after receiving a tremendous reception from Hampshire supporters in the crowd as he made his way to the crease, mindful perhaps of how a Lord's final had always eluded him.

Hampshire's 253 for five from their 55 overs (Robin Smith run out 90) was a formidable total and required Kent to score the greatest number of runs for a side batting second in the history of the competition's final. The scene was set for an exciting Kent response but Marshall and Cardigan Connor each bowled one over before the umpires decided the light was not good enough to continue, and it didn't improve until the next day when Kent fell quickly behind the required run rate and never caught up. Marshall gave little away, made the early breakthrough by dismissing Trevor Ward and returned later to see off Graham Cowdrey and Richard Davis. All the other Hampshire bowlers chipped in and Kent subsided to 212 all out in the 53rd over. Marshall's three for 33 was not enough to win him the man of the match Gold Award, which went to Smith instead, but the celebrations continued into the night and now there was something tangible to show for all his unstinting efforts on Hampshire's behalf.

The disappointment for Marshall was that he went into playing retirement without a championship medal. Hampshire had got close to it in 1985 when they were runners-up and when he returned from the Caribbean in 1987 there was the nucleus of a strong side. It was his benefit year and with a full diary of fund-raising events to be fulfilled the fear was, as with other beneficiaries, that he might not be able to deliver when it mattered. That would have been to deny his professionalism. Marshall had a superb season personally, averaging 35 with the bat and taking 76 wickets at 19.84 in first class matches, but the team managed only fifth place behind Hadlee and Rice's Nottinghamshire and made little impression in the one-day competitions. The nearest he came to a century was at Lord's where he played on to Angus Fraser after making 99, but overall it was a season somewhat wasted.

At least his benefit went well and the public was not slow to respond to his cause. A final cheque for £61,000, while not outstanding by the standards of bigger counties, was a fair reflection of the esteem with which he was held within Hampshire where he was revered not just for his achievements and express pace but also for his commitment. Not long before Marshall's arrival as the overseas player, the sudden and acrimonious departures of Barry Richards and Andy Roberts had left a legacy of scepticism, not to say cynicism, about the true value of an imported star name. Happily Richards and Roberts were able later to become reconciled with Hampshire but Marshall's prodigious output restored faith in the concept of an overseas player so that it became hard to think of anyone who gave more to a county. Subsequent signings from abroad by Hampshire had much to emulate and it was only after his retirement that the county and its supporters realised how spoiled they had been.

Marshall did not come back in 1988 when Hampshire reached their first final, and in 1989 the best chance of any success came in the NatWest Trophy and there was an air of anticipation at Southampton when Middlesex arrived for the semi final. It was a desperately close affair in which Marshall needed to hit the last ball of the match for six, but managed only a single and Middlesex were through by three runs. The following year was much better, third place in the championship and Marshall's best as an all-rounder, but heartache once more in the NatWest Trophy when he was moved to tears as Northamptonshire won the semi final by a single run. Would he ever get to a Lord's final? Northamptonshire made 284 all out and Hampshire were in trouble at 55-3. The match looked to be over but Marshall and Gower put on 141 in 25 overs to revive their county but the acceleration required proved to be great. Marshall's first Man of the Match award for his 77 and tight bowling was no compensation for another near miss and he was visibly distressed at the awards ceremony.

In the championship he came agonisingly close to a cherished ambition of 1,000 runs in a season for the first time. He went into the last match of the season against Gloucestershire at Southampton needing 105 runs and anyone who had ever cared about him rooting for him to succeed. Sadly he managed only 21 and 46 and fell short by 38. Add that, though, to his 72 wickets and it was easy to see why he was such a major asset. Only Derbyshire's Ian Bishop finished above him in the averages but Marshall took more wickets. His greatest moment that season came at Ynysangharad Park, Pontypridd where he took eleven wickets in the match against Glamorgan and hit a crucial 51 in an eight-wicket victory. Other, wealthier counties were always fully aware of Marshall's importance to Hampshire and over the next couple of years unofficial overtures were made to him which indicated that if he was to move he could name his own price. One of those was certainly from Yorkshire as they prepared to drop their opposition to signing overseas players, but Marshall was going nowhere. He made it very clear that Hampshire was his county and he was happy to see out his career with them.

Such loyalty got its reward in 1992 at Lord's but it was an otherwise disappointing summer in terms of results and Marshall's own contribution diminished to 49 wickets and 513 runs. He did lead the side for the first time in championship matches against Yorkshire and Surrey, small but significant landmarks in his career, and while he remained the supreme professional he was not now producing the match-winning performances. Since 1993 was his last and most disappointing season on the Hampshire staff it can be seen that from the day he picked up his much-desired winners's medal at Lord's his productivity fell away. This was obviously not deliberate but the psychological affect of having fulfilled a long-held ambition took a toll of sorts and he was never the same force for Hampshire again.

The summer of 1993 will be regarded as one too many. At 34 he was simply not able to touch the peaks of his prime and in many ways it was sad to see him struggle so hard to so little effect. Players who might have been petrified of him a year or two before were getting on the front foot and hitting him for boundaries and, like a boxer who had taken on one fight too many, there were times when it was almost embarrassing to watch him attempting to intimidate and destroy when he was patently unable to do either. His final tally of 28 wickets at 30.67 did him little credit and in retrospect it would have been better if he had quit Hampshire the year before while he could still be remembered for his many great moments, not the few bad ones at the end. The popular theory was that he was simply too old, so it is therefore odd that with new ambitions and new incentives in South Africa he enjoyed a profitable and contented renaissance where the years fell away and the wickets tumbled once more.

The facts would appear to indicate that age had nothing much to do with his demise in 1993; he had merely grown stale in the Hampshire cause and required only fresh goals to revive him. His admiring captain Mark Nicholas summed up his overall contribution in the club's handbook when it became clear he would not be coming back in 1994: "He has never given less than everything for his team. He is self-interested in the acceptable way of top sportsmen but when it is not his day, and others are wreaking their havoc, he is as pleased as punch. In 14 years I do not remember him once giving short change and, along with Mike Procter and Richard Hadlee, whom Marshall greatly admires, he has been the best overseas player in English cricket. To be so, he has remained supremely fit and his sharp mind has ensured the preservation of those supple, rubbery limbs." He left Hampshire with the grateful thanks not only of his captain but those of his colleagues and those of his club's supporters who quickly became convinced that his like would not be seen again.

The summer of 1995 was spent playing for Scotland in the Benson and Hedges Cup and in the Lancashire County League for Denton. Many of his West Indian teammates and friends had spent time in the leagues and all had enjoyed the responsibility and commitment required of the overseas professional. Joel Garner had played for Littleborough and had helped convince him he would relish the atmosphere where it was so vital the professional made a telling contribution. Many other prominent West Indian players of the past had extended careers in the league, not least Ramahdin and Valentine, the 50s spin kings, Learie Constantine and Everton Weekes. Viv Richards was also to conclude his career in the same type of competition. As usual, Marshall made many friends and responded by giving everything, even against weekend amateurs, because that was his nature and that was what he had been hired to do.

He took the opportunity also to gain a coaching qualification and to take the first steps along that path by helping out with some bowling coaching in the Old Trafford nets. Peter Martin, later to play for England, attributed much of his advancement at that time to the advice he received from Marshall: "He taught me so much about so many facets of bowling. To hear it from him was an education and I will always be thankful for what he did for me."

Coaching was obviously next on the agenda, though it was going to have to wait while he saw out his career in South Africa, but that duly done, he quickly came in demand. Natal wanted him, so did Hampshire and since their seasons did not cross he could have done both jobs comfortably enough. However, the West Indian Cricket Board were also aware of his natural ability to coach and persuaded him to take over a team declining from the great standards it had set in the 1980s, in tandem with Clive Lloyd as manager. The great players do not always make the best coaches; it is said they do not understand that players with lesser ability cannot do without difficulty what they could do without thinking. The best coaches have often been moderate players themselves and have a better comprehension of what it is like to have to work for success. That is the theory and there have been enough examples in the past to support it, but Marshall's rapport with players, his easy approach and his technical knowledge soon won him the respect of those whom he had been placed in charge.

The West Indian job, prestigious as it was, clashed with a proposed similar role with Natal but he was able to take up Hampshire's offer in the knowledge that there would be time enough for both. The disappointment for Marshall and all those who hoped he would succeed was that the West Indians were down to a rump of three great players (Lara, Ambrose and Walsh) while Hampshire were about to undergo a similar metamorphosis as capable, proven players gave way to the young and untested. As a result, his coaching career did not sparkle with trophies. Hampshire's improvement was only gradual and not without some major setbacks, but in the Caribbean, Marshall and Lloyd, two of the greatest names of West Indies cricket, were forced to preside over an alarming drop in the region's status within world cricket. Hard as they looked, the seemingly endless well of talent had dried up. Where once there had been fast bowlers to spare, now there was none of international calibre or consequence. They could not find any opening batsmen; they couldn't find a wicket-keeper; they couldn't find a spinner. Above all, they couldn't find anyone to support the ageing Ambrose and Walsh as they reached their dotage, and from being the best team in the 1980s the prospect began to emerge of entering the new millennium as one of the poorest.

Marshall and Lloyd came in for their share of criticism around a slightly startled and disturbed Caribbean. Why couldn't they put together a team good enough to look the world in the face? There was no easy answer:

years of neglect at the top level, poor pitches, a shift among the young in their affections for the televised American sports, a lack of desire and ambition among those who did play the game. There was no one single answer to the problem, only that there were suddenly very few players of outstanding ability coming through the system. Marshall and Lloyd gave all kinds of opportunities to players who in another, recent era would not have been considered. Others, long forgotten like Clayton Lambert, were suddenly recalled and the number of one and two cap players began to rival England's. Marshall even tried to excuse the modern-day player by pointing out that the West Indies team of the 1980s had been exceptional, one of those freaks of nature whereby a gaggle of truly great players come together at the same time to form a phenomenal team. Greenidge and Haynes, for instance, were outstanding opening batsmen in their own right; to have them together for 15 years or more was an astonishing stroke of good fortune. To follow them with the likes of Viv Richards, Lloyd, Lara and Richardson in the middle order, and then have four or more fast bowlers of exceptional ferocity and quality forming the tail, was something followers of West Indian cricket had come to take for granted. They would not have been replaced easily at the best of times, and these were not the best of times.

Marshall was not prepared to offer further excuses; he believed that those West Indian cricketers of the 1990s did themselves no favours with a sloppy, uncaring approach and no apparent desire to listen, learn and improve. He found, as did Lloyd, that there was not only not much high-class talent emerging but also very little ambition. Judged therefore by the highest standards set in the 1980s by the teams led by Lloyd and Richards, the Marshall coaching years were difficult and not particularly successful, but his record is not as bad as his detractors might indicate. Starting in 1996-97 in Australia, the West Indies lost 3-2; no disgrace there. In 1997 also there was a win and four draws in the five-match series with India and a win and a draw in a two-match series in the Caribbean to mark Sri Lanka's first visit. It worsened in Pakistan in 1997-98 where the home side won every match in a three-Test series but improved in the spring of 1998 when England were resoundingly beaten 3-1 over six Tests. The nadir was in South Africa, where he had so many friends and admirers, in a 5-0 thrashing and it was then that the calls for his head and that of Lloyd accompanied general discontent and a desire for changes at all levels. The 2-2 draw in a fantastic series against Australia in the Caribbean in 1999 only partially redeemed his reputation and there's no doubt that the World Cup in England the following summer would have been his last chance to turn fortunes around. He never got that opportunity.

4.

Postscript

HOW GOOD WAS MALCOLM MARSHALL? Wes Hall said he was the greatest fast bowler of all time during his memorable sermon, but did the emotion of the occasion cloud his judgement, or was he right? The facts tend to support the belief that he was the best of his era, the 1980s, but beyond that analysis tends to become as subjective as Wes Hall's.

The history of the game is littered with the names of players about whom a similar claim could be made, a few of them from the West Indies. At his very best he was a lethal and cunning fast bowler who was close also to being a very good batsman. It annoyed him, as much as anything could annoy him for long, that he was not considered as a bowling all-rounder, and to those who doubted him he would point to the fact that only his great hero Gary Sobers had beaten him to the all-rounders' double of 1,000 runs and 100 Test wickets among West Indians. (Surprisingly, perhaps, Curtly Ambrose became the third). What also irritated him was that he never got a Test century; that 92 early in his career in Kanpur being his best in ten half centuries, and had he reached the magic three figures there might have been a greater statistical evidence to back his contention that he deserved all-rounder status.

As a bowler in limited overs competitions he was by no means outstanding; few match-winning performances and not many collections of four wickets or more in an innings. His final tally of 157 wickets in internationals came at 26.96 each with a best of four for 18. Even for Hampshire in one-day games he was more restrictive than devastating. His supporters will claim that by tying up one end he got wickets for other bowlers, but that is only partially true. He didn't particularly like limited overs cricket and regarded the first class game as a proper guide to his ability and that of others. His view was that with the many restrictions on bowlers

214

(no bouncers, fielding markers) the game was heavily loaded in favour of the batsmen.

Finally, if there was another regret it was that he was not more successful as a coach. He would have liked to have been able to translate his great success as a player to those who followed him in the West Indian maroon, but it was not to be, largely through circumstances beyond his control. A low point was the players' strike over money at Heathrow Airport which delayed the departure to the ill-fated tour of South Africa. He would never have been involved in anything so undignified in his day.

As a person it was hard to find anyone with a bad word about him. He was not just liked, as we have said so often in this book, he was loved for his qualities of kindness, humility, honesty and fun. He could be vain, a little intolerant about those slower to follow his tactical appreciation, but if that is the worst that could be said about someone it is hardly worth saying. As so many people said without prompting, he was a good man and his loss was deeply felt by all who knew him and by some only by repute. To be struck down at 41 was a terrible blow to his family, but he bore his illness with the same quiet dignity and strength of character he had shown as a player. If there was one, minor consolation it was that at least he was able to fulfil his great talent as a cricketer.

My own involvement with him as his ghost writer and, I hope, friend began when Vincent Nurse, then his agent, asked if I could get him a column in a national newspaper to coincide with the West Indies tour to England in 1984. I remember going to the Daily Mirror offices in Holborn one winter Sunday afternoon to sell them the idea, and even now I'm not convinced that one or two decision-making executives were completely sure who he was. By the end of that summer they knew all right. He wrote for the Daily Mirror from all parts of the globe for the next eight years, his trenchant views never based on prejudice.

I was party to one surreal incident in the making of 'Marshall Arts' in 1986 in Barbados. Down the hill from the Marshall home was a rough-hewn cricket pitch and as Marshall drove up to the house from the coast, in the heat of the afternoon an ageing white man was smiting each delivery from local youths into the rough ground beyond what passed for a square "That's Boycott," said an astonished Marshall as he drove me past. Quite what Boycott was doing there was never certain but an hour later, as we came back down the hill, he was still at the crease, using his bat as a prop to rest on and mopping his brow while the youths scoured the undergrowth for lost balls. Marshall stopped the car and leaning across me in the passenger's seat, wound down the window and shouted: "Boyks, I'm coming to get you. Do you hear me? I'm coming to get you." Boycott only slowly realised to his horror just who it was shouting at him, and the prospect of taking on the world's fastest bowler on a piece of ground normally used by the village sheep and goats clearly did not appeal. "No, no Maco," he insisted with only a hint of panic. "No need for that, I'm joost finishing." With that he tucked his bat under his arm and beat a hasty retreat. Marshall re-started the car and as we moved off it was possible to see in the wing mirror a slightly unnerved Boycott striding off to his own vehicle, occasionally looking over his shoulder.

Mark Nicholas said in his eulogy that in time we must all party in Malcolm's honour because that is what he would have wanted. He finished that eulogy with some famous lines written by the actress Joyce Grenfell, among which were: "If I should go before the rest of you, bring not a flower, nor inscribe a stone. Nor when I'm gone speak in a comely voice but be thy usual selves, the selves that I have known. Weep, if you must, for parting is hell but life goes on, so sing as well." He leaves a legacy of world-wide admiration and respect and a family who doted on him. As Wes Hall so thunderously put it: "Malcolm Denzil Marshall is safe and all is well with his soul."

First Class Career Statistics

Compiled by Jim Baldwin

FIRST CLASS CRICKET

Debut: Barbados v Jamaica at Bridgetown 1977-78
HS: 120* Natal v Western Province at Pietermaritzburg 1993-94
BB: 8-71 Hampshire v Worcestershire at Southampton 1982

TEST CRICKET

Debut v India (Second Test)at Bangalore 1978-79
HS: 92 v India (First Test at Kanpur 1983-84
BB: 7-22 v England (Third Test) at Manchester 1988

FOR HAMPSHIRE

Debut v Glamorgan at Southampton 1979
HS: 117 v Yorkshire at Leeds 1990
BB: 8-71 v Worcestershire at Southampton 1982
Most Runs in a Season: 962 (Ave. 45.81) in 1990
Most Wickets in a Season: 134 (Ave. 15.73) in 1982

FOR BARBADOS

Debut v Jamaica at Bridgetown 1977-78
HS: 89 v Jamaica at Bridgetown 1988-89 and
89 v Guyana at Bridgetown 1990-91
BB: 6-38 v Trinidad at Port-of-Spain 1979-80

FOR NATAL

Debut v Eastern Province at Port Elizabeth 1992-93
HS: 120* v Western Province at Pietermaritzburg 1993-94
BB: 6-45 v Transvaal at Johannesburg 1992-93

FIRST CLASS CAREER STATISTICS

Bowling:

	Runs	Wkts	Ave.	BB	5WI	10WM
West Indies (Tests)	7876	376	20.95	7-22	22	4
West Indies (First Class)	2489	152	16.38	7-56	9	1
Hampshire	15401	826	18.65	8-71	45	7
Barbados	3146	180	17.48	6-38	8	1
Natal	2118	96	22.06	6-45	1	0
Other First Class	518	21	24.67	4-39	0	0
TOTALS	31548	1651	19.11	8-71	85	13

Batting:

	Inns	NO	Runs	HS	Ave.	50+
West Indies (Tests)	107	11	1810	92	18.85	10
West Indies (First Class)	48	9	913	76	23.41	5
Hampshire	269	37	5847	117	25.20	31
Barbados	49	7	1270	89	30.24	9
Natal	36	9	891	120*	33.00	5
Other First Class	7	0	273	109	39.00	1
TOTALS	516	73	11004	120*	24.84	61

INDIVIDUAL PERFORMANCES

Centuries(7):

120*	Natal v Western Province	at Pietermaritzburg 1993-94
117	Hampshire v Yorkshire	at Ledds 1990.
116*	Hampshire v Lancashire	at Southampton 1982.
112	Hampshire v Leicestershire	at Leicester 1990.
112	Hampshire v Kent	at Bournemouth 1983.
109	West Indies Under-26 v Zimbabwe XI	at Bulawayo 1981-82.
100*	Hampshire v Surrey	at Southampton 1983.

Ten Wickets or more in a Match (13):

11-89 (5-34 and 6-55) West Indies v India(Third Test) at Port-of-Spain 1988-89.

11-92 (5-45 and 6-47) Hampshire v Glamorgan at Pontypridd 1990.

11-107 (7-48 and 4-59) Hampshire v Sussex at Eastbourne 1982.

11-120 (4-40 and 7-80 West Indies v New Zealand(Third Test) at Bridgetown 1984-85

11-125 (6-71 and 5-54) West Indians v East Zone at Jamshedpur 1978-79.

11-128 (8-71 and 3-57) Hampshire v Worcestershire at Southampton 1982.

10-76 (3-38 and 7-38) Hampshire v Surrey at The Oval 1982.

10-92 (6-32 and 4-60) West Indies v England(Second Test) at Lords 1988.

10-107 (3-60 and 7-47) Hampshire v Derbyshire at Portsmouth 1990.

10-107 (5-69 and 5-38) West Indies v Australia(Third Test) at Adelaide 1984-85.

10-109 (6-55 and 4-54) Hampshire v Kent at Maidstone 1982.

10-124 (4-39 and 6-85) Barbados v Windward Islands at Bridgetown 1985-86.

10-124 (6-73 and 4-51) Hampshire v Essex at Southend 1983.

Career Record of First-Class Matches - Season-by-Season
Bowling:

Season	Country	Runs	Wkts	Ave.	BB	5WI	10WM
1977/78	West Indies	97	7	13.86	6-77	1	-
1978/79	India	717	37	19.38	6-42	3	1
1978/79	Sri Lanka	93	5	18.60	4-32	-	-
1978/79	West Indies	401	25	16.04	6-82	2	-
1979	England	1051	47	22.36	5-56	1	-
1979/80	Australia	144	7	20.57	3-66	-	-
1979/80	New Zealand	149	7	21.29	5-43	1	-
1979/80	West Indies	273	18	15.17	6-38	1	-
1980	England	1170	66	17.73	7-56	3	-
1980/81	Pakistan	465	25	18.60	5-9	1	-
1980/81	West Indies	541	28	19.32	6-75	1	-
1981	England	1321	68	19.43	6-57	5	-
1981/82	Zimbabwe	192	7	27.43	4-49	-	-
1981/82	Australia	105	11	9.55	5-31	1	-
1982	England	2108	134	15.73	8-71	12	4
1982/83	West Indies	1045	42	24.88	5-37	1	-
1983	England	1327	80	16.59	7-29	5	1
1983/84	India	641	34	18.85	6-37	2	-
1983/84	West Indies	480	21	22.86	5-42	2	-
1984	England	646	40	16.15	7-53	4	-
1984/85	Australia	699	36	19.42	5-38	4	1
1984/85	West Indies	486	27	18.00	7-80	1	1
1985	England	1680	95	17.68	7-59	5	-
1985/86	West Indies	835	50	16.70	6-85	1	1
1986	England	1508	100	15.08	6-51	5	-
1986/87	Pakistan	327	17	19.24	5-33	1	-
1986/87	New Zealand	289	9	32.11	4-43	-	-
1986/87	West Indies	54	7	7.71	4-35	-	-
1987	England	1508	76	19.84	5-49	1	-
1987/88	West Indies	750	42	17.86	5-24	3	-
1988	England	553	42	13.17	7-22	3	-
1988/89	Australia	651	18	36.17	5-29	1	-
1988/89	West Indies	350	20	17.50	6-55	3	1
1989	England	1067	64	16.67	6-69	4	-
1989/90	West Indies	339	12	28.25	3-57	-	-
1990	England	1381	72	19.18	7-47	4	2
1990/91	Pakistan	166	6	27.67	4-24	-	-
1990/91	West Indies	772	43	17.95	4-27	-	-
1991	England	782	30	26.07	4-33	-	-
1992	England	1348	49	27.51	6-58	1	-
1992/93	South Africa	451	28	16.11	6-45	1	-
1993	England	859	28	30.68	5-62	1	-
1993/94	South Africa	698	19	36.74	3-35	-	-
1994	England	60	3	20.00	3-60	-	-
1994/95	South Africa	566	35	16.17	4-40	-	-
1995/96	South Africa	403	14	28.79	4-48	-	-
TOTALS:		**31548**	**1651**	**19.11**	**8-71**	**85**	**13**

Batting:

Season	Country	Inns	NO	Runs	HS	Ave.	50+
1977/78	West Indies	1	0	0	-	0.00	-
1978/79	India	12	2	148	59	14.80	1
1978/79	Sri Lanka	3	0	12	9	4.00	-
1978/79	West Indies	5	1	38	17	9.50	-
1979	England	25	2	197	38	8.57	-
1979/80	Australia	3	1	39	23*	19.50	-
1979/80	New Zealand	3	1	20	13*	10.00	-
1979/80	West Indies	4	1	142	55	47.33	1
1980	England	22	3	462	72*	24.32	3
1980/81	Pakistan	8	0	70	24	8.75	-
1980/81	West Indies	9	2	239	49*	34.14	-
1981	England	23	3	425	75*	21.25	1
1981/82	Zimbabwe	4	0	175	109	43.75	1
1981/82	Australia	2	0	66	66	33.00	1
1982	England	31	3	633	116*	22.61	2
1982/83	West Indies	15	1	323	71	23.07	1
1983	England	16	4	563	112	46.92	4
1983/84	India	8	0	305	92	38.13	3
1983/84	West Indies	4	0	45	19	11.25	-
1984	England	9	0	103	34	11.44	-
1984/85	Australia	9	2	212	57	30.29	2
1984/85	West Indies	4	0	90	63	22.50	1
1985	England	33	2	768	66*	24.77	5
1985/86	West Indies	11	2	204	76	22.67	2
1986	England	23	2	263	51*	12.52	1
1986/87	Pakistan	6	2	48	16*	12.00	-
1986/87	New Zealand	4	0	83	45	20.75	-
1986/87	West Indies	-	-	-	-	-	-
1987	England	22	5	610	99	35.88	3
1987/88	West Indies	13	2	373	77	33.91	4
1988	England	10	1	289	76	32.11	2
1988/89	Australia	11	1	129	31	12.90	-
1988/89	West Indies	5	1	173	89	43.25	1
1989	England	21	5	412	68*	25.75	2
1989/90	West Indies	8	1	136	59	19.43	1
1990	England	24	3	962	117	45.81	8
1990/91	Pakistan	5	0	92	27	18.40	-
1990/91	West Indies	12	2	305	89	30.50	2
1991	England	11	2	196	67	21.78	1
1992	England	25	5	513	70	25.65	2
1992/93	South Africa	8	0	87	35	10.88	-
1993	England	16	2	250	75*	17.86	1
1993/94	South Africa	11	4	420	120*	60.00	3
1994	England	-	-	-	-	-	-
1994/95	South Africa	10	3	209	82*	29.86	1
1995/96	South Africa	7	2	175	99*	35.00	-
TOTALS:		**516**	**73**	**11004**	**120***	**24.84**	**61**

MACO

For West Indies in Test Cricket - Season-by-Season

Bowling:

Season	Opponents	Ovs	Mdns	Runs	Wkts	Ave.	BB
1978/79	India	77	11	265	3	88.33	1-44
1980	England	172.3	42	436	15	29.07	3-36
1980/81	Pakistan	98.3	12	319	13	24.53	4-25
1980/81	England	21	2	64	3	21.33	2-48
1982/83	India	174.2	39	495	21	23.57	5-37
1983/84	India	234	64	641	33	18.85	6-37
1983/84	Australia	158.5	24	480	21	22.85	5-42
1984	England	167.4	50	437	24	18.21	7-53
1984/85	Australia	215.2	45	554	28	19.78	5-38
1984/85	New Zealand	170.1	30	486	27	18.00	7-80
1985/86	England	169.3	36	482	27	17.85	4-38
1986/87	Pakistan	114	27	266	16	16.63	5-33
1986/87	New Zealand	119	21	289	9	32.11	4-43
1987/88	Pakistan	91.4	14	284	15	18.93	5-65
1988	England	203.1	49	443	35	12.66	7-22
1988/89	Australia	192	42	488	17	28.71	5-29
1988/89	India	111.2	18	290	19	15.26	6-55
1989/90	England	59	17	132	3	44.00	2-55
1990/91	Pakistan	65.2	14	166	6	27.67	4-24
1990/91	Australia	156.2	24	437	21	20.81	3-31
1991	England	172.1	36	442	20	22.10	4-33
	TOTALS: 2942.5	**617**		**7876**	**376**	**20.95**	**7-22**

Batting:

Season	Opponents	Matches	Innss	NO	Runs	HS	Ave.
1978/79	India	3	5	1	8	5	2.00
1980	England	4	5	0	90	45	18.00
1980/81	Pakistan	4	5	0	13	9	2.60
1980/81	England	1	1	0	15	15	15.00
1982/83	India	5	6	1	74	27	14.80
1983/84	India	6	7	0	244	92	34.86
1983/84	Australia	4	4	0	45	19	11.25
1984	England	4	5	0	47	29	9.40
1984/85	Australia	5	6	1	174	57	34.80
1984/85	New Zealand	4	4	0	90	63	22.50
1985/86	England	5	5	1	153	76	38.25
1986/87	Pakistan	3	5	1	32	13*	8.00
1986/87	New Zealand	3	4	0	83	45	20.75
1987/88	Pakistan	2	4	1	75	48	25.00
1988	England	5	6	1	135	72	27.00
1988/89	Australia	5	8	0	76	23	9.50
1988/89	India	3	4	1	84	40*	28.00
1989/90	England	2	4	1	19	8*	6.33
1990/91	Pakistan	3	5	0	92	27	18.40
1990/91	Australia	5	7	1	145	51	24.17
1991	England	5	7	1	116	67	19.33
	TOTALS: 81	**107**	**11**		**1810**	**92**	**18.85**

Limited Overs Cricket

FOR WEST INDIES IN LIMITED OVERS INTERNATIONALS

Debut v England (Prudential Trophy) at Leeds 1980
Highest Score: 66 v Pakistan at Gujranwala 1986-87
Best Bowling Performance: 4-18 v Australia (World Series Cup) at Melbourne 1991-92

FOR HAMPSHIRE IN ONE-DAY CRICKET

John Player Special League/Refuge Assurance League/Axa Equity & Law League

Debut v Middlesex at Lords 1979
Highest Score: 59 v Yorkshire at Southampton 1993
Best Bowling Performance: 5-13 v Glamorgan at Portsmouth 1979

Benson & Hedges Cup

Debut v Derbyshire at Derby 1979
Highest Score: 34 v Essex at Chelmsford 1987
Best Bowling Performance: 4-20 v Essex at Southampton 1992

Gillette Cup/Nat West Trophy

Debut v Gloucestershire at Bristol 1979
Highest Score: 77 v Northamptonshire at Southampton 1990
Best Bowling Performance: 4-15 v Kent at Canterbury 1983